# Canada and the
# KOREAN WAR

# Canada and the
# KOREAN WAR

**DIRECTORATE OF HISTORY AND HERITAGE
DEPARTMENT OF NATIONAL DEFENCE**

ART GLOBAL

Canadian Cataloguing in Publication Data

Main entry under title:
Canada and the Korean War
Includes index
ISBN 2-920718-85-1

1.Korean War, 1950-1953 - Participation, Canadian. 2. Canada. Canadian Army - History - Korean War, 1950-1953.
3. Korean War, 1950-1953 - Pictorial Works. I. Canada. Dept. of National Defence. Directorate of History and heritage.

DS919.2.C36 2002          951.904'24'0971          C2002-940248-4

Publisher: Ara Kermoyan

Project director: Stephen J. Harris

Copy editor: Jane Broderick

Dust-cover illustration:
inspired by the United Nations
Service Medal (Korea)

End paper:   Edward Zuber, 1932-
             *Incoming,* 1978
             CWM – 90033

Published by Editions Art Global and the Department of National Defence in co-operation with the Department
of Public Works and Government Services Canada. All rights reserved. No part of the publication may be reproduced,
transmitted, in any form or by any means, electronic, mechanical, photocopying, recording, or otherwise, or stored
in a retrieval system, without the prior written permission of the Minister of Public Works and Government Services,
Ottawa, Ontario K1A 0S5 Canada

© Her Majesty the Queen in Right of Canada, 2002
Catalogue number: D61-13/2001E

Art Global
384 Laurier Avenue West
Montreal, Quebec H2V 2K7 Canada

ISBN 2-920718-85-1

Printed and bound in Canada

Art Global acknowledges the financial support of the Government of Canada, through the Book Publishing Industry
Development program, for its publishing activities.

Cet ouvrage a été publié simultanément en français sous le titre de :
*Le Canada et la Guerre de Corée*
ISBN 2-920718-84-3

# TABLE OF CONTENTS

## PREFACE AND ACKNOWLEDGEMENTS

*Having served in Korea as commanding officer of the 3rd Battalion, Princess Patricia's Canadian Light Infantry, Lieutenant-Colonel Herbert Fairlie Wood subsequently became the author of the official history of the Canadian Army in Korea, entitled* Strange Battleground: The Operations in Korea and Their Effects on the Defence Policy of Canada *(Ottawa: Queen's Printer, 1996). The book is easier reading than its somewhat cumbersome title might suggest, but it is – as with most official histories, especially those that discuss the effects of policy – essentially history from the top down.*

*However, Colonel Wood had a profound understanding of what the army was like from the bottom up, the result of some twenty-five years of service, and he seems to have felt an urge to tell Canadians about that, as well, before his death in May 1967 at the early age of 52. To do so, he turned to fiction with a humorous twist in the story of a very ordinary other rank in the Canadian Army Special Force raised for service in Korea.* The Private War of Jacket Coates *(Toronto: Long, Don Mills, 1966), was dedicated to "Fred Azar, – good soldier, firm friend, who will understand Jacket Coates."*

*Anyone who knew the late Warrant Officer Class II Alfred A. Azar will realize at once why he would have understood, for Freddie was Wood's model for Jacket Coates. Although he served throughout the Second World War, Freddie was never a front-line soldier – after all, in modern times most soldiers are not, no matter what they may claim! – but then, neither is the fictitious Jacket Coates, even though he happens to be serving in an infantry battalion.*

*Chance has put him where he is, and Jacket is simply the proverbial old soldier or old salt who knows how to work the system – skiving away in anonymity (he hopes), generous to a fault, cracking bad jokes with a solemn, long-suffering expression on his face, a twinkle in his eye, and his mind too often set on pretty women or petty larceny. Without resorting to fiction, from a perspective of half a century this "unofficial" (and incomplete) history tries to look at a "sour little war" through the eyes of Jacket Coates and his ilk, as well as those of more serious mien who rightly occupy the front and centre of the stage.*

In the following chapters some quotations are in Roman *type, some (together with book and journal titles) in Italic. The former are quotations from secondary sources or the speech of politicians and diplomats who were not directly and immediately involved with the Korean experience: the other, more numerous, italic quotations are taken from personal recollections or documents prepared by people who were there, "on the ground" so to speak.*

*The armed forces were, and still are, irresistibly attracted to acronyms and abbreviations, so that quotations from official documents such as war diaries, and sometimes from reminiscences, are full of such jargon. In the interests of both clarity and sanity, these bugbears have been written out in full unless the meaning is unmistakeably clear. Sometimes punctuation has been altered slightly, and material in square brackets has been added to amplify somewhat cryptic observations perhaps penned under great pressure. Few of us historians would write half as well as we do if people were habitually shooting at us.*

*The spelling of Korean place names is an etymological minefield, since the Korean tongue bears little or no resemblance to any other known language. Even the commonly accepted name for the country is Japanese in origin, the old Korean name being some unpronounceable mixture of Tancook or Hancock, perhaps with an apostrophe or two thrown in for good measure. The style adopted here is that employed for the maps in the official history of* The United States Army in the Korean War *series, which seems superior to that of* Strange Battleground *and the official RCN history, Thor Thorgrimsson's and E.C. Russell's* Canadian Naval Operations in Korean Waters, 1950-1955 *(Ottawa: Queen's Printer, 1965). However, when place names appear in quotations the author's spelling as been retained.*

*Like all our commemorative histories, the production of* Canada and the Korean War *has been materially assisted by several members of the Directorate of History and Heritage staff as well its friends. My sincere thanks are due, in alphabetical order, to Hugh Halliday, Steve Harris, Andrew Horrall, Ara Kermoyan, Sergeant Carl Kletke, Madeleine Lafleur-Lemire, Major Paul Lansey, Major Michael McNorgan, Sergeant Ed Pinto, Cameron Pulsifer, Bill Rawling, and Michael Whitby.*

*Serge Bernier, Director*
*Directorate of History and Heritage*

Opposite: Private John Hoskins, 2 PPCLI, on Hill 419, 24 February 1951. (PA 116785)

Overleaf: Private Heath Matthews, 2 RCR. (PA 1288825)

Edward Zuber, 1932–
*Korea, Land of Morning Calm*
CWM-90024

# CHAPTER I

# *"Land of the Morning Calm"*

BRITISH COLONEL E. C. W. MYERS, 1 (Commonwealth) Division's senior military engineer, or sapper, during the Korean War, offered an intriguing overview of that third-world country whose Japanese name translates as "Land of the Morning Calm." He found it an often disagreeable, sometimes delightful, domain of extremes.

*Korea needs seeing to believe. It is hardly accurate to call it a Sapper's paradise, because one should not need to eat salt pills in paradise to avoid heat exhaustion in the summer; on the roads through paradise one should not alternatively be in a thick cloud of dust or wallowing through deep or slippery mud; one should not have 12 inches of rain in 10 days in mid-summer nor almost unbearably cold winds and temperatures throughout the winter months; the flood water breaking one's bridges and roads in summer; ice breaking them up in the thaw in the spring.... There is nearly always too much or too little of everything. Even the countryside, a monotonous cruelly barren brown in winter when not lightly covered in snow, is incredibly beautiful in the summer evenings, with its colourful foreground of wild flowers, many shades of green cultivation, and numerous types of trees in the plains and valleys, its sandy foot-hills often thickly covered with chestnut, pine and scrub and its rugged blue-tinted mountains in background.[1]*

The British War Office offered a practical description that may well have been more useful to a Western soldier encountering this alien environment for the first time.

Korea is a mountainous country about the size of Great Britain.... Much of it is without trees, the ground being covered mainly by coarse grass and bushes.

Most of the rivers are shallow and easily fordable in the dry season, those in the North freeze up for the winter, during the rains however, both spates and severe flooding are prevalent. The larger rivers may be from a quarter to half a mile [approximately a half to one kilometre] wide or even more.

About a fifth of the country is cultivated and about half this is made up of [rice] paddy fields which occupy much of the valleys; the lower hill slopes are terraced and also planted with rice. Cross country mechanized movement is impossible in the hills at any time and, during the rainy season, is impracticable in the lowlands and valleys, owing to the flooding of the rice fields and irrigation ditches.[2]

Along the same lines, Brigadier John M. Rockingham, first commander of the Canadian Army's UN contribution to the war, 25 Canadian Infantry Brigade Group (25 CIBG), recognized an infantryman's war when he saw one and got to the nub of the matter immediately.

> *There is nothing new about tactics in Korea. All established principles will apply, but require different application from that in countries where the terrain is flatter and the roads more numerous....*
>
> *Troops should be trained to climb hills of 2000 to 3000 feet [600 to 900 metres] with a 50 pound [23 kilogram] load on their backs; hills which are very close to perpendicular. Leg and back muscles become very stiff if these climbs are attempted without proper training, and there is danger of affecting the climber's heart. The essential state of training is to be able to arrive on the top of such a hill in condition to fight immediately.*[3]

As might be expected, Lieutenant-Colonel James R. Stone, commanding the 2nd Battalion of Princess Patricia's Canadian Light Infantry (2 PPCLI), the first Canadian Army unit to arrive in Korea, had serious administrative concerns when he and the unit arrived there, on 18 December 1950.

> *The brothel areas of Pusan, not being "Off Limits," have been doing a roaring business since the Battalion arrived.... An attempt is being made to appeal to the men on both moral and disease grounds, but in all possibility neither will have any effect....*
>
> *Korea is a land of filth and poverty. Social amenities of a desirable type are lacking and nothing but hard work will alleviate the boredom that will soon set in. ...the alcoholics in the battalion are already drinking the very poor liquor brewed in local bathtubs. Diseases, except venereal ones, probably will not be a problem during the winter, but as all fertilizing of fields is done with human excreta there is no doubt that there will be a health problem in the spring and summer.*[4]

When he wrote his report Stone had already arranged for the battalion to move up-country and get the hard training it still needed, primarily in the form recommended by Rockingham. That would also help banish the threat of boredom. Moreover, the North Koreans and Chinese, in turn, would ensure that the more fortunate among his men would experience both hard living and hard fighting before they saw Canada again. As for the unfortunate ones, two officers and 53 other ranks out of the 34 officers and 873 other ranks who had just landed would never come home, and another 11 officers and 147 men would be wounded,[5] a quite startling casualty rate for what would be officially described as a "police action." And that was only one battalion out of the nine that served in the Korean campaign, together with their supporting arms (armour, artillery, sappers and signals) and services (transport, ordnance, medical and dental, engineer workshops, provost and so forth).

A little less than six months before Colonel Stone put pen to paper in Pusan, on 29 June 1950 a presidential press conference had been held in Washington, DC, to hear what the president of the United States had to say about North Korea's four-day-old invasion of capitalist South Korea. It could hardly be described as an unprovoked attack – although that was a popular and over-used description at the time! – for each country had provoked the other with zealous enthusiasm a number of times over the preceding several years.[6] This particular provocation, however, was clearly a full-scale invasion, not a mere incursion as so often in the past – and the United States had already become involved.

> REPORTER: Are we, or are we not, at war?
> PRESIDENT TRUMAN: We are not at war. The members of the United Nations are going to the relief of the Korean Republic to suppress a bandit raid.
> REPORTER: Mr. President, would it be correct, against your explanation, to call this a police action under the United Nations?
> TRUMAN: Yes, that's exactly what it amounts to.[7]

Labelling American intervention as a "police action" seems to have been a spur-of-the-moment decision on the president's part. It is unlikely that he was simply relieving himself from the constitutional necessity of winning Congressional approval before committing US forces, as some have claimed, for Congress had already extended the draft – selective conscription of 18-year-old males for military service – by 314 votes to 4, and the next day the Senate would pass a bill providing for military assistance to Korea by 66 votes to none.[8] As for what the Korean eruption really was, Averell Harriman, Truman's shrewd and strong-minded adviser for national security affairs, was more truthful in labelling it "a sour little war."[9]

Louis St. Laurent, the prime minister of Canada, took the presidential line when he told the House of

Commons about "our relationship to the present situation in Korea" on 30 June, the day after Truman's press conference.

> Any participation by Canada... – and I wish to emphasize this strongly – would not be participation in war against any state. It would be our part in collective police action under the control and authority of the United Nations for the purpose of restoring peace to an area where an aggression has occurred as determined...by the security council, which decision has been accepted by us.[10]

But an unidentified commentator in National Defence Headquarters – the handwriting suggests the vice-chief of naval staff, Rear-Admiral F. L. Houghton – clearly inclined to the Harriman interpretation, minuting on a typescript of St. Laurent's statement, "How can you do this without going to war against the aggressor? We are as dishonest as Hitler was, or N. Korea [is]."[11]

Whether police action or sour little war, it would prove to be the third most costly conflict in Canadian history, fought over a remote Asian peninsula with a population of 30 million – nearly double that of Canada at the time. How did it come about that first Canadian sailors, then Canadian soldiers and finally a few Canadian airmen found themselves fighting (and sometimes dying) on, or in the vicinity of, a country that few Westerners had ever even heard of a week before St. Laurent raised the issue in Parliament?

When the future of Korea had first been discussed by US President Roosevelt, British Prime Minister Churchill and Chinese Generalissimo Chiang Kai-shek,* at their meeting in Cairo in 1943, Korea was a Japanese possession, and it had been so since its annexation by the latter during the Russo-Japanese War of 1904–1905. At their meeting, however, the three statesmen agreed that, in due course, Korea should become free and independent once again. The USSR's Marshal Stalin had not been included in that decision-making process, since the Soviet Union was not then at war with Japan. But at Potsdam, in late July 1945, when he committed his country to declaring war on the Japanese at some time in the indefinite future, Stalin formally agreed with Roosevelt and Churchill that, once they had been defeated, "there should be a trusteeship for Korea under the United States, China, Great Britain, and the Soviet Union."[12] The clear implication was that independence would follow in due course.

The Soviet declaration of war did not come until 8 August 1945, just two days after the first atom bomb was dropped on Hiroshima and one day before the second fell on Nagasaki – cataclysmic events that ensured a quick end to the Far Eastern fighting. When the end came, on 2 September, the Allies' terms of surrender stipulated that Japanese forces north of the 38th Parallel capitulate to the Russians (who shared a very short border with Korea in the northeast corner of the peninsula, the rest of the country bordering on China, a land still enmeshed in civil war) and those to the south of it to the Americans, with both powers then maintaining a garrison in their respective zones until a permanent settlement could be arranged.

The Russians moved in immediately by road and rail, but it took the Americans a month to arrive on the scene by ship. Perhaps surprisingly, given the way in which the Cold War subsequently developed, during that hiatus the Russians adhered to the Potsdam agreement and made no attempt to cross the 38th Parallel. When the Americans did appear, all was briefly lovey-dovey. "In the afterglow of victory it was not anticipated that there would ever be any need to control movement between the two zones, so it seemed irrelevant that the line was totally indefensible from a military point of view."[13]

But agreement on unification proved impossible and, while Russians and Americans, Korean nationalists and Chinese communists (for Chiang Kai-shek was losing his hold on mainland China to Mao Tse-tung) squabbled interminably, the 38th Parallel developed into a closed, impenetrable frontier. The American zone encompassed some 40 per cent of Korea's land mass and was home to two thirds of the population. It had few natural resources and much agriculture, while the Soviet zone was rich in resources and boasted most of what little industry there was.

Within their respective zones, the Russians quickly established their authority but the Americans became mired in internal political bickering and power struggles. Finally, in September 1947, the United States proposed, and the General Assembly of the United Nations called for, a nation-wide election. In the West, however, the Cold War was getting chillier and, not surprisingly, the Soviets objected. They wanted no elections until all occupying forces, Russian and American, had left the country, when, they believed

---

*Chinese names are recorded in the anglicized form commonly employed at the time.

Prime Minister Louis St. Laurent greets officers of the 3rd Battalion, Royal 22e Regiment, in Korea. (PA 128830)

Brooke Claxton, minister of national defence, with Lester B. Pearson, 1 September 1950. (PA 121698)

The North's invasion produced the inevitable flow of refugees streaming south. (PA 128864)

Kim Il-sung, leader of the Democratic
People's Republic of Korea — the North.
(PPCLI Museum)

Syngman Rhee, president of the
Republic of Korea — the South.
(PPCLI Museum)

(probably rightly), their well-organized Korean Communist Party would be able to dictate the disposition of events.

At the same time as the General Assembly was calling for elections, the US joint chiefs of staff, chaired by General Dwight D. Eisenhower, were deciding that, given their limited resources, the United States had "little strategic interest" in Korea.

In the event of hostilities in the Far East, our present forces in Korea would be a military liability and could not be maintained there without substantial reinforcement prior to the initiation of hostilities. Moreover, any offensive operation the United States might wish to conduct on the Asiatic continent [an oblique reference to American support of Chiang-Kai-shek's nationalists, still struggling for dominance with Mao Tse-tung's communists] most probably would by-pass the Korean peninsula.[14]

Without the concurrence of the Russians, in May 1948 an election in South Korea was marked by the violent deaths of nearly 600 potential voters in assassinations and political riots.[15] Nevertheless, a UN Temporary Commission On Korea (UNTCOK) decided that the election had been "a valid expression of the free will of the electorate in those parts of Korea which were accessible to the Commission," despite the expressed doubts of Canadian, Australian and Syrian delegates.[16]

With US support, 70-year-old Syngman Rhee was chosen president of the new republic. In hindsight, that was a mistake. Stubborn and troublesome, he quickly proved to be a poor administrator who continually alarmed his American patrons by public threats to reunite his country by force. His régime was plagued by mutinies and rebellions – some communist-inspired, some simply the result of corrupt and inept government, and most by a combination of the two influences. By June 1949, Rhee was busy suppressing risings in five of his eight southern provinces.[17]

Meanwhile, a rival government had been set up in the North, and the Democratic People's Republic of Korea was proclaimed in September 1948 with Kim Il-sung as premier. With Kim firmly in the saddle, his Soviet masters now began withdrawing their troops, so that by the end of the year there was only a cadre of advisers left to train North Korea's growing army in the use of Soviet tanks, artillery and aircraft. The Americans, who had carefully avoided supplying Rhee with any heavy or sophisticated weapons

systems for fear that he might try to make good on his threats against the North if they did, also pulled out all but a few advisers, leaving Rhee with an army more suited to the maintenance of an uncertain civil order than fighting a war.

As the half-century turned, Korea was seen by Washington as being outside the boundary of America's forward defences. In January 1950 President Truman's secretary of state, Dean Acheson, was proclaiming that his country's "defensive perimeter...runs along the Aleutians to Japan and then goes to the Ryukus...to the Philippine Islands."[18] Korea lay beyond that line – a position which could not help but encourage Kim Il-sung's ambitions. Given such apparent indifference, he had every reason to believe that he could get away with a unilateral reunification imposed by force.

Just what part did Canada play in all this? Very little. Ottawa's first involvement had come in late October 1947, when J. A. Bradette, a back-bench Liberal MP but current spokesman for the Canadian delegation to the United Nations, had spoken out in support of the American position on Korean elections. He boldly trod where no Canadian politician had trod before in declaring that Canada was "particularly interested in the future of Korea because of its position on the northern Pacific" – a view that half a century later has become ritualized as Canada's solicitude for the Pacific Rim. At the time, however, Prime Minister Mackenzie King, reading Bradette's words, told his secretary, Jack Pickersgill, "This United Nations is going to destroy us yet. Just imagine, *Bradette* making speeches about Korea!"[19]

Nevertheless, Bradette's initiative resulted in Canada being offered, and taking, a place on UNTCOK over Mackenzie King's half-hearted opposition. "In sum," the historian Denis Stairs has written, "the American government had turned to the United Nations as a means of implementing policies which it had been unable to execute through its own efforts,"[20] and now, despite the prime minister's reservations, Canada was merely abetting the Americans. In his prime, King's scepticism would surely have been decisive, but now he was getting old and tired: he resigned a year later, to be succeeded by Louis St. Laurent, an enthusiastic supporter of the United Nations and UNTCOK who won the 1949 general election with a substantial majority. In early 1950, for better or worse, Canada was aboard the UN bandwagon, arm in arm with Uncle Sam.

Confident that neither the United States nor the United Nations would intervene, Kim saw a lamb fat for the slaughter. On Sunday 25 June 1950 at 0400 hours local time, North Korean artillery and mortars began to fire on targets all along the 38th Parallel and, two hours later, some 110,000 troops, supported by about 1,400 assorted artillery pieces and 126 T-34 tanks,[21] began to invade South Korea. There was (and is) no evidence that this attack was instigated by the Soviet Union or China, although it seems likely that both Moscow and Peking (later Beijing) had been informed of Kim Il-sung's intentions in advance and acquiesced in his decision.

To oppose Kim's legions, Syngman Rhee mustered an ill-led, ill-trained and ill-equipped army numerically about two thirds as strong as his enemy's. The Americans had left him only 50,000 rifles and light machine-guns, "a small amount of artillery," and a few soft-skinned vehicles. Nearly half his men were armed with ex-Japanese weapons.[22] Rhee's forces were very soon fleeing south in total disarray.

Word of the attack reached Washington early on Saturday evening, 24 June, and New York (where the United Nations was headquartered) shortly afterwards.* The UN Security Council (the Soviet Union, with a permanent seat and a veto, was currently boycotting its meetings over the issue of who should hold the Chinese seat, Nationalists on Formosa – now Taiwan – or Communists on the mainland) met on Sunday afternoon and, led by the Americans, called for "the immediate cessation of hostilities" and for the North Koreans "to withdraw forthwith."[23] North Korea, of course, took no notice.

In 1950 politicians and civil servants kept their personal lives strictly separate from their professional ones; weekends were sacred and telephones were generally viewed as regrettable necessities of the working world. Thus Ottawa's power brokers were late in hearing the news. Mary Macdonald, secretary to Lester Pearson, the secretary of state for external affairs, just happened to be listening to a CBC Sunday afternoon radio programme at her Lac Gauvreau cottage, in the Gatineau Hills north of Ottawa, when it was interrupted for the announcement.

Neither Pearson nor his acting under-secretary, Escott Reid, had a telephone at their respective

cottage homes, but Reid's place was within walking distance. Ms. Macdonald tramped over to pass the word, only to find that Reid and his son had gone out for a row on the lake. Commandeering another rowboat, she set off in hot pursuit. She finally managed to catch up and tell him what was happening. Apparently Reid was not too concerned. After all, this was a weekend – a time for boating and fishing and watching the sun go down from a deckchair on the dock, not for racing in to Ottawa to deal with international crises.

Not even for driving over to Lester Pearson's cottage on a neighbouring lake. Instead of going himself, he sent Macdonald on a 25-kilometre drive through the Gatineau Hills to tell Pearson what she had heard. Then she had to drive him another three kilometres to the nearest telephone, in order that he might call Louis St. Laurent at Saint-Patrice-de-Beaurivage, south of Quebec City, where, happily, the prime minister did have a telephone. Prime minister and secretary of state agreed, however, that nothing needed to be done – or, indeed, could be done – until office hours on Monday morning.[24]

Even then, Ottawa thought that the United States was unlikely to take or call for any concrete military action.[25] But the next day, 27 June, the Security Council, led by the Americans and still lacking the Russians, resolved that "Members of the United Nations furnish such assistance to the Republic of Korea as may be necessary to repel the armed attack and to restore international peace and security in the area."[26] For the first time in history, an international body had voted for force to be used to repel aggression, and President Truman promptly ordered American air and naval forces to "give cover and support" to the retreating South Koreans. Two days after that, on 29 June, he authorized General Douglas MacArthur, who commanded all US forces in the Far East from his headquarters in Tokyo, to use American ground troops as well.

In Ottawa, where Parliament was about to prorogue for the summer vacation, the matter was debated on the 29th and the opposition parties, Conservatives, New Democrats and Social Credit, united in agreeing to support the government in whatever action it might deem necessary. The motives of the opposition parties are not entirely clear, but apparently everybody felt that if Canada supported the United Nations (and, by extension, the Americans) then it might be possible to influence – or moderate – American policy to some

---

*Korean time was 10 hours ahead of Eastern Standard Time in Washington, New York and Ottawa, and 11 hours ahead of Eastern Daylight Time. In this narrative, events will be recorded according to local dates and times.

slight, if indeterminate, degree. Perhaps the situation might yet be salvaged.

Canada did not participate in the UN expedition to Korea because of any intrinsic concern for Korea and Koreans, but because of an interest in the UN, first, and in relations with the United States, second. The possibility that Korea was a prelude to a general Communist attack else where on the vast periphery of the Soviet Union was…sufficient to bring the Canadian government to the contemplation of war. But it was the prospect of war in Europe that moved them, and not war on the continent of Asia.[27]

The next day, after St. Laurent had given the speech quoted earlier, MPs left Ottawa for the electorally greener fields of their constituencies. Apparently there was no expectation on anyone's part that Canada would move beyond offering moral support and perhaps very, very nominal participation in any military venture. While Washington clearly believed that the North Korean attack was a subset of the Cold War, orchestrated by Moscow, and needed to be handled as such, Ottawa (without much actual knowledge to base its view on, since Canada relied upon Britain and the United States for most of its diplomatic intelligence) was hoping to treat it as the one-off adventure of Kim Il-sung that history would, in fact, show it to be.

On 1 July elements of 24 (US) Division, part of the American occupation force in Japan, began landing at Pusan, in the southeast corner of the peninsula, and started to move north as quickly as road and rail conditions permitted, while two more occupation divisions began preparations to follow it. On 5 July the leading Americans encountered their first North Koreans near Osan, some one hundred kilometres south of Seoul. Then, outnumbered and outfought, they promptly joined their South Korean allies in fleeing back towards their starting point. Retreat was inevitable, for five years of occupation duties in Japan had left the Americans almost as ill-led and ill-trained as the South Koreans, they had negligible armour and artillery, and their hand-held anti-armour weaponry (bazookas) was inadequate to deal with T-34 tanks.

In the air, however, the Americans did have a distinct edge from the beginning, and once enough tactical aircraft appeared on the scene the T-34s and much of the enemy artillery was destroyed by airborne weaponry – 20mm cannon, 5-inch anti-tank rockets and napalm bombs. They also wrecked the North Koreans' relatively meagre motorized transport, posing major problems of re-supply, and finally enabling the Americans and South Koreans to hold a rectangular enclave in the southeastern corner of the peninsula – the Naktong Perimeter (named after the Naktong river that formed the bulk of its western boundary) based on the port of Pusan, stretching some 160 kilometres from north to south and half that distance east to west.

On the same day, 5 July, that the first Americans met the enemy, HMCS *Cayuga, Athabaskan* and *Sioux* sailed from Esquimalt, bound simply for "western Pacific waters." They were formally offered to the United Nations on 12 July, the day they arrived at Pearl Harbor, and the crew of *Cayuga* would be the first Canadians to engage the enemy, a month later; but the story of those three ships and their successors in the Korean campaign will be told in Chapters 2 to 8. The RCAF was also early on the scene, although none of its units would be engaged against hostile air forces at any time. No. 426 (Transport) Squadron was attached to the US Military Air Transport Service and assigned to carry mail between North America and Japan on 20 July 1950, and 21 RCAF pilots would serve with US Air Force squadrons in Korea, accounting between them for 20 enemy fighters destroyed or damaged. Their stories will be told in more detail in Chapter 9.

On 14 July the secretary-general of the United Nations, the Norwegian Trygve Lie, asked if the Canadian government would "examine its capacity to provide an increased volume of combat forces, particularly ground forces."[28] The furnishing of soldiers posed a real problem, however. There were not nearly enough men to provide a Korean contingent from existing resources, and the difficulty was compounded by the growing likelihood that Canada would also have to find soldiers for the inchoate NATO command being formed for the defence and garrisoning of Western Europe – a likelihood that became a certainty by mid-August.[29] The only solution was to recruit and train additional troops, and on 7 August the prime minister announced the raising of an infantry brigade "to be available for use in carrying out Canada's obligations under the United Nations Charter or the North Atlantic Pact" – whichever of the two seemed most important at the moment when the brigade would be considered fit to fight. The recruitment and training of the Special Service Force destined for Korea, and its subsequent adventures, will be recorded in Chapters 3 to 7 and Chapter 10.

HMCS *Cayuga* and *Sioux* on passage to the Far East.

## CHAPTER II

# *"First at Bat"*

IN THE SUNNY LATE AFTERNOON of Wednesday 5 July 1950, four Canadian warships steamed westward through the spectacular beauty of Juan de Fuca Strait, a cruiser, HMCS *Ontario*, leading three destroyers. *Ontario* would be with them for only a brief period, but the destroyers were off to war under unique circumstances and to spur them on came a message from the chief of naval staff in Ottawa: "First at bat as usual. Good luck in your mission."[1]

First at bat indeed – but only in the usual Canadian context! When North Korean artillery batteries had fired their first rounds across the border into South Korea 12 days earlier, the crews of the destroyers were not even in the stadium, let alone in the "On Deck" circle. HMCS *Sioux*, in dry dock for routine maintenance, was not scheduled to come out until 30 June, and would then require further work alongside; *Athabaskan* was in the midst of her annual leave period with the last of her crew not expected back until 6 July; and *Cayuga* had only just emerged from dry dock and had not yet begun the task of storing ship.[2]

Nevertheless, on 30 June the senior naval officer on the Pacific coast, Rear-Admiral H. G. DeWolf, had been formally instructed to put the three ships at five days' notice for sailing to join United Nations ships gathering in the Far East to meet the Korean emergency. In *Athabaskan*, Commander Robert P. Welland recorded in his monthly report of proceedings:

> *The complement of 15 Officers and 178 men was increased to 16 Officers and 262 men: wartime allowances of ammunition were received and stowed, including live squid [bombs for the forward-throwing anti-submarine mortar]: spares of every kind were provided on a lavish scale. It is a tribute to the Dockyard that when "ATHABASKAN" sailed the only article that had been asked for and not received was a supply of C.S.A. for the smoke generator, and that was to follow.*[3]

Even though the three destroyers sailed on time swollen with men and supplies, it had been a near-run thing. The navy was in the midst of a serious personnel crunch and in order to bring *Cayuga*, *Athabaskan* and *Sioux* – the only operational destroyers on the station – up to wartime strength, the barracks and other ships based on Esquimalt were stripped of personnel.[4] Moreover, at a time when budgets were tight, the navy did not have a lot of supplies to go around and the rushed deployment to Korea left many storeroom shelves empty. That said, the three ships were well suited to the task that lay before them. *Cayuga* and *Athabaskan* were the two newest destroyers in the fleet, commissioned in 1947 and 1948 respectively, and boasting superior electronics. The older *Sioux*, dating from February 1944, was a veteran of much hard steaming in the latter part of the Second World War but had also been modernized extensively. In fact, not only did she possess modern radars and armament, but she was the first RCN destroyer with upgraded accommodation that included cafeteria messing and tiered bunks in place of the traditional hammocks.[5]

The officer leading the deployment was 37-year-old Captain Jeffry V. Brock, one of the more controversial figures in Canadian naval history, who took command of *Cayuga* and the flotilla only the day before they sailed – the change in command was routine and had been promulgated weeks before. As the commanding officer of both British and Canadian escorts and escort groups during the Second World War, he had displayed considerable tactical prowess and would do so again in Korea. The controversy lay in his personality, which can perhaps best be described through an account of a meeting he attended in London in the mid-1950s that included the Canadian chief of naval staff, Vice-Admiral Harry DeWolf, and the British First Sea Lord, Admiral of the Fleet Lord Louis Mountbatten. After Brock made his presentation to the two legendary senior officers and withdrew, Mountbatten, no shrinking violet himself, observed to DeWolf, *"He's a brash young man isn't he!"*[6] Brash, forthright and lacking humility well describe Brock, but those traits aside, and no matter what one thinks of him, he was to perform capably in his role as Commander Canadian Destroyer Division Pacific (CANCOMDESPAC) and in doing so set a lofty standard, not just for those who followed him in Korea but for those who would lead similar Canadian naval deployments in the future.

"It is evident from the nature of the North Korean invasion of the South," the Australian official history of the Korean War has concluded, "that Kim Il-sung gave little thought to the strategic importance of the sea."[7] That was an error on his part, for command of the sea played a decisive role in shaping the course of the war, enabling United Nations troops to launch direct assaults on, or be evacuated from, any port or ports anywhere on the peninsula.

The maritime environment varied greatly between the two coasts, and that shaped the deployment of UN forces. The east coast, bordering the Sea of Japan, was distinguished by a narrow coastal plain with deep water close inshore; the west coast and the Yellow Sea featured a wider littoral, shallow water, many islands, fast tidal currents, and shifting shoals and sand banks. Navigation there was far more challenging, and the milieu favourable to mining. As a result, although ships shifted from one coast to the other, the cruisers, destroyers and frigates that made up the Commonwealth's contribution generally operated off the west coast, while US Navy task groups, formed around large aircraft carriers, cruised the Sea of Japan.

The Canadians were not given much opportunity to adjust to their new surroundings. On 31 July, within 24 hours of putting into Sasebo, Japan, *Athabaskan* was dispatched to escort an American troop ship carrying reinforcements to embattled Pusan. Meanwhile, Brock made the rounds at headquarters, meeting his new masters and confirming where his ships stood in the command structure. *"Each ship individually joined T.G. 96.5 under Rear Admiral HARTMAN, USN for service with T.E. 96.50 (Captain JAY) and T.E. 96.53 (Rear Admiral ANDREWS, RN)."*[8] Amongst this confusing nomenclature delineating task groups (TG) and smaller task elements (TE) was the critical designator "individually," which meant that the Canadian ships would be deployed piecemeal and not as a national force with some inevitable loss of prestige and less effective public relations.* *Cayuga's* first operational task was to escort an oiler refuelling British and Dutch ships engaged on the West Coast Blockade patrol. Although the North Korean navy, such as it was, had been largely destroyed in the first days of the conflict, there was still a mild threat of air or submarine attack. The North Korean air force had been aggressive in attacking UN naval forces in the early stages of the war before it had lost the air superiority battle but it still posed a potential danger to ships exposed without air cover. This was borne out on 23 August when two Shturmovik fighter-bombers attacked the British destroyer *Comus* off Inch'on, causing serious damage. It proved an isolated incident but *Comus* could do little to defend itself and it is unlikely that a Canadian destroyer would have fared any better. Brock later

---

* When Canada next faced a similar situation, during the 1991 Gulf war, Cabinet insisted that our three-ship force stay together, even though that meant operating in a support role far from the likelihood of serious action.

reported to naval headquarters: *"It is fortunate that the enemy did not possess sufficient air strength to enable him to place the blockading and bombarding forces in any real danger...[as the] efficiency of the Long and Close range AA armament [in RCN destroyers] was dangerously low when the division was first committed to the Korean campaign."*[9]

The submarine threat was more problematic. North Korea had no ships of that type, but there was a concern over the course of the war that the Soviets would deploy submarines in the theatre or that the Chinese would build up a force of submarines. Vice-Admiral Charles Turner Joy, the UN naval commander, initially directed that his forces attack any unidentified submarine, but cooler minds persuaded him that an attack on a Soviet submarine could have serious political ramifications. Joy thus ordered his forces to attack only submarines in a position to attack UN ships. Although several attacks were carried out by UN escorts throughout the conflict, there is as yet no definitive evidence that any were against actual submarines.[10]

After five trips escorting transports to Pusan, *Cayuga* took her first stab at shore bombardment, a task which was to was become one of the most frequent and satisfying for Canadian sailors. It would seem quite a simple operation to bring a warship within range of a static target and blast away from relatively close range until it was destroyed or at least neutralized. In the first place, the enemy sometimes fired back; witness the Australian destroyer HMAS *Bataan* that was straddled several times from four miles range on 1 August by a shore battery northwest of Inch'on. Furthermore, the potential use of mines by the enemy complicated the task of ships moving close inshore into what were sometimes obvious firing positions. But the challenges associated with shore bombardment extended beyond the complications introduced by the enemy, and because it was such an important feature of Canadian naval operations in Korea it should be looked at in some detail.

The armament and fire control systems in the Canadian destroyers serving in Korea varied – for example, *Sioux* had three 4.7-inch guns in single turrets while *Cayuga* and *Athabaskan* had six 4-inch in three twin turrets. These were formidable weapons, capable of firing armour-piercing or high-explosive shells as far as 15,000 metres. The sophisticated firing data that took range, ship's motion, target inclination, wind speed, air temperature, barometric pressure and other variables into account was calculated by the Admiralty Fire Control Clock, an analogue computer located in the transmitting station deep in the hull. Under centralized control, this information was fed to the gunnery control crew in the director tower atop the bridge superstructure, who controlled the fire of the turrets being used – as the director tower rotated onto the target, the turrets designated to engage followed automatically. When all guns were laid, elevated and loaded, the gunnery officer ordered "Shoot" – under local control, the individual turrets fired visually.

Although the Canadian ships all had radar-controlled gunnery systems, that form of control was seldom used for shore bombardment. Instead, gunnery was directed either visually from the ship – direct fire – or from spotters ashore or in aircraft overhead indirect fire. These systems could achieve great accuracy, and well-trained gunnery teams could loose between 12 and 15 rounds per minute at a target.

Effective gunnery requires constant exercising, but Brock complained to headquarters that on arrival in Korea *"control teams were unpractised [sic] at this particular phase of gunnery [bombardment], so that it was not until two or three actual bombardments were carried out that a satisfactory state of efficiency was achieved. This would seem to indicate a requirement for a bombardment range on the West Coast, and for bombardment training to be an important part of a ships gunnery exercises."* There were other problems. The American and British navies utilized different target-spotting systems, forcing the Canadians to become proficient in both. Ultimately, *Cayuga's* gunnery team developed a unique spotting disk, a device that solved this difficulty and that was adopted throughout the RCN. There was also trouble with ammunition. The cordite propellant came from different production lots, each very slightly different from the others, which affected uniformity, a key element of accurate fire control.[11] There were other minor irritants that affected bombardment operations but ultimately experience provided the remedy, and the Canadian destroyers built a reputation for providing prompt and accurate shooting.[12]

On 15 August 1950 *Cayuga* fired the first Canadian shots in anger in Korea. Yosu, a small port on the southern tip of the peninsula, west of Pusan, had recently been taken by the North Koreans and UN commanders wanted its port facilities demolished before any use could be made of them by the enemy. *Cayuga*, accompanied by a British frigate, anchored four miles offshore and, after a spotter aircraft from the carrier HMS *Theseus* arrived, she fired some 94

Rear-Admiral H. G. DeWolf wishes the commanding officers of the Canadian destroyers luck upon their departure for Korea in July 1950. From left, Captain H. F. Pullen of the cruiser *Ontario*, which accompanied the destroyers on the first leg to Hawaii, Captain Jeffry Brock, Commander Paul Taylor and Commander Bob Welland. (DND E-11853)

Korea was a gunners' war: *Cayuga*'s forward 4-inch fires a salvo. (CA-168)

Mines posed a constant threat. Here, sailors from *Cayuga* inspect a typical example (DND CA-80) while *Sioux* destroys another. (DND CA-116)

rounds over a 50-minute period. Firing and spotting procedures were judged to be good, but large spreads developed (probably due to the cordite problem) and, although several hits were noted in the target area, results were assessed as only *"fair."*[13]

There is an interesting aside to this operation. In late August, Rear-Admiral William Andrewes, second in command of the Royal Navy's Far East Station and commander of the United Nations' west coast support group, responded to a query from his commander-in-chief in Singapore:

> *You asked recently whether we are wearing the United Nations Flag and if so, what are the regulations; I replied that we are not wearing it and indeed none of us were very clear as to how it should be worn.*
>
> *I find now that our Canadian ships have orders or permission to wear the United Nations flag at the foremasthead and H.M.C.S. CAYUGA wore it the other day when bombarding "just for the hell of it." Personally I have not sighted it since this war started though this must have been due to not keeping a good look out as I am told that it flies over General MACARTHUR's Headquarters in TOKYO.*[14]

Whether Brock had noticed that MacArthur was flying the UN flag when he visited his headquarters in Tokyo we do not know, but that may have given him the idea. *Cayuga* appears to have been the first warship to fly the UN flag in Korea and thus perhaps the first warship ever to fly it at all.

Rear-Admiral Andrewes had more pressing issues to contend with than flags and national pride. In a meeting in Tokyo on 8 August, Admiral Joy expressed concern about the effectiveness of the west coast blockade. *"There is little doubt,"* Andrewes reported, that Joy *"is being pressed continuously to intensify the blockade and the reasons are not far to seek"*:

> *Frequent reports from returning aircraft indicate that large numbers of Junks are sighted, here one day, there another. Immediately it is thought that they are a "supply Armada." A ship goes [to the scene], a number are searched, they are found harmless.... So I feel, and Admiral JOY really intimated, that he is continually faced with doubts about the blockade on both sides [of Korea] but more especially the West. He said plainly that he "understood perfectly" but that it was hard to convince the Commander-in-Chief [MacArthur].*

> *The enemy was getting supplies. All roads and bridges, railways and rolling stock had been knocked out by air, but still supplies were getting in. It must be by sea.... Of course I could not deny the likelihood of some sea supplies evading the very thin patrols we have had. But still I do not think it is much.*[15]

Andrewes was plagued by a shortage of destroyers and he proposed to use strike aircraft from the light fleet carrier HMS *Triumph* *"to back up the blockade in the west."* Joy agreed, which shaped the immediate future of *Athabaskan* and *Sioux*. *Triumph* sailed from Sasebo on 12 August, screened by the cruiser HMS *Kenya* and the destroyers *Sioux*, *Athabaskan* and HMS *Comus*. Reconnaissance flights were flown off when the force reached the west coast but nothing much was sighted until the 14th, when several small vessels were reported in the Taedong estuary, about halfway between the major ports of Inch'on and Chinnamp'o. *Triumph* launched an air strike that damaged several vessels with high-explosive 3-inch rockets – each with a warhead the equivalent of a 6-inch shell – and 20mm cannon fire, but little else was found in the way of targets, leading Andrewes to conclude that *"with the lack of sea traffic, lack of serviceable shipping in port and general lack of activity, any supply running by the enemy down the West Coast must be on a very small scale."*[16]

Screening carriers during flight operations has never been popular among destroyermen. The Canadians in Korea not only found the work tedious, but the constant manoeuvring to keep station as the carrier turned into the wind to launch and recover aircraft and then shifted back to base course was a bane to watchkeepers, signals staff, helmsmen and engine-room personnel. Everyone had to stay on their toes lest their ship suffer the embarrassment of being caught out of position or, worse still, cause a collision. The Canadians derogatorily coined such duty as the Corpen Club, for the Course Pennant flown from the carrier before course alteration signals. Lieutenant A. L. Collier, *Cayuga's* navigating officer, recalls, *"You were Corpening yourself to death with all the alterations of course and screen orientations and everything else.... We were burning up fuel and spent the whole time going and changing stations because the areas there are very confined and every time they flew off a strike, [or were] changing over their CAP [combat air patrol] we were just going around in circles."*[17] Later, Brock persuaded the British to adopt the US Navy's looser, more flexible circular screen in which destroyers did not have to match every move of the carrier but merely had to adhere to its general course.

Thus, there was a measure of relief on 15 August when *Triumph* headed back to Sasebo and *Sioux* and *Athabaskan* turned to blockade operations. Their instructions were to enforce the blockade of the west coast occupied by the North Koreans; to prevent infiltration by sea on coasts held by South Koreans; and to provide fire support as required against North Korean maritime forces or land targets.[18] Under these general headings, *Sioux* headed inshore in company with the cruiser HMS *Kenya*. Excerpts from Commander P. D. Taylor's Report of Proceedings for the six-day deployment describe well the challenges associated with such missions:

*Tuesday, 15th August*
...H.M.C.S. SIOUX *and* H.M.S. KENYA *proceeded to a position off Kai To [in order to] investigate coastal shipping reported by aircraft patrols to be at anchor in that area. Nothing was seen in the area from seaward.* H.M.S. KENYA *sent one boat inshore for a closer look at 1025 [hours]; the boat returned at 1257 with nothing to report....*

*[At] 1725 investigated Junk off Kai To; harmless fishermen. No number, considered friendly. Rejoined* KENYA *1804....*

*2110 stopped to board a large junk, this proved to be another fisherman from Chin Ju heading for unoccupied islands to the south. Junk was searched and told to proceed to Ochon To....*

*Wednesday, 16th August*
*This day the ship patrolled with* H.M.S. KENYA *West of the Te Chong Islands....*

*1517 rejoined* KENYA, *speed 31 knots to proceed in search of aircraft reported ditched...1535 Aircraft [number] 8150 reported all crew of 5150 safe in life raft. 1835 sighted two life rafts.* KENYA *proceeded to rescue crew. The remainder of the night was spent in company with* KENYA *patrolling to seaward south of the Te Chong Islands.*

*Thursday, 17th August*
*This morning the ship in company with* KENYA *proceeded south to rendezvous with [Royal Fleet Auxiliary]* WAVE CHIEF *off Clifford Is... All ships took fuel from Wave Chief during the afternoon,* SIOUX *proceeded alongside at 1500 and rejoined the screen at 1657 having received 293 tons of oil fuel and 20 tons of water.*

*On completion of fuelling* H.M.C.S. ATHABASKAN *came alongside* SIOUX *to turn over notes and information on the Kunsan patrol.*

*1805 the ship detached from* CTU *96.53.3 to take over the Kunsan Patrol.* SIOUX *patrolled between Ochon To [more correctly, perhaps, Oeyon-do], Yon To and Orchong To [Och'ong-do] throughout the night.*

*2300 exchanged identities with [patrol vessel]* ROK *310, during this exchange of recognition signals the* ROK *vessel used a standard Navy 12" searchlight which caused unnecessary illumination.... Nothing further of consequence occurred during the night....*

*Friday, 18th August*
*0438 Radar contact was identified as a junk which was boarded and considered harmless on search. Junk was ordered to proceed to Ochon To for screening by* ROK *forces....*

*1003 proceeded to investigate 3 junks in company, these proved to be starving refugees in pitiful condition, junks were given food and told to proceed to Ochon To.*

*1230 Investigated junk which proved to be a fisherman; bread and tinned beef given to junk who was ordered to Ochon To....*

*Saturday, 19th August*
*...At 1040 the ship stopped off Ochon To and the boat was sent inshore as on the day before....* R.O.K. *Commander requested that the ship bombard Communist forces in the Popsong'po area, Communist machine guns reported active against his craft in that area.*

*The boat returned and was sent back inshore at 1300 with technicians to repair motor generator in* ROK *704.*

*1530 sighted* ROK *310 with boat in tow, 310 slipped the boat about ? mile South-east of Yon To and proceeded alongside* H.M.C.S. SIOUX....

*At 2137 off Yon To* ROK *310 was observed to be firing tracer presumably at a junk inshore.*

*Sunday, 20 August*
*The ship carried out the usual patrol during the dark hours of the early morning. At 0215 a persisting bright glow was observed inshore in the direction of Kunsan, it is thought that* ROK *310 was attacking in the area of the river mouth.*

*0330 the ship proceeded south to the vicinity of Popsong'po with the intention of bombarding that town in accordance with the request of* R.O.K. *forces. At first light the ship was in position 283 [degrees], Popsong'po Weather signal station 6000 yards [distant]. At 0645 fire was opened at a range of 6800 yards.*

Under-way replenishment enabled UN warships to remain on station without returning to harbour. Here, *Cayuga* takes on provisions from HMAS *Warramunga*. Note the mast of another destroyer doing likewise on the starboard side of the Australian ship. (DND CA-340)

Chinnamp'o junks carrying refugees seek protection under the guns of UN destroyers that, later, shoot-up the port facilities. (DND CA-316 and CA-315)

Navigation was a tricky business in Korean waters. In *Cayuga*'s operations compartment, sailors plot contacts from a radar display. (DND CA-359)

Lieutenant Andy Collier, who successfully navigated *Cayuga* on the difficult passage into Chinnamp'o. (DND CA-334)

*During the afternoon the ship patrolled to the westward of Yong To....*

*1730 made rendezvous with TU 96.53.2 which Unit took over the West Coast Blockade.*

*2115 turned over Kunsan Patrol notes...to H.M.S. CONSORT who proceeded to the Kunsan area at 2125(K). TU 96.53.1 and TU 96.53.3 sailed for Sasebo....*[19]

While *Sioux* was carrying out her patrol with *Kenya*, *Athabaskan* cruised an area to the south during which she carried out several bombardments and put ashore a small landing party in support of an assault on the island of Taku Chaku. Then, on 21 August, after damaging a radio reporting station on the islet of Yo Dolmi, in the approaches to Inch'on, with gunfire, Commander Welland audaciously put a small demolition party ashore to finish the job.[20] Towards the end of the month, *Cayuga* and *Sioux* screened *Triumph* as she flew off air strikes and then carried out their own routine blockade patrols off Kunsan and Inch'on.

History has demonstrated time and again that when one side's naval forces hold command of the sea to the extent they did in Korea, they offer military commanders a vital advantage over their enemy – strategic mobility. One leader who understood that was the UN and US supreme commander, General Douglas MacArthur. In his 1942–45 southwest Pacific campaigns, MacArthur had used the strategic mobility provided by the potent naval and maritime air strength at his command to bypass and isolate some Japanese-held islands while attacking and taking others. Now, as his Eighth Army prepared to recover the ground lost to the North Koreans in the early summer of 1950, he recognized the potential for an amphibious counter-stroke that, if successful, would compel the North Koreans to make a hasty withdrawal from ground to the south of the selected landing place.[21]

He settled on Inch'on, the port for Seoul, the latter attractive politically as the capital of South Korea and militarily as a vital transportation centre. But Inch'on had myriad stumbling blocks from a naval point of view. Indeed, one USN planner recalled, *"We drew up a list of every natural and geographic handicap – and Inchon had 'em all."*[22] The approaches to the port were through two narrow channels that joined at Palmi-do island, which lay at the mouth of the narrow Salee river, 16 kilometres downstream from Inch'on. Both the channels and the river could easily be blocked by mines, and they were all so narrow that

if a ship should be sunk or run hard aground, those ahead of it would be trapped like wasps in a bottle. The normal harbour current at Inch'on was a dangerously quick two to three knots and sometimes reached eight knots. The anchorage was small; there were few docks and piers and no landing beaches in the usual meaning of that term – only sea walls, piers, rocks and patches of sand. Perhaps the most critical factor of all was a tidal range of nearly 10 metres.[23]

With Operation CHROMITE scheduled for 15 September and final approval not coming until 23 August, there was not much time to pull it together. From a naval perspective, there would be a USN Assault Force to put the 1st Marine Division ashore, followed by the 7th Infantry Division and other elements of X (US) Corps. Rear-Admiral Andrewes was appointed to command Task Force 91, designated the Blockade and Covering Force, comprising a light carrier, a cruiser, eight destroyers, and 15 South Korean submarine-chasers and minesweepers. When they entered the assault area these would split into Task Group 91.1, which would provide cover and bombardment support west and north of Inch'on, and 91.2, which would maintain the southern element of the blockade and secure a Logistic Support Area (LSA). The three Canadian destroyers and several South Korean vessels, designated the Blockade Force, Southern Group, were commanded by Captain Brock.

Anticipating at least some enemy activity against his forces, Brock initially planned *"to keep one ship inshore for a period of about three days, leaving two as covering and containing forces and for escort duty."* But the enemy never showed up. *"No submarines nor enemy surface craft were detected at any time, and only friendly aircraft appeared."* With often just one supply ship requiring protection in the LSA, Brock elected to send two destroyers inshore. Nothing much was going on there either. *"Inshore blockade,"* he wrote in his monthly report, *"apart from the very considerable navigational hazards involved, was uneventful. Numerous Junks and fishing vessels were sighted, amongst the islands, and most were investigated. No traces of contraband were found, nor any indication of Communist coastal activity."*[24]

CHROMITE proved a dramatic success that fully justified MacArthur's confidence. After naval gunfire and close air support blasted Wolmi-do into virtual submission on 13 September, US and Korean marines landed on three beaches at or near Inch'on two days later. Light opposition was soon overwhelmed and by nightfall the harbour area was secure, while the city itself was under UN control the next day. X corps seized the vital airfield at Kimp'o on 17 September and entered the outskirts of Seoul five days later. Fighting in the city was intense, and casualties heavy, but the capital was completely in UN hands by 28 September. Meanwhile, the rest of Eighth Army had broken out of the Naktong perimeter and, moving rapidly northwest, linked up with X corps some 60 kilometres south of Seoul, near Osan, on 27 September.

With no real threat to the LSA, the main duty of TG 91.2 was to mount the inshore blockade and harass the enemy ashore. *Athabaskan's* patrol from 22 to 29 September demonstrated just how effectively destroyers could intervene in the land battle when things were quiet at sea. On the night of 22 September she stood by an American destroyer landing a party of US Marines near Namp'o. The next day *Athabaskan* and a South Korean patrol boat entered the small port of Pory'on-po, just north of Kunsan, and, in Commander Welland's words, *"bombarded gun pits and lookout points on the hillsides at point blank range, employing the 40mm armament as well as the 4 inch."*

*A group of about ten warehouses housing troops and stores, and the small harbour...in which were two motor junks were taken under fire at a range of 3200 yards. The 4 inch [high-explosive Direct Action] shell bursting inside the buildings soon brought them down in ruins, but the target didn't catch fire and burn until the 40mm incendiary shells took effect. ROK 704 with his 3 inch gun wrecked the junks. One gun pit some distance inland was seen to fire an automatic weapon before it was taken under fire with the main armament.*[25]

On the morning of 25 September, *Athabaskan* and two ROK patrol boats carried out a reconnaissance in force against the enemy-held islands of Youjiki-do and P'iun-do, which commanded the entrance to Kunsan. *Athabaskan* landed a party of 30 volunteers on the latter but found it abandoned except for old people and children. The situation was different on Youjiki-do, where machine-gun fire prevented a landing. Two days later, after it was learned that the North Koreans had reinforced the garrison, *Athabaskan* and the Australian destroyer *Bataan* were ordered to bombard the island. With aerial spotting unavailable, *Athabaskan's* gunnery officer, Lieutenant C. A. Sturgeon, proceeded close inshore in a small boat and controlled the fire from both ships by voice radio. Welland recalled that *"the shoot for both ships was highly success-*

*ful; one target after another being systematically wiped out."*

On 28 September, the final day of the patrol, Welland proceeded north towards Inch'on after firing upon targets together with *Bataan*. When he was rounding one island, lookouts sighted *"hundreds of civilians"* digging trenches and preparing defensive positions. *Athabaskan* closed to 4,000 metres and fired 40 rounds of 4-inch ammunition that destroyed a number of trenches and bunkers. Human casualties were apparently minimal for, as Welland happily asserted, *"The United Nations policy of avoiding casualties was made easy on this occasion by the white clad Koreans themselves who displayed more speed than dignity in clearing the area long before the first salvo landed."* Then *Athabaskan* put into Inch'on where she refuelled, embarked Rear-Admiral Andrewes and his staff, and proceeded to Sasebo.

Although seaborne bombardment could play an effective role in harassing the enemy ashore, Andrewes questioned whether his ships should keep it up.

*I have for some time been a little worried about wastage of ammunition through ships carrying out what might be termed "casual" bombardments. To enliven a dull patrol it had become almost a habit for Commanding Officers to carry out bombardments of gun positions and strong points on the various islands, and coastline of the mainland. An unplanned and unobserved bombardment is not of great value and at the present time might do more damage to SOUTH KOREAN property than the harm to the enemy might warrant. I accordingly issued the following signal (timed 261202Z September): "When planning bombardments Commanding officers should consider carefully the expected damage and casualties which will be inflicted on the enemy and balance this against the damage to South KOREAN property and expenditure of ammunition."*[26]

Reducing the frequency of bombardments also meant reducing the threat from mines. After his preliminary operation against the islands of Youjiki-do and P'iun-do on 25 September, Welland had intended to take *Athabaskan* upriver to attack Kunsan, only to discover a mine blocking the channel. When he sent the ship's boats out to mark its location early the next day, they discovered two more. *"That rather put me off going into the river,"* Welland later recalled.

*...we anchored and got the sonar operating and with this, we managed to detect what we thought were about six or eight mines in this river. You know you get a little blippy echo back, and if [you're] patient enough you can sort them out. We waited until low water and the mines came to the surface, as the tides changed when it was low-water slack, the mines came to the surface and we destroyed them with the motor-boats firing machine-guns at them.*[27]

Welland's caution was justified. Mines could easily sink or cripple a warship the size of a destroyer and, with no navy or air force to speak of, they were the only real deterrent the enemy had against warships conducting a close blockade. The mining of the destroyer USS *Brush* on 26 September, which killed 13 sailors and wounded 34 others, emphasized the extent of the danger, and although no Canadian warships were mined over the course of the war, they had to remain constantly vigilant. Brock reported: *"The sudden laying of mines around the coasts of Korea by Communists has cast a new light on the Naval warfare, and has demonstrated conclusively the power that mines have of stopping coastal shipping."*[28]

Events now moved quickly. Despite threats of Chinese intervention, MacArthur received permission from the American joint chiefs of staff and the United Nations to push on north with the intention of reunifying the country by conquest. Flushed by victory, he now had in mind another major landing at the east coast port of Wonsan. Again navy planners argued against the operation and again they lost. However, this time MacArthur was embarrassingly wrong and probably saved from disaster only by the pace of the ground advance. On 10 October, the very day the 250-vessel assault force sailed for Wonsan, South Korean troops captured the city by land, but a dense minefield blocked the harbour and the minesweeping operation proved lengthy and hazardous – two USN minesweepers were lost with heavy casualties. It was not until 26 October that they could land, "to be greeted by grinning ROK's and jeering pilots of the First Marine Air Wing...."[29] Nevertheless, on the other side of the peninsula, P'yongyang had fallen on 17 October, and nine days later ROK troops reached the Yalu river. Victory looked to be at hand.

The Canadian destroyers still had plenty of work. *Athabaskan* had been assigned to the Wonsan landing not because she was needed, but because when operating north of the 38th Parallel the high command liked to include ships from as many countries as possible. Not surprisingly given the history of the operation, Commander Welland complained that Wonsan consisted of *"one anticlimax after another,"* and the only gloss that Captain Brock could put on the destroyer's seemingly endless steaming up and down the Sea of Japan with the amphibious force waiting for the harbour to be cleared of mines was that *"much valuable experience in fleet work was gained by 'Athabaskan' during these operations, on a scale never likely to be duplicated in peacetime exercises."*[30]

While *Athabaskan* criss-crossed the Sea of Japan, *Cayuga* and *Sioux* continued the west coast blockade and Brock was horrified by the plight of the Korean fishermen he encountered. During the run-up and aftermath of CHROMITE, fishermen inhabiting the coastal islands had been prevented from earning their livelihood, first by the North Koreans who thought they were supplying intelligence to UN forces, and then by South Koreans and UN authorities who feared they might be minelaying.[31] They were starving and Brock was determined to do something about it.

*In visiting these Western Korean Islands, the destitute state in which the natives had been left by the Communists came to my attention, and so on return to Sasebo at the end of September, I proposed a rehabilitation scheme to help them return to their self sufficiency, involving the visiting of each island, the assessment of damages inflicted, and donation of food and medical supplies, garrisons of ROK troops and police, and the establishing of fishing sanctuaries.*[32]

Senior officers lauded Brock's initiative, which he dubbed Operation COMEBACK, and although circumstances prevented him from leading the relief effort subsequently carried out by South Korean naval forces, he did conceive the organization and put it on the road to success.

Even though actual war-fighting was minimal, operations such as the three Canadian destroyers had been involved in took their toll. During one stretch in September, for example, *Sioux* was at sea for 22 days, and in a seven-week period in October and November *Athabaskan* burned 3,100 tons of fuel – 100 tons more than her entire annual peacetime allowance.[33] Such a high operational tempo, with machinery strained to the limit and sailors standing watch after watch, was enough to run down a ship and its company. Sasebo was too crowded, too squalid and too close to the war zone to provide much respite, so

UN destroyers routinely stopped vessels in search of contraband or information.
After *Nootka* interrogated the crew of this junk, they exchanged bread for fresh fish. (DND NK-702)

Admiral Andrewes sent his ships in rotation to Hong Kong where there was a dockyard and recreational opportunities ashore for the sailors. The Canadians' turn came in November, and their rest period provides us an opportunity to step away from operations and briefly consider issues related to logistics, health and morale.

Effective logistical support is essential in keeping ships at sea, but in Korea, according to Captain Brock, the Canadian destroyers fell under the definition of beggars and borrowers. With no afloat logistics capability of their own, limited strategic air lift and no bases in-theatre, they had to acquire much materiel from American and British sources. This did not present a problem in the short term as there were arrangements in place between the RCN and USN for common logistical support and because *such stores as the Royal Navy could spare were unhesitantly [sic] placed at the disposal of H.M.C. Ships.*[34] That said, it was still often difficult to obtain purely naval stores from navies who were understandably reluctant to part with equipment or spares they might soon need themselves. Replacing RCN pattern clothing was a particular problem as this could only be obtained from Canada at the other end of a three-month supply line.

Sailors could endure delays in acquiring kit or canteen items – "SNAFU," they might grumble – but they were not nearly as patient when it came to mail delivery. The personal lifeline to home was critical to morale. Men needed to know what their families or girlfriends were up to and, just as importantly, needed to know that the home front knew what they were up to, but for the first two months of the deployment to Korea mail delivery was sporadic at best and was prone to long delays. Brock, who as the administrative authority had to bear the brunt of the criticism, pointed the finger squarely at the Fleet Mail Offices.

*It appeared [he complained to headquarters] that attempts were being made to follow slavishly a set of inadequate peace-time regulations regarding mails to and from ships cruising [in peacetime], and to overlook such aspects as operational commitments, wireless silence, communication difficulties, movements of ships without notice, separation of Canadian units, etc.*[35]

In other words, they were at war, and peacetime red tape should not thwart the needs of fighting sailors. As it was, the start of routine RCAF flights to Korea solved the mail problem, but a sour taste was nonetheless left in the mouths of Canadian sailors.

At least the crews stayed healthy. Their messing was excellent; indeed Brock thought his men had the best food of any Commonwealth navy in Korea and that this was largely responsible for the good health of Canadian sailors. Not surprisingly, the major medical problem was venereal disease. Brothels were plentiful in Sasebo and the incidence was high. Medical stores had been augmented before they left Esquimalt to treat the range of tropical diseases that might be encountered, but most complaints involved the usual colds, skin infections and influenza.

When the three ships sailed from Hong Kong on 16 November 1950 after their rest and recuperation, there was below-deck scuttlebutt about being home for Christmas. Such rumours were not far off the mark. *"The war appeared to have been going so well,"* Rear-Admiral Andrewes wrote in his November report, *"that preliminary arrangements could be made to release a part of the British, Commonwealth, and Allied ships employed on the West Coast of KOREA."*[36] As part of these arrangements, preliminary plans were being formulated to send two of the RCN destroyers home *"very soon,"* with the third following shortly in their wake.[37]

The collapse of the North Korean army had already caused a reorganization of the west coast blockade force. Andrewes withdrew the carrier *Theseus* and the cruiser *Kenya* to Hong Kong, leaving *Ceylon*, seven destroyers and four frigates to carry out the blockade. All three Canadian ships remained with the west coast squadron for the time being,[38] and on 20 November they began what likely would have been their last patrol had the land war not changed dramatically for the worse. On 25 November the Chinese "People's Volunteer" Army, which had been trickling across the Yalu for some weeks, gathered itself and launched a massive counter-attack against the Eighth Army.

Within hours of the Chinese attacks the UN forces were in retreat on all fronts. In a summation contrasting sharply with his enthusiastic "on the verge of victory" report just a few weeks earlier, Admiral Andrewes described a situation teetering on the edge of disaster.

*By 4th December, 1950, the Chinese Communist drive in North KOREA had driven a wedge between the United States Eighth Army in the West and the Tenth [US] Corps in the East. The Eighth Army was retreating southward and PYONGYANG was about to fall into enemy hands. A section of the Eighth Army was in danger of being cut off north of the CHOPPEKI Peninsula, and plans were being made for the evacuation of United Nations Forces from the port of CHINNAMPO. In the east the First Marine Division had been cut off near CHOSIN reservoirs, and was fighting its way south towards HUNGNAM to join up with the remainder of the Tenth Corps. It was planned to withdraw these troops by sea from HUNGNAM and land them again at PUSAN.*[39]

In a hurriedly drawn-up plan, amphibious group commanders were given control of naval forces at maritime evacuation points. On the west coast Rear-Admiral Thackrey, USN, was in charge of the arrangements at Inch'on, while further north Captain S. G. Kelly, USN, commanded the evacuation at Chinnamp'o. Rear-Admiral Andrewes's cruiser and destroyer force was to lend support when required, while *Theseus* provided air cover. Brock, with *Cayuga, Athabaskan* and *Sioux*, the Australian destroyers *Warramunga* and *Bataan*, and the American destroyer *Forrest Royal*, was in command of TE 95.12 in Area SHELTER, at the western entrance to the Chinnamp'o river, ready to answer any call for assistance from Captain Kelly, who had taken five transports upstream on 4 December.

As with Inch'on, the problem at Chinnamp'o was exacerbated by its geographical setting. Serving as the port to P'yongyang (just as Inch'on did to Seoul), the city lay about 35 kilometres from the sea, at the end of a shallow, narrow, serpentine channel, through which USN and ROKN minesweepers had swept an even narrower channel. Early on 4 December, Brock received orders from Andrewes to be prepared to cover Kelly's transports at Chinnamp'o and provide fire support to the withdrawing ground forces as the evacuation proceeded. That evening he was informed that his ships would be required in Chinnamp'o no later than noon the next day.

Brock promptly signalled Kelly: *"Indicate degree of urgency for destroyers support [in] inner harbour. Will attempt night passage of river if essential otherwise arrive early morning."*[40] Meanwhile, he called a meeting of his commanding officers, all of whom apparently counselled against a night passage – something no UN ship had previously attempted. However, while Brock waited for a response from Kelly, a panicked signal arrived from one of the American ships now lying alongside at Chinnamp'o. *"We are uncovered,"* it complained. *"Take necessary action immediately."* A signal from Kelly shortly afterwards, reporting that the situation in Chinnamp'o *"may reach emergency basis,"* seems to have confirmed his fears. Brock took this to mean that the situation was grave and he ordered his

force upriver immediately. Commander Welland noted bluntly that the passage was one that *"a prudent navigator would regard with misgivings [even] with a high tide or a sunny day."*[41] Brock's ships would have neither.

At 2230 hours the six destroyers set off upstream at five knots an hour, in the order *Cayuga, Athabaskan, Bataan, Forrest Royal* and *Sioux*, with *Warramunga* proceeding separately. The tide was approaching high water and, according to Welland, it was *"one of the blackest nights I have seen."*[42] *Warramunga* ran aground shortly before midnight, and after working herself free she withdrew to the SHELTER area in order to check for damage. About half an hour later *Sioux* also ran into trouble, touching bottom *"although well within the limits of swept channel."* Commander Taylor skilfully worked his ship free, only to run afoul of a channel marker that had broken loose from its mooring and drifted into the channel. The damage caused heavy vibration in the starboard shaft and, not wanting to break down completely and block the channel, Taylor reluctantly followed *Warramunga* back to sea. Brock was now down to four destroyers.

The burden of getting their ships safely to Chinnamp'o fell on the navigation officers, and it fell heaviest on Lieutenant A. L. Collier, navigator in *Cayuga* at the head of the line. *"It was pitch-black,"* he recalled:

*I was, as you'd expect, in the [Operations] room, you couldn't see anything up top. What concerned us was that most of the buoys marking the swept channel were spherical buoys, so they didn't really show up on radar very well and they were kind of hard to see. We saw the odd one going in but it was basically navigating up, for all of us, using our old 293 radar, following one after the other.*[43]

Throughout the four-hour passage, Collier obtained some 132 fixes, about one every two minutes. *"We only got a bit of a scare once,"* he remembered, *"when the ship didn't seem to be answering her helm fast enough, that was mainly because of the [rising] flood tide. She just caught it a bit."*

Astern of *Cayuga, Athabaskan* had a navigational advantage over her sister ship. Prior to leaving Esquimalt, her navigator, Lieutenant R. H. Leir, RCN, had grabbed a crated LN 16 high-definition navigational radar set from stores, but had been unable to get it fitted until just before Chinnamp'o. Its effectiveness was still an unknown quantity when the ships left SHELTER (which may have been why *Athabaskan* did not lead), but Leir took full advantage of it in the run-up to Chinnamp'o, using it to acquire close-range bearings that the Type 293 surface-warning radars in the other destroyers missed. In his report, Welland noted that 189 radar fixes were charted during the passage – some 50 more than in *Cayuga* – providing firm evidence of the effectiveness of the set.[44] The lesson was not lost and all future RCN contributions to the Korean War would be fitted with high-definition navigational radar.

When *Cayuga, Athabaskan, Bataan* and *Forrest Royal* anchored off Chinnamp'o shortly before 0300 hours on 5 December, the urgency that had sparked their hazardous passage was nowhere in evidence. Lights, not guns, blazed ashore, and when Brock contacted Captain Kelly to suggest they hold a planning meeting at once, the American told him to wait until after breakfast. *"That made old Brock pretty furious, I'll tell you,"* recalled Collier.[45] As it turned out, no Chinese were yet within 30 kilometres of the city, although they were still pressing south.[46]

If the transports were to clear the estuary by nightfall, they would have to depart by mid-afternoon. Once they had left, Brock's ships would shoot up any materiel left on the waterfront so that it would not fall into enemy hands. The plan went awry only when it became apparent in the early afternoon that the harbour would not be clear of the many vessels carrying refugees trying to escape Chinnamp'o and pass down the swept passage in time for Brock to conduct his bombardment on schedule. The situation was resolved by sending *Athabaskan* downriver to establish a defended anchorage some eight kilometres west of the city. That would allow the remaining destroyers to conduct the bombardment later in the evening and then take refuge with *Athabaskan* overnight.

After destroying three pillboxes overlooking the selected anchorage, *Athabaskan* spent a busy afternoon ensuring the safety of both the anchorage and the escape route.

*The townspeople fearing the destruction of their city were fleeing in every manner of craft, mostly sailing junks. As mines have been laid from junks it was considered prudent to search these laden craft in the event of such a plan. Both the ship's motor cutters were detached on this duty and before darkness fell their crews had boarded 35 craft. The boarding Officer on pulling aside a tarpaulin in one overcrowded junk was greeted with a complaining "MOO" from a black and white cow. There were no mines.*[47]

At Chinnamp'o the last of 7,700 soldiers were embarked at 1700 hours and 35 minutes later Brock opened fire on targets along the harbour front, including railway lines, oil tanks, supply dumps and factories. The result was spectacular.

*The fires started by the military [demolition squads] were sufficient, in the dusk, to indicate very clearly the target areas, and more fires were started by the opening broadsides. As darkness fell, the fires became more and more brilliant, making the whole waterfront as bright as day; great balls of fire rose from the explosions to dissolve into the huge pall of black smoke which was drifting slowly to the southeast. Whenever a fresh oil tank was hit, which was often, sprays of molten glowing metal were radiated in all directions, adding spectacularly to the show. Fires were observed and explosions heard until 0615...the following morning.*[48]

At 1845 hours the three destroyers joined *Athabaskan*, and next morning, with the smoke from Chinnamp'o still billowing skyward, they transited the Daido-ko into the Yellow Sea. They were greeted with great acclaim. Rear-Admiral Andrewes informed them the operation *"was a fine feat of seamanship, on the part of all concerned, and its bold execution was worthy of the finest traditions of the Naval Service."*[49] Brock was universally praised for his leadership and was made a member of the Distinguished Service Order. Collier was awarded a Distinguished Service Cross, and several others were also decorated. Chinnamp'o marked a professional high point in seamanship and was perhaps the Royal Canadian Navy's finest moment in the Korean War.

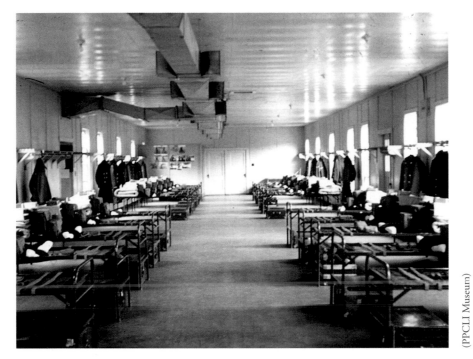

Quarters at Currie Barracks, Calgary, where many Special Service Force recruits were trained.

(PPCLI Museum)

## CHAPTER III

# *The Special Force*

ON 30 JUNE 1950, the day that Parliament prorogued for its summer vacation, the Active Force component of the Canadian Army numbered 20,369 all ranks, mustered in three infantry regiments each of one battalion: the Royal Canadian Regiment (RCR), the Princess Patricia's Canadian Light Infantry (PPCLI) and the Royal 22e Régiment (Vingt-deuxième, or Van Doos – R22eR), two armoured regiments, the Royal Canadian Dragoons (RCD) and Lord Strathcona's Horse (LdSHs); their supporting arms, in the form of one regiment of artillery, the Royal Canadian Horse Artillery (RCHA), field engineers (RCE) and signallers (RCSigs); together with transport (RCASC), ordnance (RCOC), engineer workshops (RCEME), and smaller medical, dental, provost and intelligence units that serviced what was colloquially known as "the sharp end."

Some officers and men from every branch of the service were committed to essential staff, administrative and training functions, and there were probably not enough left to form a brigade group – the smallest formation that could hope to operate independently in time of war – for the defence of Canada, never mind send an expeditionary force halfway around the world. In the words of Lester Pearson, secretary of state for external affairs:

> Canadian defence policy...had been based on the concept of providing a small, highly-skilled regular army, charged with responsibility of doing its immediate share of North American defence, especially in the Arctic, and designed to be capable of rapid expansion in the event of a general war.... The furnishing to the United Nations on short notice of expeditionary forces capable of quick deployment in distant areas... had not...entered into our planning.[1]

"Rapid expansion" and "quick deployment" were relative terms. Even recruiting and training an infantryman, the core of any combat force, took six months. It took twice as long to train a competent gunner, field engineer (called "sappers," because originally their prime responsibility had been to dig siege trenches, or saps) or signaller.

A contribution of one infantry battalion, which might possibly have been spared from the Active Force, would have seemed laughable and, lacking any supporting arms and services of its own, it would have had to depend entirely upon the uncertain favour of some larger, foreign force – American or British – for even the most minor items of logistical support. The United States, anxious to see other national contingents fighting under the United Nations banner for political and propaganda reasons, would no doubt have been willing to equip and support a Canadian battalion, but in 1950 it would have been impracticable for the Canadian Army to rely entirely upon American resources. The Imperial tie was still too strong outside of Ottawa and Quebec and, practically, every aspect of equipment and training would have had to be radically altered.

The British, with a larger army but also with far larger responsibilities, committed themselves to an independent brigade group – infantry, with their own integral supporting arms and services – by 25 July, and the chairman of the Canadian chiefs of staff, Lieutenant-General Charles Foulkes, visualized a brigade group from Canada. This hypothesis of a second brigade or brigade group from Canada and the possibility of a third from other Commonwealth countries – Australia and New Zealand came to mind, and perhaps India and Pakistan! – raised the political spectre of a Commonwealth division, but Ottawa, despite its dependence on British military doctrine and equipment, was reluctant to accept any appearance of Imperial unification. "Operations in Korea should have the aspect of *United Nations* operations," the Canadian High Commissioner in London was told. "It is in discharge of obligations under the Charter [of the United Nations] that our troops will be serving and not in any sense as members of the Commonwealth."

> We are not in favour of...a Commonwealth Division, as such, but we are in favour of troops from the various Commonwealth nations serving in the same divisional formations, and this for obvious reasons of efficiency and convenience.
>
> ...We realize that when, in fact, forces from the various Commonwealth Nations are brought together it may prove impossible to prevent the press and the public from referring to the division in which they serve as a "Commonwealth Division".... We trust...that the term will not be used officially or even unofficially by the participants. Perhaps the acceptance at an early stage of some such name as "The United Nations First Division" would help.[2]

The British, disinclined to forgo their traditional status as first among equals, proposed "First (Commonwealth) Division, United Nations Forces," and Ottawa reluctantly accepted that terminology, but, once the division was actually formed, media convenience and the insatiable military appetite for abbreviations (in this case to "1 Comwel Div") would soon eliminate the brackets and the UN suffix: 1 Commonwealth Division it would be.

The only way Canada could provide a brigade group at relatively short notice was to raise one by recruiting and training it from scratch, and the formation of the Canadian Army Special Force (CASF) was authorized by Order-in-Council on 7 August 1950. It would be an infantry brigade group composed of approximately 5,000 all ranks, recruited from Second World War veterans, the Reserve Force, the Supplementary Reserve, young men in search of adventure and perhaps older men in search of a job. All would be enlisted for a period of 18 months, or longer if "required in consequence of any action undertaken by Canada pursuant to an international agreement or where the term of service expires during an emergency or within one year of the expiration thereof."[3] In the event, the bulk of the brigade was recruited off the street from among veterans and novices in approximately equal numbers, and probably half of the rest came from the Reserves. However, a considerable proportion of senior officers and non-commissioned officers of the more technically inclined units had to be drawn from the Active Force.

The administrative process of enlisting the thousands of volunteers that promptly appeared at recruiting depots across the country commenced at a rate only slightly faster than the usual peacetime pace, but the minister of national defence, Brooke Claxton, goaded by the media, was in a hurry. After visiting the personnel depot in Toronto, he noted that "in the [first] two days they had fully processed something like 50 per day, whereas up to Wednesday night they had 657 applicants," most of them expecting to join the infantry. The selection procedure was too elaborate, he argued. Physical examinations could be carried out more speedily, and "interviews should be reduced to five or ten minutes. Documentation could well be done when the man arrived at his unit. He wanted the men attested and posted, in one day."[4]

This hastening process was a two-edged sword. It enrolled men quickly but also enabled a considerable number of thoroughly unsuitable candidates to slip through the meshes of physical and psychological testing. Among them, allegedly, were a man with an artificial leg and a man who was 72 years old,[5] and there were certainly some with minor criminal records. Major R. C. D. Laughton, appointed to command 54 Transport Company, RCASC, at Camp Borden, later remembered *"going out on the parade square to meet the beginnings of my unit...and watching the men as they walked on. One chap was in white running-shoes, with a newspaper in his hip pocket and wearing a sweat shirt."* That might not be considered unusual in the 21st century, but in 1950 it was informality carried to an extreme. *"I found out later that he was a member of the Beanery Gang from Toronto. We got chaps from that kind of background."*[6] In London, when an officer asked one group of recruits how many of them had spent time in prison, "the entire room of men stood up, except Don Hibbs. *'I'd never spent a day in jail in my life,'* Hibbs remembers thinking. *'Yet there I was, the only guy seated in a roomful of criminals!'* So he stood up to make it unanimous."[7]

Of course, time spent in jail did not necessarily mean a man would not make a good soldier, and the vast majority of applicants were physically, psychologically and morally fit for service. On 18 August the chief of the general staff reported to Cabinet that the CASF had enlisted the necessary 5,000 men and recommended that another 5,000 be recruited to provide for wastage over the next 12 months. The estimated wastage rate, based on Second World War rates, soon ceased to have any relevance, however.

> There were abnormally high discharges during the period of training in Canada and the USA, and unexpectedly low casualties and sickness when the brigade saw action in Korea. Thus, while there was a constant scramble for recruits during the training period, there was never any lack of reinforcements once the brigade took the field, except for a short period when French-speaking enlistments dropped off.[8]

Indeed, many of the later recruits had to wait until the first major troop rotation began, in October 1951 and March 1952, before they reached Korea, and some did not get there until the final rotation in 1953.

If some of the men recruited were undesirables for one reason or another, the same could not be said of their senior officers, who were, without exception, admirable men and experienced soldiers. Brigadier John Meredith Rockingham, DSO and Bar, Australian-born, aged 39, was appointed to command what was soon designated 25 Canadian Infantry Brigade Group. Rockingham, a Second World War recruit who had distinguished himself while commanding first the Royal Hamilton Light Infantry and then 9 Infantry Brigade, had returned to civilian life after the war and was currently a transport company executive in British Columbia. He had, however, retained a connection with the militia, and in 1948 had been appointed to command 15 (Reserve) Infantry Brigade.

Rockingham was allowed to choose his own officers from the Active Force or the Reserves, or to recruit them from among veterans of the Second World War, as he saw fit. The most important selections were those to command the three infantry battalions, numbered as second battalions of the three existing regiments, and for those appointments he chose one serving soldier and two Second World War veterans from civil life. The regular, Lieutenant-Colonel Robert A. Keane, DSO, aged 36, who had commanded a motorized infantry battalion in northwest Europe and now wore the badges of the RCR, was given 2 RCR. The volunteers were James R. Stone, DSO, MC, aged 41, who had risen from private soldier to commanding officer of the Loyal Edmonton Regiment, appointed to command 2 PPCLI, and Jacques A. Dextraze, DSO and Bar, aged 31, who had followed a similar route in rising through the ranks of Les Fusiliers Mont-Royal and would now command 2 R22eR.

The three were given a free hand in selecting their own officers, most of the senior ones also being veterans of the Second World War and about half of them decorated. Two thirds of the commanding officers of the smaller units and sub-units, all of which had a more technical aspect, were found from the Active Force, but they, too, were mostly decorated veterans of the previous war.

An undecorated company commander was Major John Firth of 2 PPCLI. On the outbreak of the Second World War, Second Lieutenant Firth of the Dufferin and Haldimand Rifles, a militia regiment that was not mobilized for active service, had promptly relinquished his commission to join the Royal Hamilton Light Infantry as Private Firth. By April 1943, when Rockingham had first taken command of the RHLI (for six months), Firth was a captain, and when Rockingham briefly resumed command in mid-July 1944, Major Firth led B Company until he was wounded on Normandy's Verrières Ridge later that month. When his old CO's appointment to command the Special Force was announced, Firth, now employed as a parole officer, cabled his congratulations and offered his services.

Off to Fort Lewis! 21 November 1951.
Little did these gunners know that they would face
danger later that day. (RCA Museum)

The collision at Canoe River, British Columbia, killed 17 gunners and four
trainmen. Another 49 gunners were injured. (RCA Museum)

A Canadian military band plays to 2 PPCLI, who on 25 November 1950 sailed from Seattle,
Washington, in USNS *Private Joe P. Martinez*. (PPCLI Museum)

It took 20 days to cross the Pacific. Card playing was a diversion.
(PPCLI Museum)

Brigadier John Rockingham (left foreground) and Lieutenant-Colonel J. R. Stone, 2 PPCLI
(right foreground), two experienced and forceful battlefield commanders. (PA 133399)

General Douglas MacArthur, UN Commander in Korea until his dismissal
by US President Harry Truman on 11 April 1951. (PPCLI Museum)

*Nothing happened for a few days. The railway strike was on at the time I remember. Then one day some Provincial Police officers called at my house and told me I was to report to Army Command at Oakville.*

*At Oakville somebody shook my hand and said, "Congratulations, Major Firth. You're to command a company of the Patricia's in Korea. You leave Monday." Just like that. And it was Friday! Well, I finally settled for eleven days to clear up my affairs.*[9]

Lieutenant Thomas Webb had joined the RHLI in 1946, after serving in the army during the latter part of the war but not getting overseas. *"Not being able to relate personally to the Friday night mess stories of taking the Casino [at Dieppe], landing in Normandy and so on, I decided to see what it was really like for myself."* As the Patricias' liaison officer with an American armoured/mechanized infantry group, "Task Force Dolvin," Webb would be with the first UN troops to re-cross the 38th Parallel in May 1951 during the United Nations' second offensive. He was subsequently wounded in the arm and shoulder while serving with 2 R22eR and eventually returned to Hamilton well able to hold his own in the realm of Friday night mess stories.[10] Two other officers and "about 60 other ranks" of the RHLI also joined the Special Force, and many of those who returned would have equally exciting tales to tell.

> Regrettably the hurried circumstances under which the Special Force was enlisted and the fact that recruitment was not carried out through the Reserve system, meant that the Regiment kept no nominal roll of its members who joined the force. Over the intervening years the names of those RHLI other ranks who enrolled have been lost; Webb remembers that *"at least two of them were badly wounded but I cannot recall names."*[11]

Many other illustrious militia units had similar problems.

Rockingham's brigade staff was composed mostly of officers who had filled similar appointments in wartime and subsequently passed through the Canadian Army Staff College. The first brigade major – Rockingham's right-hand man on the operational side – was Major H. F. Wood, while the first Deputy Assistant Adjutant and Quartermaster-General (a cumbersome title always abbreviated to DAA&QMG – which was little better!) responsible for administration

and logistics was Major J. P. L. Gosselin. He held the appointment only very briefly, being Dextraze's choice for second-in-command of 2 R22eR, and was succeeded by newly promoted Major C. J. A. Hamilton, who had no shortage of work to keep him occupied.

> *While the units trained under General Rockingham's critical eye, I was deeply involved in personnel staff work. The scope of the work becomes clear when it is realized that almost the strength of one infantry battalion (approximately 900 men) was sent back to Canada [from Fort Lewis] on compassionate or disciplinary grounds. Many of the recruits had forgotten to make arrangements for their wives and families back in Canada.*[12]

In total, some 45 per cent of the Force were veterans of the last war, "and of that number 20 per cent were former non-commissioned officers (NCOs)."

Training became the responsibility of the parent Active Force units and began at different times in different places, but by 15 August it was in progress everywhere. Initially, officers and other ranks were separated, so that the former's training would not be disrupted by the need to concern themselves with the welfare of the latter, while their men – with a much smaller proportion of veterans – were trained by NCOs from their respective 1st Battalions, employing what was described as the "wheel system." That proved to be a major blunder. Too many men had family and/or marital problems, frequently involving finances and pay allotments, some self-inflicted and some due to the hasty recruiting procedures. With no officer to turn to for help, the victims were inclined to go home and try to sort things out for themselves.

By 1 October 1950, 2 R22eR reported 278 out of 919 men absent without leave, and on 5 October Major-General Chris Vokes "expressed concern over the high rate of [Absence Without Leave] in the Special Force Units in Central Command after 4 days leave. He described it as a symptom of our time and he felt that the sooner the 2 [Battalion officers] assume [command] of their troops the better."[13] A week later, Dextraze reunited the Van Doos' officers and men, and the former were instructed to attend to administration in the mornings and continue their own training in the afternoons. By mid-November, as the battalion prepared to entrain for Fort Lewis, nearly all the absentees were back.[14] Although 2 RCR, with approximately 65 per cent of the battalion being veterans "above average in physique and education," had far fewer absentees, on 15 October Keane (and Stone) followed suit.

In the supporting arms, where the proportion of Regular officers and NCOs was higher, training progressed more satisfactorily. Among the gunners, the first troop exercises in unlimbering a gun and getting it into action "produced timings as low as two minutes – the same standard used as a yardstick for towed 25-[pounder] troops in the Second World War."[15] The signals squadron, with a high percentage of veterans in its ranks, some of them having earlier seen service in the communications branches of the RCN and RCAF, also had few problems. Despite the sophisticated nature of much of the trades training for linemen and radio operators, by the end of October "an effective Signals Squadron began to appear."[16]

As far as Army Headquarters was concerned, how long training should be expected to take was a matter of some dispute – and with good reason, since the skills required differed from one type of unit to another and the extent to which former experience could be brought to bear varied considerably. In the end, the decision was left to Brigadier Rockingham: when he felt his brigade was ready to go to Korea, he should say so.

There seemed no desperate hurry. The Americans now had three divisions on the ground, and they and the remnants of the Republic of Korea (ROK) army had stopped the North Koreans in their tracks some 50 kilometres west of the deep-water port of Pusan, along the line of the Naktong river, and, at their furthermost point, twice that distance to the north. Putting it another way, the defenders were still holding a rectangle of ground nearly 100 kilometres wide and 150 kilometres deep in the southwestern corner of the peninsula. The American tactical airpower and troop reinforcements now pouring in left General MacArthur confident that this enclave could be held indefinitely, leaving time for other UN contingents to prepare for, and participate in, what might well prove to be a prolonged campaign to retake all of the lost ground.

As far as the Special Force was concerned, drill, physical and weapons training, and instruction in the niceties of military law and hygiene could be carried out in the fall weather, but collective tactical training would be difficult over the winter. The only part of Canada where the weather might cooperate was the west coast, and there was no large training area there. Consideration was given to putting the final polish on the brigade in Japan, and, when MacArthur vetoed that, on Okinawa – still Japanese territory but away from the home islands. At the end of September, however, a reconnaissance by Brigadier F. J. Fleury, the head of a newly created Canadian Military Mission, Far East, declared Okinawa unsuitable.

Even before Fleury reported, the situation in Korea had changed immeasurably for the better. On 15 September MacArthur had launched two American divisions – one Marine and one Army – in an amphibious assault directed on Inch'on, a small port about halfway up the west coast of the peninsula. It was wildly successful and immediately threatened the North Korean supply line to the south, compelling the enemy to pull back his forces besieging the Pusan enclave – although they did not go easily! The Americans and South Koreans followed them north and on 27 September the southern garrison and the Inch'on force linked up. On the last day of September they crossed the 38th Parallel, and everyone, including the United Nations, which established a Committee for the Unification and Rehabilitation of Korea (UNCURK) on 7 October, ignored Chinese premier Chou En-lai's warning (to the Indian ambassador) that his forces would intervene if the UN forces did not stop there. On 19 October, the day that South Korean troops occupied the North Korean capital of P'yongyang, Chinese "volunteers" began to cross the Yalu river, which formed the North Korean-Chinese border.[17]

MacArthur, full of confidence and either unaware of the Chinese intervention or unwilling to recognize its significance, now wanted only nominal contingents from his UN allies. Apparently still in ignorance of the many weaknesses that plagued his own troops, and prophesying that the fighting would be over by (American) Thanksgiving, he announced that "we have no fear of Chinese intervention...if the Chinese tried to get down to Pyongyang there would be the greatest slaughter." He was reluctant to accept any further UN contingents when he met President Truman and his entourage at Wake Island on 14 October. "They are useless from the military point of view and would probably never see action," MacArthur told the US Army chief of staff, General Omar Bradley. Their only value, he believed, was that "from the political point of view they give a United Nations flavour."[18]

Washington and Ottawa were now thinking in terms of the UN occupation forces – not so much a matter of fighting as one of policing the status quo – and 2 PPCLI, at Camp Wainwright, Alberta, was selected for the role because its training was the furthest advanced of the three infantry battalions and it was the closest to Seattle, the embarkation port for Japan and Korea.[19] Moreover, according to the official historian, Colonel Stone, it was judged by Rockingham to be *"the most suitable CO to work in an independent role, far from Canada and subordinate to British and American formations."*[20] Of course, if MacArthur's assessment should prove correct, the rest of the brigade would have been recruited to no purpose – even 2 PPCLI would not be doing what its members had enlisted to do.

Morale plummetted.

Nevertheless, a third PPCLI battalion was formed at the end of the year and then went to join 2 RCR and 2 R22eR on the west coast of the United States, at Fort Lewis in the state of Washington, for collective training. The move was made by train – it took 2 RCR four days from Petawawa and 2 R22eR five days from Valcartier. No. 2 RCHA, commanded by Lieutenant-Colonel A. J. B. Bailey, DSO, and with a third of its strength recruited from other veteran gunners, could look forward to a shorter trip, from Shilo, Manitoba, but met with disaster on their journey west. Two trainloads of gunners – 40 officers and 639 other ranks (the guns travelled separately on a freight train) – left Shilo, but the second train never reached Fort Lewis. Having crossed Yellowhead Pass, it was involved in a head-on collision with the Vancouver–Montreal express near Canoe River, British Columbia, apparently caused by a misunderstanding over where the two trains were to pass each other.*

The two trains met on a sharp curve, which meant little warning with absolutely no opportunity to stop in time, and both engine crews were killed. The coaches of the eastbound train were steel and no one in them was seriously hurt when the leading ones derailed, but the gunners were travelling in old, wooden, "colonist" cars, some of which crashed down an embankment. Fire then broke out, complicating the rescue of the living and recovery of the dead. The regiment's medical officer was travelling on the first train and the only medical help immediately available was provided by a regimental medical orderly who did *"a yeoman's job"* in tending the injured.[21] Seventeen were killed, many of them by fire, and 33 others burned or otherwise seriously hurt. The uninjured survivors were taken back to Camp Wainwright, where losses were replaced from the Active Force

regiment and the additional battery that had been formed to handle reinforcements. Another train departed for Fort Lewis on 29 November, and this time, instead of the officers' car being the last one, as usual, *"the officers' car was [immediately] behind the engine,"* recorded Lieutenant H. A. McLellan. *"No doubt that made the troops feel a little better."*[22]

The field component of CASF was now designated 25 Canadian Infantry Brigade Group and training began forthwith. Fort Lewis, situated 28 kilometres southeast of the state capital, Olympia, enjoyed a relatively mild winter climate but its outstanding characteristic was its rainfall. The RCR reported that *"we had arrived in a nice wet soggy climate,"* and then discovered, to the commanding officer's dismay, that the *"American troops' deportment is very slack and there is already a noticeable effect upon our men.... The CO has stressed the need of rigid control.... He has emphasized his intention to make the price of poor soldiering on our troops' part very high."*[23] As for the Americans, military and civilian, once they had come to terms with the curious titles that these foreign units bore and the fact that Lord Strathcona's *Horse* and the Royal Canadian *Horse* Artillery would not be leaving great steaming piles of dung on their streets, they treated these un-American soldiers with typical western kindness and hospitality.

The infantry trained hard and played hard, beginning with route marches that steadily increased in distance, from 10 kilometres to 30. Battle inoculation included obstacle courses negotiated under live fire directed just over the infantry's heads. When out of barracks, and not lucky enough to have tents, the men lay on the ground wrapped in their gas capes or greatcoats. *"Slept outside in zero weather,"* noted Private Ken McOrmond in his diary.

*Shaved in ice-encrusted water.... Platoon attack assisted by flame-throwing carriers, called Wasps. Sure like to stay near Wasp flames where it's warm.... I swear the cold, damp ground sucks all the warmth out of a person's body.... Some have a lousy night without tents. One lad must have prayed all night, because he kept calling out "Jesus Christ!"*[24]

Originally the armoured squadron, raised from elements of the Royal Canadian Dragoons, Lord Strathcona's Horse and the Armoured Corps School, together with veterans and militia volunteers, was labelled A Squadron, 1st/2nd Armoured Regiment, and put under Major James Quinn. His second-in-command, who would subsequently command the

---

* The railway signalman accused of being responsible was successfully defended (free of charge, because he thought the accusation unjust) by a lawyer from Prince Albert, Saskatchewan, who was also a back-bench Conservative MP, one John G. Diefenbaker.

Patricias receive a helping hand.
Moving in single file across a Korean valley to their next objective, troops of the PPCLI receive help from an elderly Korean as they reach a small stream of water. After seeing a rifleman slip into the water, he gathered rocks and placed them as stepping stones. 11 March 1951. (PA 114888)

Villages like this were typical. Men of 2 PPCLI follow retreating Chinese, March 1951. (PA 115564)

squadron himself, was Major Victor Jewkes, MC, who had joined the Royal Canadian Dragoons (in which his father was the regimental-quartermaster-sergeant) as a 14-year-old boy soldier in 1928.

Many years later, Lieutenant General Quinn recalled the days when the squadron was still at Camp Borden:

*For equipment we were told we were to get the M10[,] an antitank gun with a limited-traverse 17-pounder, mounted on a tracked [Sherman] chassis with an open turret. This bit of news, together with our unit designation, quickly made us the brunt of many jokes when we were referred to as "The Half [½] Armoured Squadron."*[25]

Arriving at Fort Lewis, they were indeed issued with M-10s, which proved to be

*highly unsatisfactory; the limited traverse of the turret severely constrained tactical employment in support of the infantry, and crews felt very vulnerable when they heard stories from Korea of enemy troops attacking similar open-top vehicles with grenades and mortars.*[26]

When Lieutenant-General Guy Simonds inspected the brigade before embarkation, Quinn took the opportunity to point these problems out and ask that his unit be equipped with a tank instead of the M-10. His wishes would be met shortly after the squadron arrived in Korea.

In few theatres of war have engineers ever had as important a part to play as they did in Korea. In 1950 the battlefield was very much a third-world country, and that, together with the nature of the terrain, meant that paved roads and bridges capable of bearing heavy loads were rare. There were, in fact, only about 80 kilometres of metalled road in all of South Korea.[27] A whimsical twin-track rail line, permitting an average speed of 18 kph,[28] ran from Pusan to the capital, Seoul, and a wide-meshed network of single tracks wound through the tangled hills, linking the terminals with minor ports on both coasts and those ports with each other. But some of the officers of 57 Field Squadron, RCE (and many of the NCOs and some of the sappers, too), had served in I Canadian Corps in 1943–44, when the Italian interior had sometimes posed similar problems. Moreover, the Regulars in the squadron had practised their skills in the Canadian north, building Bailey and timber trestle bridges and bulldozing roads through the bush. They needed little training in road construction. At Fort Lewis they honed specifically

military skills of demolitions and the intricacies of mine warfare. Their duties also included constructing observation towers, preparing field-firing target areas, setting up concertina wire, demonstrating minefield and gap-marking procedures, and providing simulated battle noise.[29]

The engineers' road- and bridge-building skills would prove vital for 54 Transport Company, RCASC, which went to Fort Lewis without any vehicles. Once there, they were issued 2½-ton GMC trucks – the reliable "deuce and a half" workhorses known to several generations of Canadian servicemen – which had been in storage. There was an awkward moment when the initial Chinese offensive led the Americans to demand the return of those vehicles when they were needed to replace trucks lost in the initial Korean débâcle, but more were supplied before long.

In March they were joined by the one officer and 26 other ranks of 38 Motor Ambulance Company, RCASC.

No. 2 PPCLI staged through Fort Lewis, en route to Seattle and embarkation, arriving on 21 November and departing on the 25th. Their brief sojourn at Fort Lewis did nothing for the morale of the two battalions left behind. *"Our men are feeling none too happy,"* recorded the RCR war diarist. *"To-night a number... made complete fools of themselves in Tacoma. Some of them were staggering around the streets improperly dressed and making general nuisances of themselves. In some cases junior NCOs were seen in the same condition, making no effort to straighten [out] either themselves or the troops."*[30]

Canada's "spit and polish" regiment seems to have been more upset by improper dress than public drunkenness, but neither were acceptable to the brigade's senior officers. Rockingham was very concerned *"over the number of cases of drunkenness in the brief time since units arrived in the area. He directed that units take control of the situation and further directed that the number of late passes granted not exceed 25% of unit strength per day."*[31] Drunkenness, perhaps inevitably, led to brawling, but in that regard Rockingham put on a brave public face. After a tangle between some Van Doos and American military policemen in a Post Exchange disintegrated into a full-fledged riot, a local reporter asked him, *"'What makes those men of yours so obstreperous?'... 'Well,'* answered Rocky, *'they're fighting men. That's what they're trained to be'."*[32]

Despite the uncertainty of Korean service, in early December Ottawa decided that the reinforcement streams recruited for the three infantry units should be formed into third battalions – 3 RCR, 3 PPCLI and 3 R22eR – and follow their brethren to Fort Lewis. No. 3 PPCLI was the first of these to appear, 432 recruits arriving just before Christmas and the battalion taking the place of their 2nd Battalion comrades who had gone to Korea.

> By the New Year Third Battalion was almost up to strength and it had taken over First Battalion's task of reinforcing Second Battalion in Korea. Thus the pattern was set that was destined to prove so exasperating. No sooner had strength been accumulated than it was taken away. The next two years were a constant tug-of-war between the requirements of the battalions in the field and the endeavours to build up and to maintain an individual identity.[33]

Unit identity is important. It creates cohesion, a vital element in producing a first-class fighting unit, and the problems created by uncertain identities may have had something to do with the somewhat lower standards that beset the first and third battalions of all three regiments during their tours in Korea.

Despite its considerable size, Fort Lewis did not offer all the facilities required by the gunners to practise their arcane arts, and their live firing was done on an artillery range at Yakima, some 140 kilometres to the east. This was a summer camp for the National Guard artillery and had never been used in winter before. According to Major J. S. Orton, MC, 2 RCHA'S second-in-command:

> It had miles of rolling hills and deep valleys, similar to conditions that would be met in Korea. But the camp was designed for summer only, the buildings were not winterized, and winter temperatures dropped below freezing. A detailed recce found the following: barracks for 80% of the [Other Ranks], one large kitchen, an office building, an officers' club, a small [Post Exchange] closed for the winter and no garage for the [Light Aid Detachment]. Nevertheless, Lt-Col Bailey decided these facilities were adequate. Authority to train there for six weeks with an allotment of 13,000 25-[pounder] rounds was requested and approved.
> ...The office space was completely inadequate – a large room and a couple of small offices. The battery offices consisted of a desk in the big room. It made an interesting sight to observe three orderly room [disciplinary] cases in the same room at the same time – always at night so they would not interfere with training....
> The training programme was based on battery and regimental exercises...using live ammunition. The ranges provided unlimited space, although roads were scarce and the ground was not completely frozen.... The CO ordered batteries to be ready to fire by first light; this meant a routine of reveille at 03:00 and the day's first deployment was always a night occupation. The regiment returned to camp late in the afternoon, so maintenance and administration had to be done in the evening....
> At the end of the training period the regiment was ready for any operation Korea had to offer.... To illustrate this spirit, one only has to recall the parade in Yakima prior to our departure. A delegation of ORs asked the CO to have a mounted parade through the city to show their appreciation of the citizens' hospitality.... The troops worked all night using blowtorches to remove frozen mud from the guns and vehicles. The parade was a tremendous success.[34]

On 8 January 1951, as a belated New Year's present, Rockingham was told by Ottawa that *"the possibility of the whole Brigade going to Korea could not be ruled out."* However, that welcome news was largely negated by an additional comment, *"if we did not go to Korea, we would probably be sent to Europe about 1 April 1951."*[35]

These changes had an effect on the status, within the Canadian Army, of the Special Force. Where formerly it had been regarded as a temporary addition, to be disbanded as soon as [the] need for it had passed, it now came to be considered a more or less permanent element of the Active Force.... However, the short terms of service under which the troops of the [Special] Force had enlisted made assumption of this new role difficult.... Re-engagement of these soldiers under Active Force regulations was required....

In execution the conversion plan did not enjoy a great success. Although Brigadier Rockingham set an example*...less than a third of the rank and file followed his lead. Peacetime soldiering had little appeal for these men. By the end of July, 1952 only 2,711 had joined the Active Force.[36]

---

* So did Lieutenant-Colonel Dextraze, who would rise to the rank of general and become chief of defence staff (1972–77).

The Fort Lewis training schedule culminated in a series of live-fire exercises dubbed by someone (Rockingham?), IGNES BELLUM – a snippet of dubious Latin that the graceless soldiery promptly translated into IGNORANT BEDLAM. IGNES BELLUM began with an infantry company in the advance, supported by an allotment of heavier weapons from the support company and a battery of field artillery. Each company was allotted one half day. The brigade war diary singled out the Van Doos – who had so often been singled out earlier for drunkenness and brawling – noting that the *"troops of 2 R22eR distinguished themselves by their vigour, enthusiasm and keenness and their high morale was the subject of very favourable comments from the Controllers."*[37] Next, in IGNES BELLUM II, came battalion attacks, each supported by all three batteries and a troop from the armoured squadron, followed by occupation of a defensive position. This time the Van Doos did not do as well: *"As was to be expected on this, the first real battalion scale exercise...there were many weaknesses, and it would have been possible for an enemy patrol to steal at least three Bren Guns, among other things...it is felt that the unit has learned its lesson...."*[38]

It had been intended that in IGNES BELLUM III the entire brigade would be exercised together, but only six hours after the last battalion, 3 PPCLI, completed IGNES BELLUM II, on Wednesday 21 February, *"the Brigadier received a telephone call from Lt-Gen Charles Foulkes [chairman of the chiefs of staff] to say that 25 Brigade would be going to Korea, any time after two weeks,"* recorded the brigade's historical officer, Captain G. D. Corry.[39] The third exercise was promptly cancelled. Personnel problems waiting their turn now needed to be solved at once, and vehicles and crew-served weapons had to be stripped down, cleaned and waterproofed, ready for the voyage to Korea.

This call from General Foulkes, apparently the delayed result of the Chinese intervention that had driven the UN forces back to a line about 60 kilometres south of the 38th Parallel in early January, followed by their fruitless "fourth-phase offensive" of mid-February 1951, pre-empted the earlier resolution by Ottawa to leave the decision in Rockingham's hands. He now "made plans to go to Ottawa for a conference with...Generals Foulkes and Simonds" – the latter being the army's chief of staff. "He left for Vancouver on Friday, spent some time with port authorities in Seattle, and went via TCA [Trans Canada Airlines] to Ottawa Saturday night."[40]

The following Wednesday, 28 February, Rockingham telephoned from Ottawa with the "definite" news that the brigade would not be leaving before 31 March, and IGNES BELLUM III – "the final controlled field firing scheme," involving "the three battalions...supported by 'A' Sqn, 1/2 Armd Regt and 2 RCHA" – was back in the timetable. "The exercise was done in three phases: 3 PPCLI attacked first, 2 RCR passed through, and 2 R22eR leap frogged to take the final objective." There was even time for Exercise SCRAMBLE to begin.

*This was intended to be a four day progressive scheme in which the Brigade would operate under operational conditions. Unfortunately the cold weather turned to rain and exposed the troops to the worst possible living conditions. In view of this and the little training value which would have been obtained had the exercise been continued, the Brigadier called a "cease fire" at 0200 [hours] on Monday [12 March 1951]. However even in this short time it was proved that the Brigade as an entity could move and operate in the field.*[41]

On 23 March Rockingham and Brigadier W. J. Megill (who had been appointed to command the brigade's Replacement Group) left for Korea on a personal reconnaissance, while the troops at Fort Lewis began a strenuous programme of physical conditioning, featuring hill climbing and forced marches, to prepare themselves for the rugged terrain and arduous battle conditions of Korea.

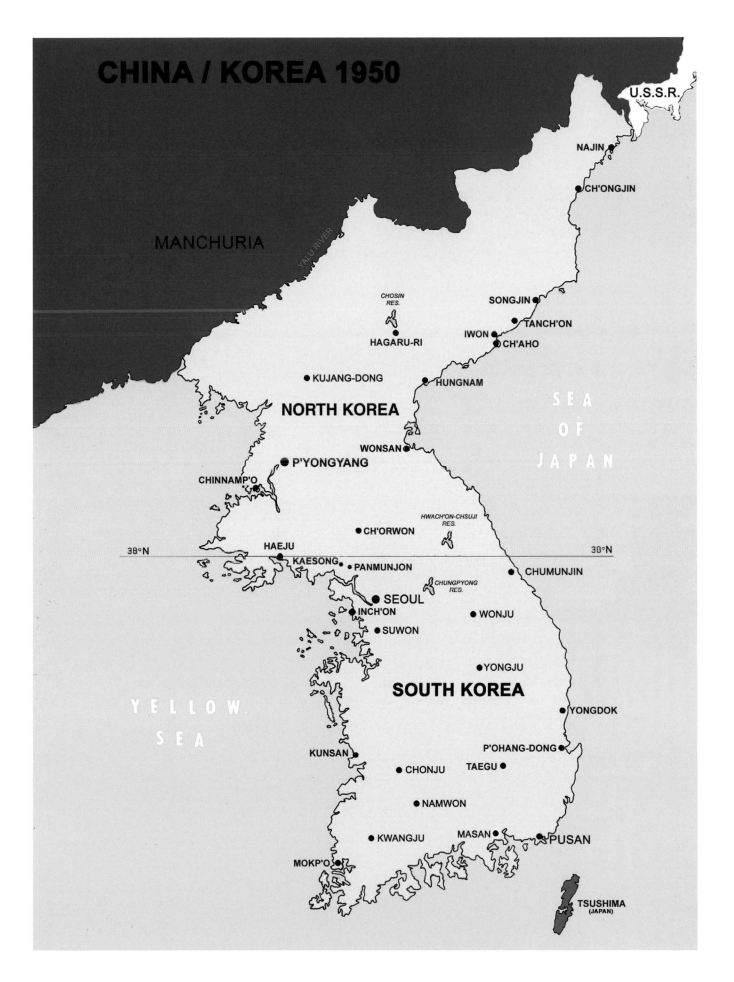

CHINA / KOREA 1950

U.S.S.R.

MANCHURIA

YALU RIVER

NAJIN

CH'ONGJIN

CHOSIN RES.

SONGJIN

TANCH'ON

HAGARU-RI

IWON

CH'AHO

KUJANG-DONG

HUNGNAM

NORTH KOREA

SEA OF JAPAN

WONSAN

P'YONGYANG

CHINNAMP'O

HWACH'ON-CHSUJI RES.

CH'ORWON

38°N                                                                              38°N

HAEJU

KAESONG    PANMUNJON

CHUMUNJIN

CHUNGPYONG RES.

SEOUL

INCH'ON

WONJU

SUWON

YONGJU

SOUTH KOREA

YONGDOK

YELLOW SEA

P'OHANG-DONG

KUNSAN

CHONJU

TAEGU

NAMWON

KWANGJU

MASAN

PUSAN

MOKP'O

TSUSHIMA (JAPAN)

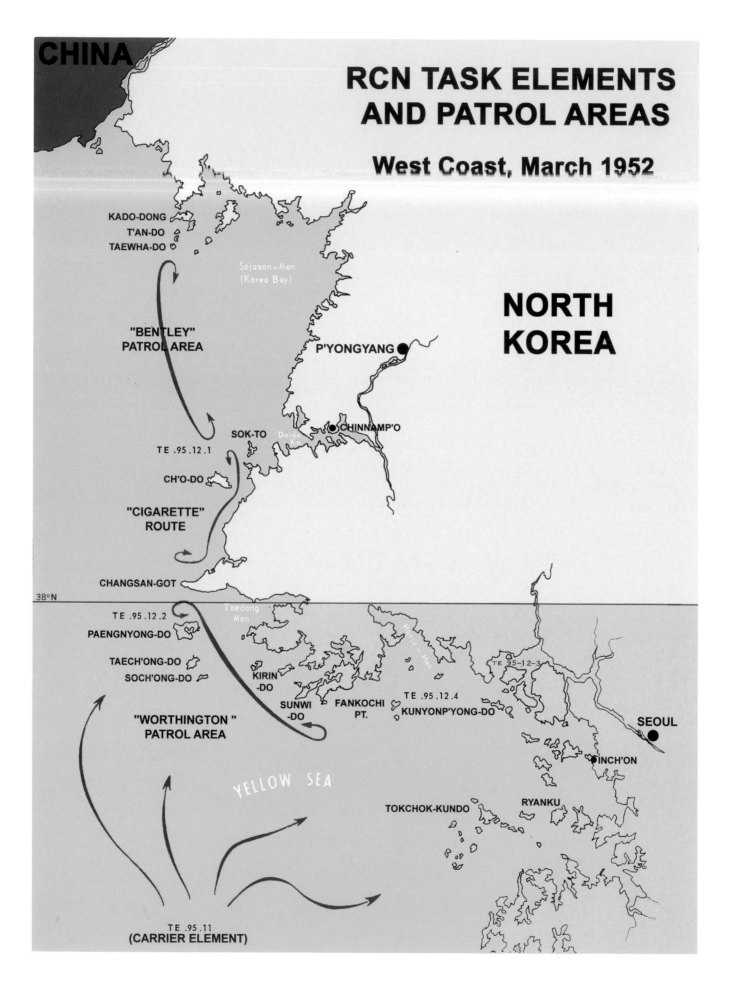

CHINA

# RCN TASK ELEMENTS AND PATROL AREAS

## West Coast, March 1952

KADO-DONG
T'AN-DO
TAEWHA-DO

Sojoson—Man
(Korea Bay)

**NORTH KOREA**

"BENTLEY" PATROL AREA

P'YONGYANG ●

TE .95 .12 .1

SOK-TO

Daido Ko

● CHINNAMP'O

CH'O-DO

"CIGARETTE" ROUTE

CHANGSAN-GOT

38°N

Taedong Man

TE .95.12.2

PAENGNYONG-DO

TAECH'ONG-DO
SOCH'ONG-DO

KIRIN -DO

Haeju — Man

TE 95-12-3

TE .95.12.4

SUNWI -DO

FANKOCHI PT.

KUNYONP'YONG-DO

SEOUL ●

"WORTHINGTON " PATROL AREA

● INCH'ON

YELLOW SEA

RYANKU

TOKCHOK-KUNDO

TE .95 .11
(CARRIER ELEMENT)

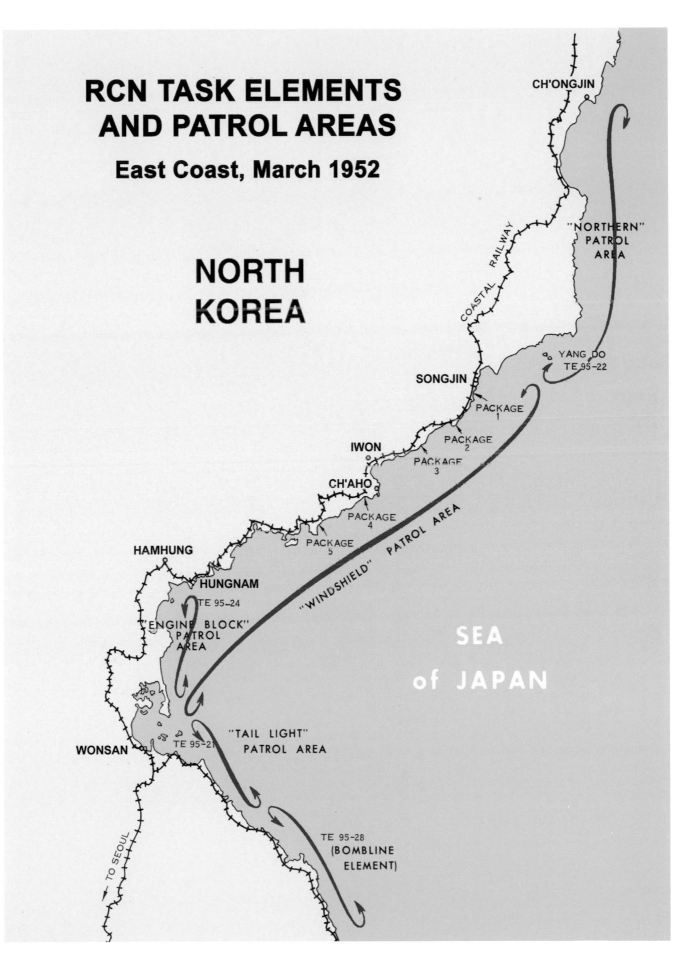

**RCN TASK ELEMENTS AND PATROL AREAS**

East Coast, March 1952

NORTH KOREA

CH'ONGJIN

"NORTHERN" PATROL AREA

COASTAL RAILWAY

YANG DO
TE 95-22

SONGJIN

PACKAGE 1

PACKAGE 2

IWON

PACKAGE 3

CH'AHO

PACKAGE 4

PACKAGE 5

HAMHUNG

"WINDSHIELD" PATROL AREA

HUNGNAM

TE 95-24

"ENGINE BLOCK" PATROL AREA

SEA of JAPAN

TE 95-21

"TAIL LIGHT" PATROL AREA

WONSAN

TO SEOUL

TE 95-28 (BOMBLINE ELEMENT)

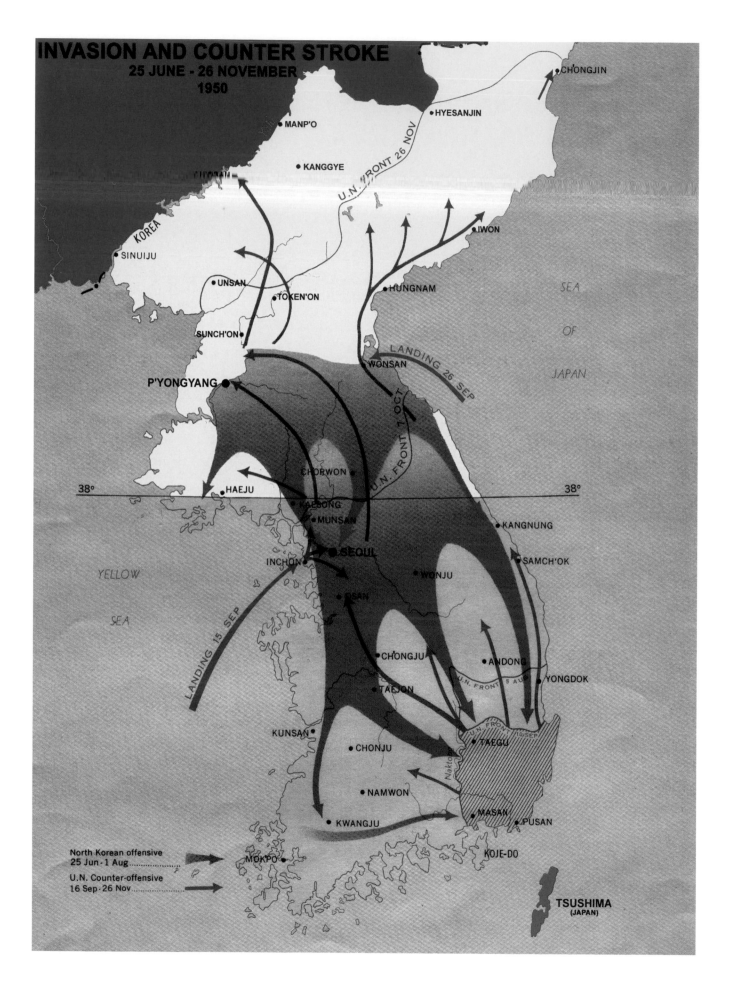

# INVASION AND COUNTER STROKE
## 25 JUNE - 26 NOVEMBER
### 1950

CHONGJIN

MANP'O
HYESANJIN

KANGGYE

CH'OSAN

KOREA

SINUIJU

IWON

UNSAN

TOKEN'ON

HUNGNAM

SUNCH'ON

WONSAN

P'YONGYANG

SEA

OF

JAPAN

LANDING 26 SEP

U.N. FRONT 26 NOV

U.N. FRONT 7 OCT

CHORWON

38°                                                                            38°

HAEJU

KAESONG

MUNSAN

KANGNUNG

SEOUL

INCHON

SAMCH'OK

WONJU

OSAN

YELLOW

CHONGJU

ANDONG

SEA

YONGDOK

TAEJON

U.N. FRONT 5 AUG

LANDING 15 SEP

KUNSAN

U.N. FRONT 10 SEP

TAEGU

CHONJU

Naktong

NAMWON

MASAN

PUSAN

KWANGJU

KOJE-DO

North Korean offensive
25 Jun - 1 Aug............

U.N. Counter-offensive
16 Sep - 26 Nov............

MOKPO

TSUSHIMA
(JAPAN)

52

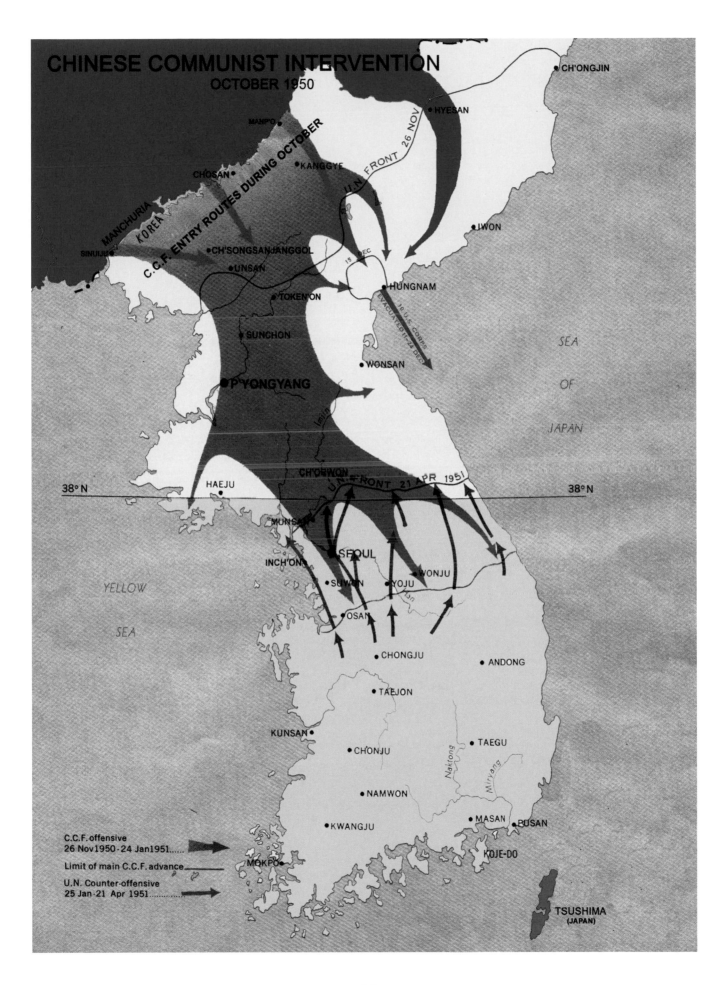

# CHINESE COMMUNIST INTERVENTION
## OCTOBER 1950

CH'ONGJIN

MANP'O

HYESAN

U.N. FRONT 26 NOV

CHOSAN
KANGGYE

MANCHURIA

KOREA

C.C.F. ENTRY ROUTES DURING OCTOBER

IWON

SINUIJU
CH'SONGSANJANGGOL

UNSAN

15 DEC

HUNGNAM

TOKEN'ON

EVACUATED 11-24 DEC

10 U.S. CORPS

SUNCHON

SEA

WONSAN

OF

P'YONGYANG

JAPAN

Imjin

CH'ORWON

U.N. FRONT 21 APR 1951

38° N                                                    38° N

HAEJU

MUNSAN

SEOUL

INCH'ON

WONJU

YELLOW

SUWON

YOJU

OSAN

SEA

CHONGJU

ANDONG

TAEJON

KUNSAN

CH'ONJU

Naktong

TAEGU

Miryang

NAMWON

MASAN

BUSAN

KWANGJU

KOJE-DO

C.C.F. offensive
26 Nov 1950-24 Jan 1951......

Limit of main C.C.F. advance_____

MOKPO

U.N. Counter-offensive
25 Jan-21 Apr 1951............

TSUSHIMA
(JAPAN)

53

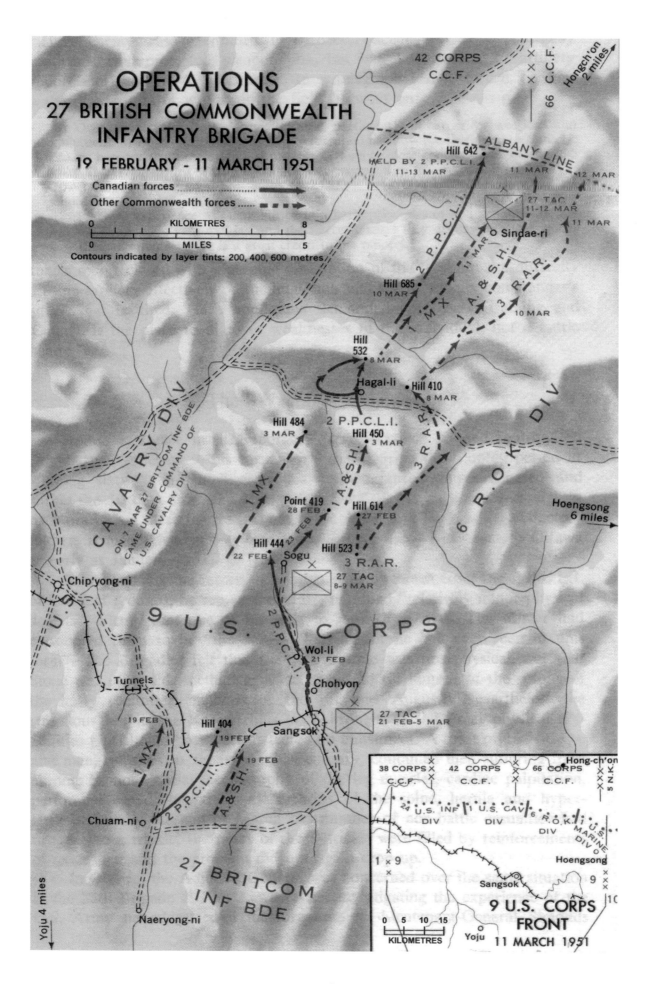

# OPERATIONS
## 27 BRITISH COMMONWEALTH INFANTRY BRIGADE
### 19 FEBRUARY - 11 MARCH 1951

Canadian forces ............→
Other Commonwealth forces ......→

KILOMETRES
0 ————————— 8
MILES
0 ————————— 5
Contours indicated by layer tints: 200, 400, 600 metres

42 CORPS
C.C.F.

×
×× C.C.F.
66 ×
Hongch'on
2 miles

ALBANY LINE

Hill 642
HELD BY 2 P.P.C.L.I.
11-13 MAR
11 MAR
12 MAR

2 P.P.C.L.I.
11 MAR

27 TAC
11-12 MAR

○ Sindae-ri
11 MAR

Hill 685
10 MAR

1 A. & S.H.

3 R.A.R.

'M X'
10 MAR

Hill 532
8 MAR

○ Hagal-li

Hill 410
8 MAR

Hill 484
3 MAR

2 P.P.C.L.I.

Hill 450
3 MAR

3 R.A.R.

G R.O.K. D I V

Point 419
28 FEB

1 A. & S.H.

Hill 614
27 FEB

Hoengsong
6 miles

Hill 444
22 FEB

23 FEB

○ Sogu

Hill 523

3 R.A.R.

27 TAC
8-9 MAR

C A V A L R Y   D I V

ON 7 MAR 27 BRITCOM INF BDE
CAME UNDER COMMAND OF
1 U.S. CAVALRY DIV

○ Chip'yong-ni

9   U.S.   C O R P S

2 P.P.C.L.I.

Wol-li
21 FEB

Chohyon ○

27 TAC
21 FEB-5 MAR

U.S.

Tunnels

19 FEB

Hill 404
19 FEB

1 M X

Sangsok ○

2 P.P.C.L.I.
19 FEB

A. & S.H.

○ Chuam-ni

27 BRITCOM
INF BDE

Yoju 4 miles

Naeryong-ni

### 9 U.S. CORPS FRONT
### 11 MARCH 1951

38 CORPS ×
C.C.F.

42 CORPS ×
C.C.F.

66 CORPS ×
C.C.F.

× Hong-ch'on

×
× 5 N.K.

24 U.S. INF
DIV

1 U.S. CAV
DIV

6 R.O.K.
DIV

1 U.S.
MARINE
DIV

1 × 9
×

○ Hoengsong

9 ×××

○ Sangsok

9

10

0  5  10  15
KILOMETRES
○ Yoju

54

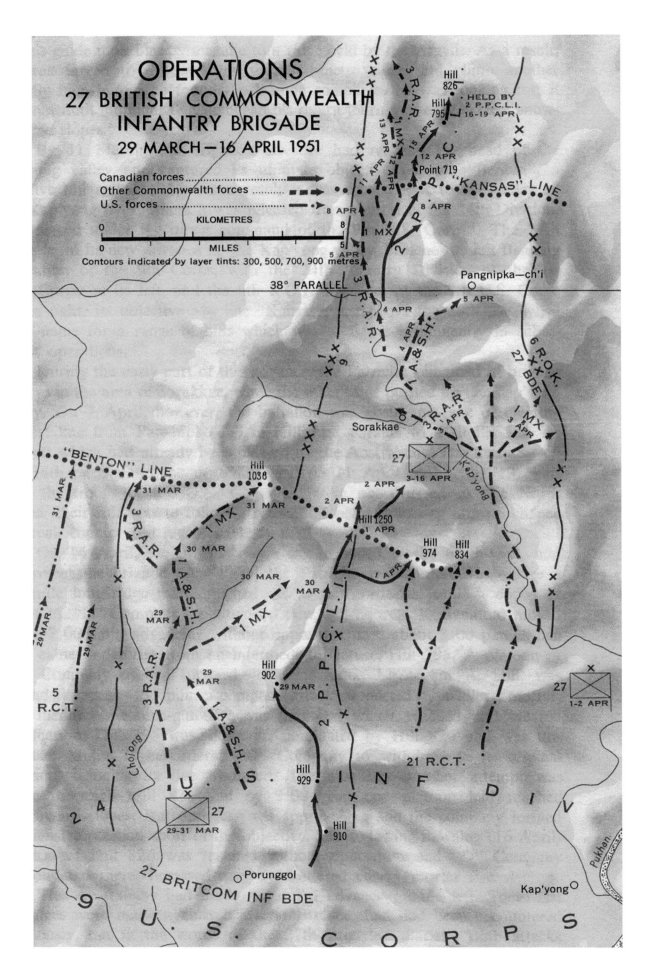

# OPERATIONS
## 27 BRITISH COMMONWEALTH
## INFANTRY BRIGADE
### 29 MARCH – 16 APRIL 1951

Canadian forces ............................
Other Commonwealth forces ...........
U.S. forces ....................................

KILOMETRES

0 ————————————————— 8

0 ————————————————— 5
MILES

Contours indicated by layer tints: 300, 500, 700, 900 metres

38° PARALLEL

Hill 826

HELD BY 2 P.P.C.L.I. 16-19 APR

Hill 795

"KANSAS" LINE

Point 719

12 APR

8 APR

Pangnipka—ch'i

6 R.O.K.

27 BDE

3 R.A.R.

"BENTON" LINE

Hill 1036

31 MAR

1 MX

31 MAR

2 APR

Sorakkae

3 R.A.R.

27

3-16 APR

Kap'yong

31 MAR

3 R.A.R.

1 A.& S.H.

30 MAR

2 APR

Hill 1250
1 APR

30 MAR

30 MAR

1 MX

1 APR

Hill 974

Hill 834

29 MAR

29 MAR

1 A.& S.H.

29 MAR

2 P.P.C.L.I.

27

1-2 APR

5 R.C.T.

3 R.A.R.

29 MAR

1 A.& S.H.

Hill 902

29 MAR

21 R.C.T.

I   N   F       D   I   V

Choiong

U

27

29-31 MAR

Hill 929

Hill 910

2   4

Porunggol

Kap'yong

27 BRITCOM INF BDE

9       U.   S.       C   O   R   P   S

Pukhan

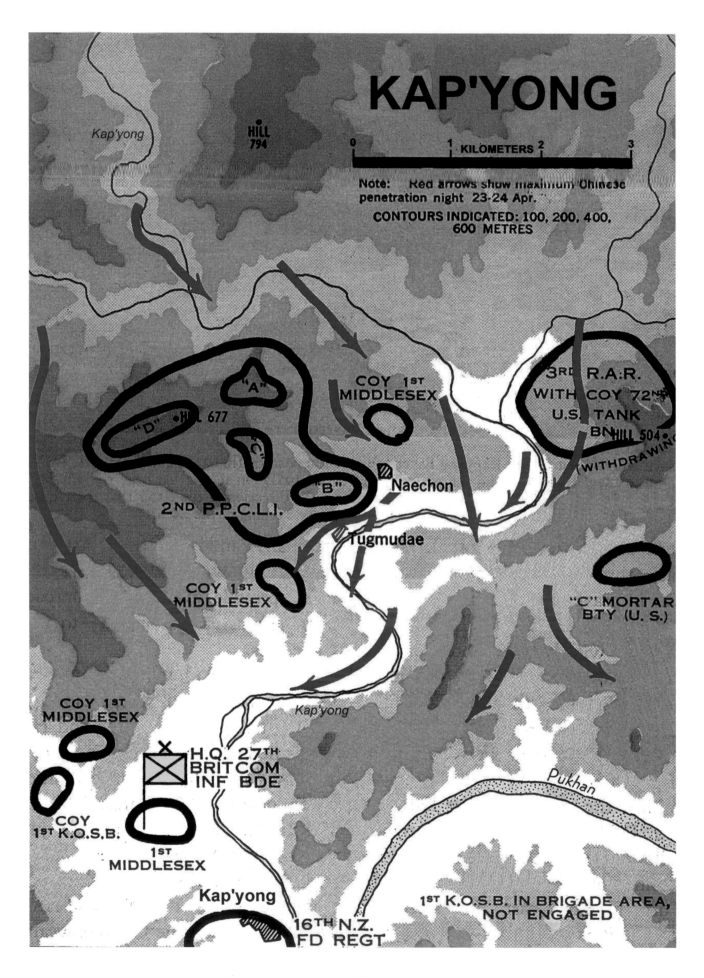

KAP'YONG

Kap'yong

HILL
794

0       1   KILOMETERS   2      3

Note:   Red arrows show maximum Chinese
penetration night 23-24 Apr.

CONTOURS INDICATED: 100, 200, 400,
600 METRES

"A"

"D"   HILL 677

"C"

COY 1ST
MIDDLESEX

3RD R.A.R.
WITH COY 72ND
U.S. TANK
BN HILL 504
(WITHDRAWING)

"B"

Naechon

2ND P.P.C.L.I.

Tugmudae

"C" MORTAR
BTY (U.S.)

COY 1ST
MIDDLESEX

COY 1ST
MIDDLESEX

Kap'yong

Pukhan

H.Q. 27TH
BRIT COM
INF BDE

COY
1ST K.O.S.B.

1ST
MIDDLESEX

Kap'yong

1ST K.O.S.B. IN BRIGADE AREA,
NOT ENGAGED

16TH N.Z.
FD REGT

56

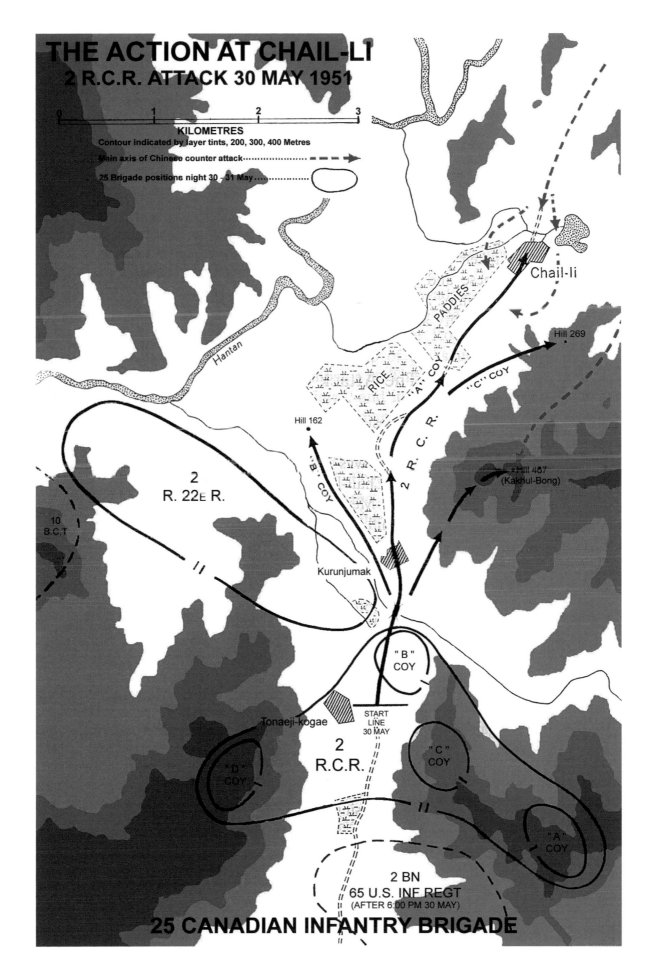

# THE ACTION AT CHAIL-LI
## 2 R.C.R. ATTACK 30 MAY 1951

0      1      2      3

**KILOMETRES**

Contour indicated by layer tints, 200, 300, 400 Metres

Main axis of Chinese counter attack ......................➤

25 Brigade positions night 30 - 31 May ....................

Chail-li

PADDIES

Hill 269

RICE

"A" COY

"C" COY

Hill 162

2 R. C. R.

"B" COY

2
R. 22E R.

Hill 467
(Kakhul-Bong)

10
B.C.T

Kurunjumak

"B"
COY

Tonaeji-kogae

START
LINE
30 MAY

"C"
COY

2
R.C.R.

"D"
COY

"A"
COY

2 BN
65 U.S. INF REGT
(AFTER 6:00 PM 30 MAY)

## 25 CANADIAN INFANTRY BRIGADE

Hantan

OPERATIONS
"MINDEN" AND "COMMANDO"
11 SEPTEMBER — 5 OCTOBER 1951

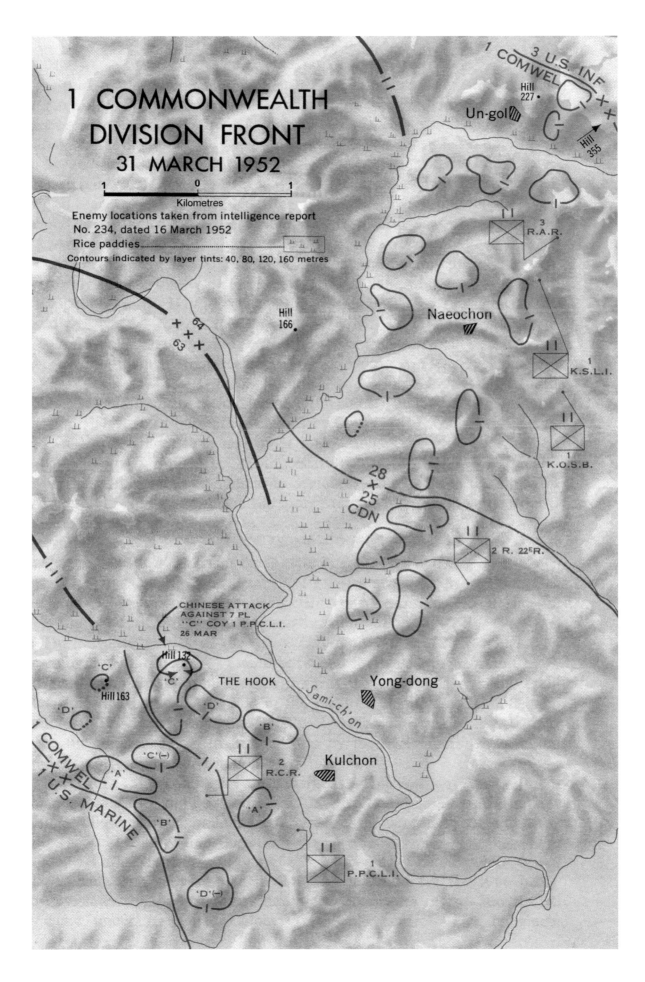

# 1 COMMONWEALTH DIVISION FRONT
## 31 MARCH 1952

Enemy locations taken from intelligence report
No. 234, dated 16 March 1952
Rice paddies..................
Contours indicated by layer tints: 40, 80, 120, 160 metres

Kilometres

3 U.S. INF.
1 COMWEL

Hill 227

Un-gol

Hill 355

3 R.A.R.

Hill 166

Naeochon

1 K.S.L.I.

64
63

1 K.O.S.B.

28
25 CDN

2 R. 22ᴱ R.

CHINESE ATTACK
AGAINST 7 PL
"C" COY 1 P.P.C.L.I.
26 MAR

Hill 132

'C'
Hill 163

'C'

'D'

THE HOOK

'D'

'B'

Yong-dong

Sami-ch'on

'D'

'C' (−)

'A'

'B'

'A'

Kulchon

1 COMWEL
1 U.S. MARINE

2 R.C.R.

'D' (−)

1 P.P.C.L.I.

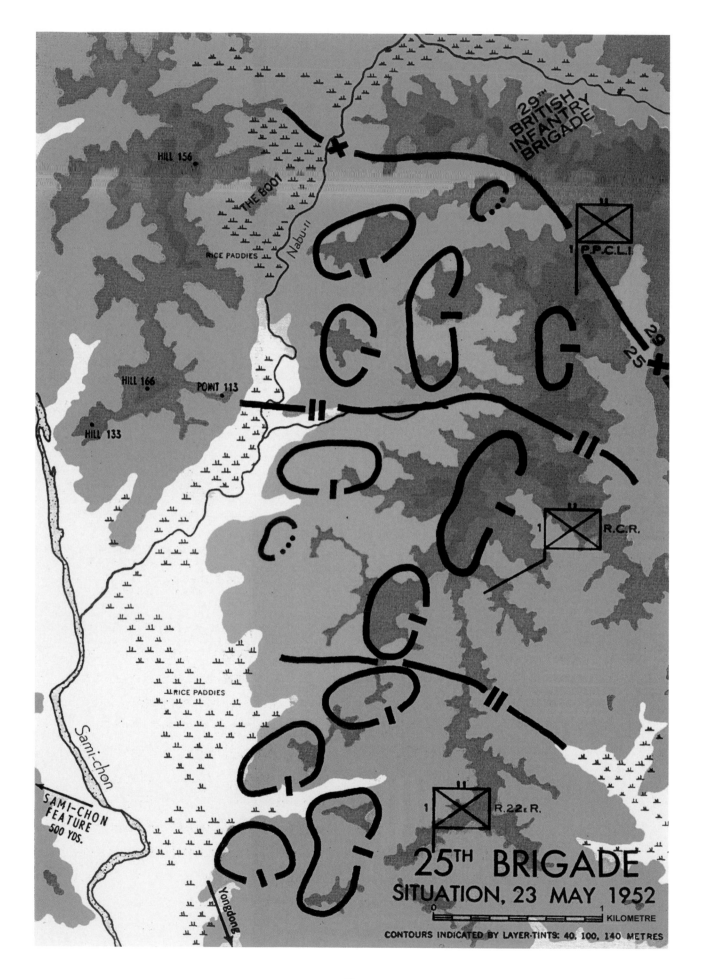

29ᵀᴴ BRITISH INFANTRY BRIGADE

HILL 156

THE BOOT

RICE PADDIES

Nabu-ri

1 P.P.C.L.I.

29
25

HILL 166

POINT 113

HILL 133

1 R.C.R.

Sami-chon

RICE PADDIES

SAMI-CHON FEATURE 500 YDS.

1 R.22ᵉR.

Yongdong

25ᵀᴴ BRIGADE
SITUATION, 23 MAY 1952

0                                    1 KILOMETRE

CONTOURS INDICATED BY LAYER-TINTS: 40, 100, 140 METRES

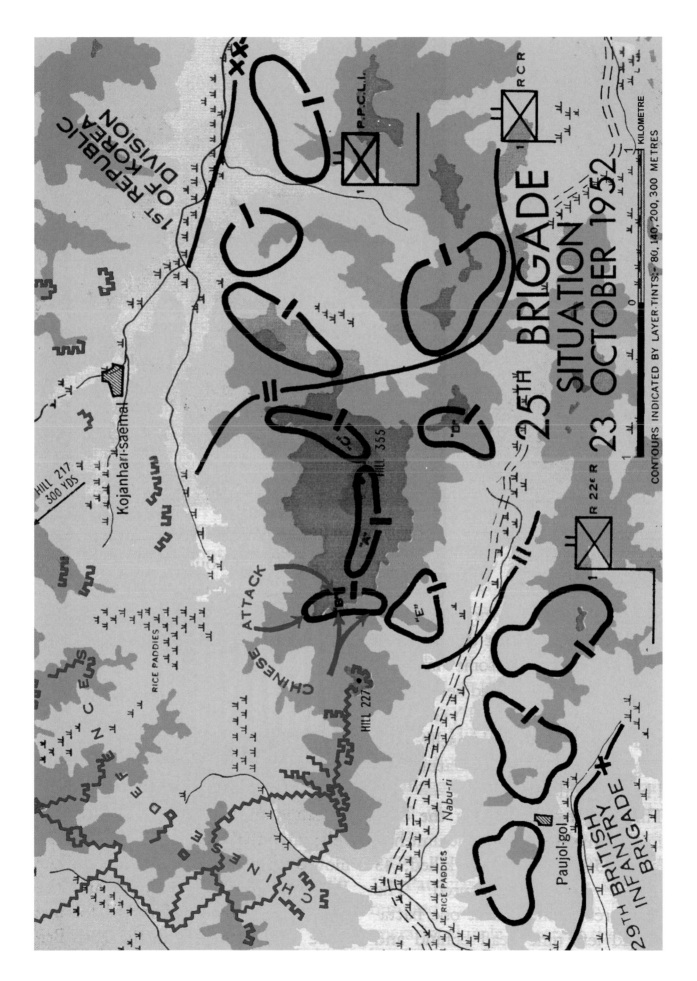

1ST REPUBLIC OF KOREA DIVISION

P.P.C.L.I.

1 RCR

Kojanhari-saemal

HILL 217
300 YDS

HILL 355

25TH BRIGADE
SITUATION
23 OCTOBER 1952

R 22€ R

CONTOURS INDICATED BY LAYER-TINTS:- 80, 140, 200, 300 METRES

KILOMETRE

DEFENCES

RICE PADDIES

CHINESE ATTACK

HILL 227

Nabu-ri

RICE PADDIES

Paujol-gol

BRITISH
29TH BRITISH
INFANTRY
BRIGADE

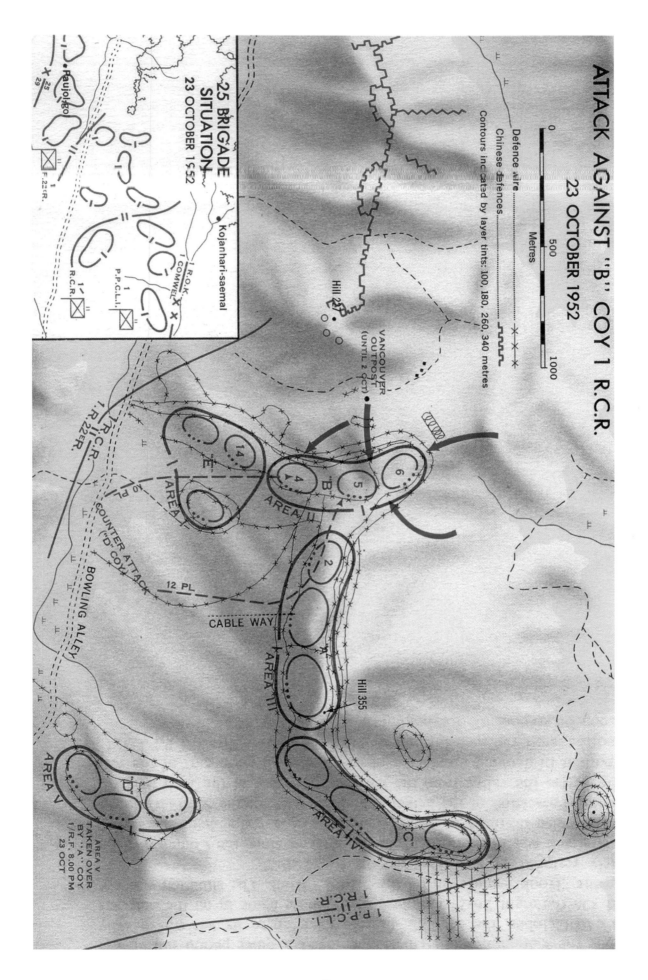

ATTACK AGAINST "B" COY 1 R.C.R.
23 OCTOBER 1952

Defence wire ....................
Chinese Defences ...............
Contours indicated by layer tints: 100, 180, 260, 340 metres

0   500   1000
Metres

Hill 227

VANCOUVER
OUTPOST
(UNTIL 2 OCT)

14

E

AREA I

6
"B"   5
4
AREA II

1   2

12 PL

CABLE WAY

COUNTER ATTACK
("D" COY)

BOWLING ALLEY

1 R.C.R.
1 R.22eR.

Hill 355

AREA III

AREA IV

"C"

AREA V

"D"

AREA V
TAKEN OVER
BY "A" COY
1/R.F. 8.00 PM
23 OCT

1 R.C.R.
1 P.P.C.L.I.

25 BRIGADE
SITUATION
23 OCTOBER 1952

Kojanhari-saemal

Paujol

25
29

1 F.22eR.

1 R.O.K.
COMWEL

1
P.P.C.L.I.

1
R.C.R.

62

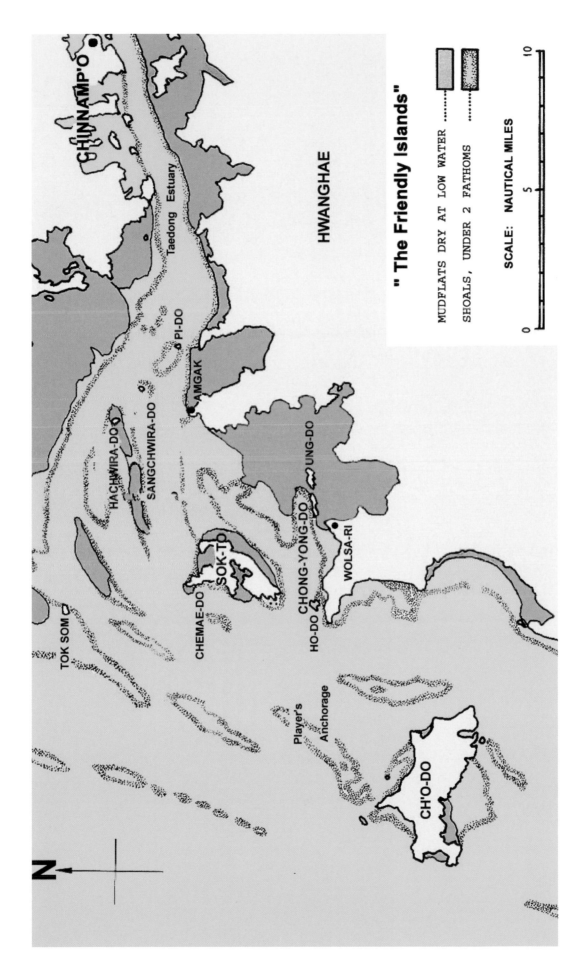

" The Friendly Islands"

MUDFLATS DRY AT LOW WATER ·········

SHOALS, UNDER 2 FATHOMS ·········

SCALE: NAUTICAL MILES

0      5      10

CHINNAMP'O

Taedong Estuary

HWANGHAE

PI-DO

AMGAK

HACHWIRA-DO

SANGCHWIRA-DO

UNG-DO

CHEMAE-DO

SOK-TO

CHONG-YONG-DO

TOK SOM

HO-DO

WOLSA-RI

Player's Anchorage

CH'O-DO

N

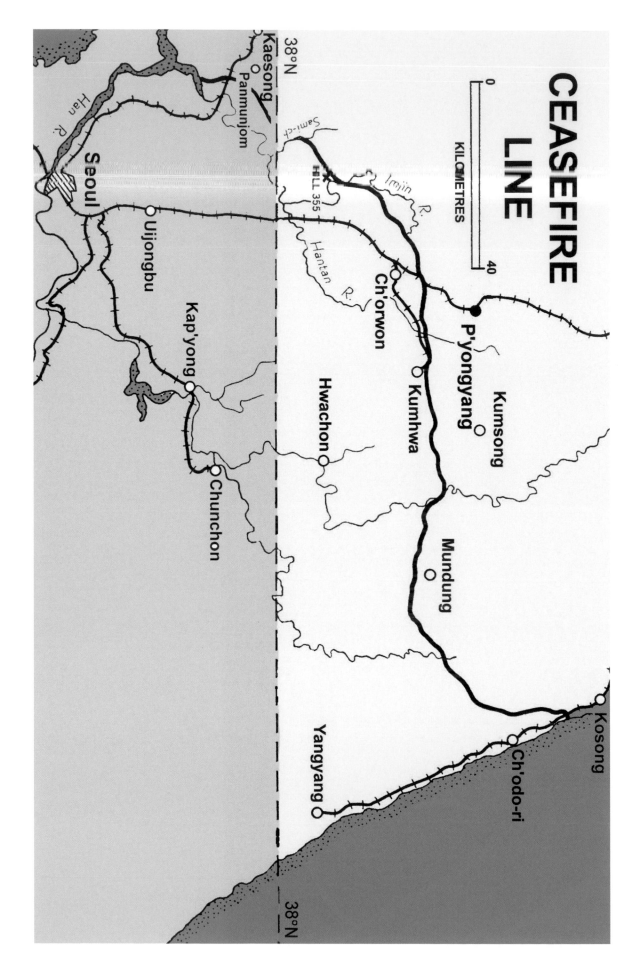

# CEASEFIRE LINE

KILOMETRES
0 — 40

Kaesong
Panmunjom
Han R.
Seoul
Sami-ch'
Imjin R.
HILL 355
Hantan R.
Ch'orwon
P'yongyang
Kumhwa
Kumsong
Hwachon
Mundung
Uijongbu
Kap'yong
Chunchon
Yangyang
Ch'odo-ri
Kosong

38°N

38°N

Edward Zuber, 1932–
*Holding at Kapyong*
CWM-90041

## CHAPTER IV

# *North to Kap'yong*

When 2 PPCLI reached Pusan on 18 December 1950, they had been afloat for 23 days except for very brief shore leaves – a few hours at most – at Yokohama and Kobe, and despite shipboard physical training the voyage had left the men in something less than first-class condition. Most especially, their feet had softened and their legs weakened. Stone was determined to correct that. Route marches and hill climbs (in accordance with Brigadier Rockingham's expressed beliefs) alternated with the uncrating and distribution of kit and lectures on this new and strange environment. *"It had a raggety-taggety frontier air about it, with strange-looking people scurrying about."*[1] But the overwhelming impression was one of smell. "It was a smell of excrement, sweat, garlic, charcoal cooking fires and human despair."[2] Those parts of Korea that could be cultivated were mostly rice paddies, and human manure was the universal fertilizer.

The Canadians were immediately issued much American equipment. *"The quantity of equipment on issue...is tremendous,"* noted the battalion diarist, *"although certain items are not the best available...particularly noticeable with respect to the sleeping bags, tentage, and cooking equipment."*[3] The cold, damp Korean winter, similar if rather more extreme than

that which their comrades were experiencing at Fort Lewis, would soon reveal various shortcomings in the kit they had brought with them as well. Water-absorbent, Second World War-vintage battledress and greatcoats were far from ideal, their boots were totally inadequate in winter (although it would take some time for that to be revealed) and some of their weapons were equally unsatisfactory for the kind of war they would soon be fighting. The weapons issue was, of course, vital, and their 2-inch and 3-inch mortars, badly outranged by the enemy's equivalents, were replaced with superior American 60mm and 81mm weapons. The 75mm recoilless rifle, designed as an anti-armour weapon but, in the absence of enemy armour, a useful implement for "bunker-busting," was another addition. Most important of all – good communications being vital for warfare in which small groups (platoons, companies and battalions) were often in widely separated perimeters because of the jagged, irregular terrain – and perhaps the most difficult to master, was the American SCR 300 radio, to be used at company/battalion level, which had a far more reliable performance in hilly country than the British-designed #31 sets with which the Canadian Army was equipped. Platoons had to make do with the British #88 set, which *"fit awkwardly into an ammunition pouch on one side with the battery in the other ammunition pouch."* But:

*The most reliable method of communication was still the hand-cranked telephone hooked up to a rudimentary switchboard. There were, of course, problems with telephones, namely the need to lay communications cable. In some positions there would be miles of signal wire cable lining trenches or strewn all over the place. It was simpler and safer after a shelling or relief in the line to lay new cable rather than try to find which of the existing cables still worked... Everyone had back-up visual signals using different colours of Very flares in case of a breakdown in communications.*[4]

The Patricias were to join the British 29 Brigade, currently in reserve at Suwon but liable to be sent into the line at any time. Explaining that his battalion was far from adequately trained, Stone *"queried the advisability of moving within 50 miles [80 kilometres] of an unstable front with green troops, particularly as the general idea was for us to patrol against guerrilla forces in the area,"*[5] and requested an interview with Lieutenant-General Walton "Bulldog" Walker, the Eighth Army commander, whose nickname was explained by his facial features and who has been labelled "tough, aggressive, and somewhat flamboyant in the style of Patton."[6]

For all practical purposes this was an American war, to be fought according to American principles and desires, but the Americans needed the support of their United Nations allies and Stone was the on-scene representative of a diplomatically important, if militarily insignificant, power. The next day he was flown to Eighth Army headquarters at Seoul, and the following morning, 21 December, he explained to General Walker the circumstances under which his unit had been recruited and their very limited degree of training. They were not yet fit to fight and Stone was unwilling to have them go into action until they were. Walker was unexpectedly *"very gracious"* and announced that *"he would not ask us to go into action until our training was completed,"*[7] although, he observed, the Canadians *"were trained as well as the US reinforcements, and the situation was desperate."*[8] (Two days later, Walker was killed in a road accident – just as his Second World War mentor, General George S. Patton, had been in Germany five years earlier.)

Afterwards, Stone met Brigadier Brodie, commander of 29 (British) Brigade, and *"discussed various points of the fighting with him."*

*It seems apparent that resolute men, dug in, in proper islands of defence can kill at will the hordes that rush the positions. However, it is also apparent that there can be no administrative tail stretching back for miles, but that everything must be tied up in Battalion defensive localities.... Infiltration between [defended] localities must be expected, but with all areas defended such infiltration is not serious....*

*The Chinese have almost no artillery, very few mortars and rely on massed movement of infantry mostly, equipped with sub-machine guns to overrun opposition. Such should be a defender's paradise, provided troops are all trained marksmen and realize that if they run, they will certainly die. Practically all attacks have taken place before first light, therefore, there must be means of illuminating the battlefield to give men an opportunity to see their targets.*[9]

Stone returned to Pusan and arranged to conclude training his men at Miryang, some 55 kilometres northwest of the port, with the battalion camp established in an orchard.

*Army headquarters had sent us to the valley partly because Miryang was considered to be the Communist capital of South Korea. It was believed that there were several thousand communist guerrillas lurking in the hills surrounding Miryang, and we were told that these guerrillas frequently raided the outlying villages for supplies. It was also noted at the time that the orchard was selected because there were no awful smelling rice paddies in the area.*[10]

"Several thousand" was certainly an exaggeration, but there were guerrillas in the area, as the battalion would soon discover – perhaps several hundred, but more likely several dozen.

After a mere half day off for Christmas, followed by the move to Miryang, training resumed on New Year's Day 1951 and *"began in earnest"* on the 2nd. The emphasis was on proficiency in the use of all weapons, particularly in the handling of the 60mm and 81mm mortars. Also:

*Company Commanders began their company training programs designed to emphasize hill climbing and section and platoon tactics in moun-*

*tains. Every effort was made to show the men the necessity for meeting the enemy on his ground, i.e. the high ridges dominating the valleys, in order that our more highly mechanized army may have freedom of movement in the valleys and along the roads.*

*Most officers considered the 60 mm mortars (81mm are battalion weapons\*) too accurate and heavy for practical use. Use of men (9 per mortar) to carry loads is felt to take too many men from company fighting strength. Most companies plan to carry 2 mortars in [the] platoon truck in the attack and only man-pack one. The extra men to be used to carry extra ammunition. In a defensive position all three would of course be employed....*

*Despite stiff training exercise the men's morale is quite high and their interest is still keen. Lt-Col Stone is under heavy pressure to commit the battalion early, but we are still to have five more weeks of training.*

*...Eighth Army HQ is extremely co-operative in anything that will hasten the battalion's arrival at the front.*[11]

Several of Stone's statements would need revision later in the war. The Chinese would eventually be well supplied with mortars and use them skilfully, while the Canadians would soon come to appreciate the 60mm mortar, heavy or not.

On 14 January the battalion war diary recorded that two New Zealanders, men from a field artillery regiment moving into a training area next to the Canadians, had been *"ambushed and brutally treated before being killed."* Three days later, Lieutenant H. T. Ross was wounded by a sniper in the battalion training area, gaining the unenviable distinction of becoming the first Canadian battle casualty of the Korean War.[12] (The next day, 18 January, Regimental Sergeant-Major J. D. Wood, DCM, the battalion's senior non-commissioned officer, was killed by the premature explosion of an anti-personnel mine about to be used in a weapons demonstration.)

B Company, with 150 South Korean policemen "under command," had been dispatched to scour the area to the west of Miryang, and *"during the first night two firefights occurred; on the second night three Koreans were killed in similar clashes."* Such a sweep was possibly the best form of training, but nothing stopped the arduous regular training schedules. Two

---

\* Held and used by Support Company rather than the rifle companies.

more weeks led Colonel Stone to conclude that his battalion was now fit to fight, and he reported so to Eighth Army HQ on 10 February 1951.

No. 29 Brigade had acquired a Greek battalion to bring it up to strength and the Canadians were now ordered to join 27 British Commonwealth Brigade, which had been in Korea since early September, when it had been a half-strength – two-battalion – British formation rushed from Hong Kong and flung into action as soon as it arrived, to help in holding the Naktong perimeter. At the end of that month an Australian infantry battalion, formerly a part of the Allied occupation force in Japan, had joined it, followed by a New Zealand artillery regiment and an Indian field ambulance. It was commanded by Brigadier Basil Coad, and 2 PPCLI came under his command on 17 February 1951.

The Eighth Army's new commander, succeeding Walker, was 54-year-old Matthew B. Ridgway, the Second World War leader of the 82nd Airborne Division and XVIII Airborne Corps, most recently serving as deputy chief of staff in the Pentagon. Assessing his record, the British historian Max Hastings has written, "Had he, rather than Browning, commanded at Arnhem, the outcome of that operation might have been astonishingly different – or certainly, less disastrous. He possessed almost all the military virtues – courage, brains, ruthlessness, decision."[13]

Ridgway chose to withdraw his forces to positions some 70 kilometres south of the Han river, once again abandoning the South Korean capital to the enemy. But not for long. His rationale was that "on the Yalu, the Chinese might be able to support a million men under arms," but their fragile logistics meant that "at a line through Pyongyang this figure fell to 600,000; at the 38th Parallel, it became 300,000; forty miles south of Seoul, it became only 200,000."[14] By pulling back temporarily, he reduced the threat of a major Chinese assault and ensured himself a secure base where he could re-train troops who had earlier been rushed into the line, restore morale, and better choose his own time and place to launch an offensive designed to inflict so many casualties on the Chinese that they would be compelled to retreat to positions north of the 38th Parallel.

When the offensive began, on 21 February, 27 Brigade was sandwiched between 1 US Cavalry and 6 ROK divisions. The Australians and Canadians led the brigade advance, the former on the right, the latter on the left, in the usual "two-up" formation, each with 150 Korean porters – affectionately dubbed "rice burners" by the irreverent soldiery – employed to bring supplies forward after the track from Kap'yong petered out just north of the hamlet of Sogu. The PPCLI axis of advance lay up a valley with steep hills on both sides. That first day the enemy was conspicuous by his absence, but two officers fell and injured themselves on the icy slopes, while rain and wet snow turned the valley track into a morass. *"The battalion was given a grim lesson in the dangers of sleeping on guard by the bodies of 65 coloured [American] troops...lying dead beside the road."*[15]

*The Americans had been travelling in machine-gun fitted jeeps, but they had not received proper training and so they were ill-prepared. At one point they chased a group of Chinese soldiers into the hills at the end of a valley. The Americans ended the chase around dusk when the surviving Chinese soldiers vanished into the hills. They then drove back down the valley to a deserted hamlet where they stopped, built some fires, ate supper and then crawled into their sleeping bags for the night.*

*The Americans had posted two pairs of sentries – armed with machine-guns – along the side of the road at the north and south ends of the hamlet. But sometime during the night, Chinese soldiers crept down out of the surrounding hills and killed all 65 men in the unit, including the four sentries [who, presumably, had fallen asleep]. Most of the men were killed while they slept in their sleeping bags.*[16]

There was little danger of Patricia sentries sleeping at their posts after that; most men declined to zip up their sleeping bags no matter how cold it was, and some chose not to use their sleeping bags at all but just wrap themselves in a blanket even though the weather had turned bitterly cold. Slit trenches had to be dug through a metre or more of wet snow, and sodden clothing froze to their bodies.

On the 22nd the advance resumed but the valley was becoming too narrow for two battalions abreast, so the Patricias now had it to themselves, with the Australians over the ridge on their right and a battalion of the British Middlesex Regiment on the ridge to their left. That afternoon the Canadians met their first slight opposition and, as they skirmished forward, two men were killed and one wounded.

The next morning their advance was threatened by a rocky spur extending into the valley from the left, code-named Hill 419.* Two attempts to take it were foiled by determined resistance from the enemy and some inaccurate napalming by the US Air Force. A little ground was gained, but not enough, at a cost of six killed and eight wounded, and the Patricias were ordered to dig in where they were. On their right the Australians were suffering similar troubles with similar results on the much higher Hill 614. The exact same scenario was repeated the next day, when the battalion war diary recorded that the *"line of hills which is the joint objective of ourselves and the Australians is held by two regiments of enemy."* That was probably an exaggeration, a Chinese regiment being roughly the numerical equivalent of a Commonwealth brigade, but there was no doubt that the head of the valley was strongly held.

*The battalion has been continuously engaged for two days with little sleep at night. Our battalion and the [Royal Australian Regiment] are in an extremely extended position so the CO has decided to confine our activities to fighting patrols for the next day.... The elements of 1 [US] Cavalry Division have failed to come up with the result that a 5–8,000 yard [4,500–7,200 metre] gap exists on our left.*[17]

Meanwhile, heavy rains had washed away the bridge over the Han river and rations and ammunition were soon in rather short supply. Under these circumstances, the advance came to a halt until the bridge could be replaced. On 27 February, however, the Australians attacked again and succeeded in taking their objective, so that the 419 spur then became untenable by the enemy. The Patricias occupied it the next day, finding the naked bodies of four soldiers who had been killed in the earlier attacks – many of their Chinese opponents were inadequately dressed for the weather, their logistics were always gravely stressed and no doubt they put the clothing of their victims to good use.

On 3 March the Argyll and Sutherland Highlanders joined the Middlesex battalion in the lead, while the Canadians and Australians went into brigade reserve, having advanced some 25 kilometres over difficult country in less than two weeks. The ground, however, was about to get worse, if that was possible. Since the Patricias had reached the front, the brigade had been advancing parallel to the grain of the country, up valleys that drained south into the Han: from here on, the valleys – and, more impor-

---

* The numbering of hills was based upon their height above sea level in metres.

There was very little easy ground in Korea. 2 PPCLI Advance. (PPCLI Museum)

Kap'yong. A westward view of the PPCLI position on Hill 677 from the Kap'yong valley. (PPCLI Museum)

tantly, the ridges between them – would run athwart the UN front.

On 7 March the Canadians and Australians were again in the lead when the brigade faced two more steep hills, 532 and 412 respectively. D Company lost six killed and 28 wounded in a desperate attempt to attain the Canadian objective, which it briefly occupied only to be driven back by a Chinese counter-attack. Private Len Barton distinguished himself when his platoon commander and several members of his platoon were wounded. He rallied the remainder and led their final advance despite incurring three wounds himself. He was subsequently awarded a Military Medal, becoming the first Canadian to be decorated for gallantry in the Korean War and the first since the end of the Second World War.[18]

Once again, the Patricias found themselves at the tip of a salient, the right wing of 1 Cavalry Division on the brigade's left having failed to cross the valley, while on the other flank the ROK division was some 5,000 metres back. However, on the 8th:

*At 0500 [hours] this morning B [Company], after spending an uncomfortable night during which the Chinese threw nearly 100 grenades into the [company] area, put in a bayonet attack, but only found two Chinese in the position which D Coy had been attacking all the previous day.*

*There were over 25 Chinese dead in the position and blood-stains in the snow showed the route taken by the wounded as they left during the night. B Coy proceeded to Hill 532 and had consolidated their positions by 0900 [hours]. A further 22 dead Chinese were found in the area raising the total of known [enemy] dead to 47.[19]*

When the brigade went into corps reserve on 13 March, the Patricias had lost 13 men killed in action, five more had died of wounds, and four officers and 45 men had been wounded.[20] Stone, who had experienced some of the hardest fighting of the Second World War, had no complaints about the courage of his men and praised their morale, while noting that they *"show lack of basic training, particularly in caring for weapons and equipment."*

*Much "scruff" that was hastily recruited has now been returned to Canada. Troops here are fit, morale high, show lots of guts in close contact. Lack of comfort which is general in this theatre is being compensated [for] with troops' own ingenu-*

*ity.... Officers are generally good but junior ranks show need of a company commander's school.*

*Practical experience will help but certain basic principles of military thinking are lacking. Troops are very well led and the aggressiveness they display in attack under very difficult circumstances is a great credit to the officers.[21]*

"Scruff" referred to the 146 men already evacuated to Japan and eventually sent home to Canada, a few as disciplinary problems, some simply unwilling to fight when push came to shove, and others with such genuine medical complaints as bronchitis, flat feet, atrophy of the leg muscles, cardiac palpitation, perforated ear drums, arthritis of the spine, hernias and hypertension – mostly men who should have been weeded out during the recruiting process.

The Communists, with no conceivable shortage of manpower, were nevertheless hampered by logistics problems and once again falling back. While 27 Brigade was in reserve, UN Forces liberated Seoul for a second time on 15–16 March. Just 50 kilometres further north lay the 38th Parallel, and General MacArthur was anxious to return to the Yalu. He wanted to cross that politically proscribed boundary, while the Truman administration (and all of the United States' UN allies, including Canada) favoured stopping on the Parallel and taking up a purely defensive posture. If the UN forces should "reach the position of a sort of de facto cease-fire roughly along the line of the 38th parallel...we should take advantage of that position, that military stabilization, to reopen negotiations with the people on the other side," Lester Pearson told the House of Commons on 20 March.[22]

However, tactical factors dictated otherwise. If the Yalu (and beyond) was too far, then the 38th Parallel was not far enough. There was no need to advance deep into North Korea, but the terrain along the Parallel was not as suitable for defence as that a little further north. If UN troops occupied selected positions in those hills, they would be in a much stronger position from which to repel any further Chinese thrusts.

On 24 April the Commonwealth Brigade was ordered back into the line and joined the US 24th Division advancing towards the 38th Parallel. On the 28th, with the Patricias sharing the lead with the Argyll and Sutherland Highlanders at first, and then with the Middlesex Regiment, the brigade began working north, along the ridges on each side of the Cholong valley, towards an objective code-named

Line BENTON, some eight kilometres south of the 38th Parallel. Once again, terrain and weather posed more of a problem than the enemy.

> On either side of the canyon-like valley the main ridges rose to a height of three thousand feet [1,000 metres]. The slopes were steep, seamed with gullies and warty with outcrops; the contours of the crest lines gave alternate dead and commanding ground, so that defensive positions succeeded each other. For the first ten miles [16 kilometres] there was a road of sorts in the valley. After fifteen miles [24 kilometres] it would be necessary to take to the hillsides.[23]

The ground was still frozen and the north, or forward, slopes had a metre or more of snow on them. "Steep rock faces and [awkward] packs made movement slow," but on the other hand there was only "light resistance – occasional Small Arms fire."[24]

As the Canadians reached BENTON, on 1 April, the valley on their left was pinched out by rising ground and the whole brigade was required to sidestep one ridge to the east – the PPCLI to the high ground above the Kap'yong river. Their new objective was Line KANSAS, about five kilometres north of the 38th Parallel. Opposition was stiffening and the battalion incurred a number of casualties in pushing forward to KANSAS.

A week later, on 8 April, leading elements of the brigade crossed the 38th Parallel as, in Washington, President Truman finally decided to fire General MacArthur, whose carefree interference in the politico-diplomatic aspects of the conflict was causing an international uproar. He still wanted to advance to the Yalu and was "privately" advocating the use of Chinese Nationalist troops from Formosa to further his objective of reuniting Korea,[25] a move that almost certainly would have brought greater Chinese involvement. MacArthur's answer to that would have been atom bombs dropping on Chinese territory!

General Ridgway succeeded him as commander-in-chief both of the United States' Far Eastern Command and of the United Nations Command, and Lieutenant-General James Van Fleet, another distinguished corps commander from the Second World War, was promoted to command of the Eighth (US) Army and UN Forces in Korea. Meanwhile, on the ridges overlooking the Kap'yong river 27 Brigade continued to edge forward, unaware that their opponents were preparing a limited offensive, perhaps aimed at re-capturing Seoul. The slightly easier ground on their right, over which 6 ROK Division was also advancing

– albeit more slowly – was more resolutely held by the enemy, and the same was true of the ground on their left held by 25 (US) Division. By 17 April, consequently, 27 Brigade had established a salient in the UN line.

The next day, elements of the Korean division on their right began to take over the brigade's front, and on the 19th the British and Canadians began moving back into reserve, the Patricias leading the way, so to speak. But their rest would be a short one, and not particularly pleasant. "It rained and our blankets (we were not permitted to use sleeping bags) which we covered as best we could with our ponchos[,] were wet, but we slept," according to Private G. F. Bordeleau. Someone was remembering those 65 dead Americans trapped and killed in their sleeping bags. "We spent a few days cleaning equipment and bodies. This activity, which is, for reasons unknown to me, called 'interior economy,' is designed, I believe, to make one anxious to return to the front."[26]

One of the most unfortunate aspects of operations in Korea was the difficulty in obtaining detailed information about enemy intentions at the divisional level and above. Unsophisticated armies, such as those facing the United Nations, provided few radio messages for interception and analysis, and, although the USAF ruled the skies far beyond the battlefield, the enemy's paltry mechanized logistics severely restricted the effectiveness of aerial reconnaissance. Men moving their scanty supplies on bicycles, largely by night, were hard to find in an age before infrared cameras became a military commonplace. Intelligence suggested that the Chinese were massing for another offensive, but its timing and objectives – not to mention its precise direction, through the bewildering labyrinth of hills and valleys that lay athwart the front – were uncertain. Interrogation of prisoners or deserters, who were never of high enough rank to know about anything at all beyond regimental level, and only rarely anything of value above battalion level, had its own built-in limitations.

Colonel Stone, who had caught a mild case of smallpox – mild because he and his men had all been vaccinated at Fort Lewis – and thus had been away from the battalion for just over a month, returned on 22 April, in time to meet this unexpected Chinese offensive. Late that evening "a strong enemy force launched an attack against elements of the 2nd ROK Regt," and by midnight "HQ 6 ROK [Division] could no longer give locations of their units and in the opinion of the US 9 Corps Commander the situation had collapsed beyond [the] control of the 6 ROK Div."[27] Put more crudely, the South Koreans had broken and run before the lesser thrust of a two-pronged Chinese attack that the enemy termed the "First Step, Fifth Phase Offensive."

Further west, on the Imjin river, the weight of the Chinese onrush would fall on 29 (British) Brigade, and particularly on the Gloucestershire Regiment, which would be literally wiped out. It would fall to 27 (Commonwealth) Brigade to stem a lesser, possibly diversionary, assault, and at 1100 hours on the 23rd Stone and his key officers went forward to reconnoitre the feature the Patricias had been assigned to occupy that night, a position due south of Hill 794, on the other side of the Kap'yong river, which had been assigned to the Middlesex Regiment. The Australians, who comprised the remainder of 27 Brigade, with an American tank company in support, would also be across the river, a little further back than the British and on the right of the Canadians, with the river looping south between them. The Patricias were on a spur of high ground, Hill 677, protruding into the valley of the Kap'yong, with the river – perhaps better described as a stream and not a major obstacle to an unmechanized force – flowing around the north and east sides of the spur.

Recalling the battle more than 40 years after the event, Stone remarked, *"We were able to look at the feature from the enemy side, which gave us a good idea of probable attack approaches,"*[28] implying that this was a deliberate decision on his part; but his intelligence officer, Captain A. P. P. McKenzie, writing in 1954, recorded that *"in starting out, the wrong direction was taken and the main body of the reconnaissance group proceeded by a long round about route to the Northern approaches to the position to be held by the battalion."*[29]

However they came to be there, there was much to be said for examining a position from the enemy's point of view, especially on such irregular, broken ground as prevailed in the hills above Kap'yong. As we noted earlier, Stone, on first arriving in Korea, had learned (from Brigadier Brodie and the evidence of his own eyes) that his men would likely have to fight defensively from *"battalion localities."* Here, on this particular piece of brush-covered ground, riven by gullies and knife-edged ridges, so that ranges were often extremely limited, even battalion localities – in the sense of a unified perimeter – would be impracticable. Perimeters would have to be limited to mutually supporting companies and platoons. Stone ordered that each company be prepared to stand alone, and battalion headquarters, together with the mortar and pioneer platoons, was sited behind C

Company, at the end of a steep, hairpin-cornered track climbing from the valley of the Kap'yong.

*The tactical road built by the Americans was not too suitable for the movement of the half-tracks [carrying the battalion mortars].... In some instances it was necessary to drive the front wheels of the half-track almost over the edge [of the road] and then winch the front end around to negotiate the sharper turns. The move of Battalion Tactical Headquarters was delayed by some four hours due to the difficulty of moving the half-tracks up this road.*[30]

However the machine-guns were sited, there would inevitably be much "dead ground" – hollows where the attackers would be out of sight behind crest lines and could not be reached by direct fire. That posed a particular problem in siting the medium machine-guns. *"Our six Vickers MMGs were deployed by sections, giving depth to the defence and covering the gaps between companies,"* wrote Colonel Stone, but there could be no real depth to the company perimeters and the gaps between them could not be properly defended by machine-gunners or riflemen. Dead ground would have to be covered as far as possible by the artillery and battalion mortars, their efforts directed by Forward Observation Officers (FOOs) working from the map. A company of US 120mm mortars were supporting the brigade, *"but when the battle got hot on the Australian front, the FOO from the US mortars on my front walked out and never a 'pop' did we get from his company. The New Zealand artillery regiment had far too big a front to cover, but they gave their all."*[31]

*In the late afternoon of 23 Apr 51 Forward Movement was greatly hampered by the retreating ROK units. As a result the 1 [Middlesex] arrived in its assembly area...so late as to make the occupation of their positions extremely difficult. The company of infantry detached from 1 [Middlesex] to cover the troop of 16 NZ [Field Regiment] assigned to support the 6th ROK [Division] units... was forced to withdraw with the artillery troop when the numbers of retreating ROK troops interspersed with small groups of infiltrating Chinese infantry made the artillery position untenable. The withdrawal of the 1 [Middlesex] together with the guns of the troop of the 16 NZ through the assembly area of the Middlesex...further demoralized a unit already unhappy with the prospect of action when they were on the point of*

Canadian soldiers spent much of their time defending hilltop positions. They relied on overhead cover and were well supported by battalion weapons like the 17-pounder anti-tank gun, the 75mm recoiless rifle and the Vickers medium machine gun. (PPCLI Museum)

*being relieved by 1 [King's Shropshire Light Infantry]. This apparently made it easier for them to rationalize their withdrawal without occupying their designated position on Hill 794.*[32]

In defence of the Middlesex men, it should be noted that they had incurred heavy casualties during the last lap of the UN advance and now averaged only 50 men per company, with much less than a full complement of officers. In contrast, 2 PPCLI was virtually at full strength.

The leading elements of the Chinese attackers reached the Kap'yong late in the evening of 23 April and the brunt of their initial assaults fell on the Australians. Despite being reinforced by a company of the Middlesex, the Australians were driven out of their positions with casualties amounting to 32 killed and 59 wounded, with three taken prisoner.[33] Their withdrawal left the Patricias with an exposed right flank, and during the afternoon of the 24th Stone ordered B Company to move across to the right in order to protect that flank.

*In the course of this shift a most gallant incident occurred. Tactical Headquarters was protected by a girdle of No. 36 grenades set with trip wires. A "B" Company platoon on its way to its new position strayed; someone stumbled over a tripwire and a grenade exploded, killing one man and wounding another. A second grenade lay smoking in the midst of the platoon. Cpl. S. Douglas shouted to everyone to fall flat, dashed forward and snatched up the grenade to throw it clear. It exploded, blowing off his hand but saving the others from injury.*[34]

For his courage, quick thinking and sacrifice, Douglas was rewarded with a Military Medal. A very similar act at Hong Kong in 1942 had brought Company Sergeant Major Osborn of the Winnipeg Grenadiers, who apparently fell on a fused grenade, a posthumous Victoria Cross.

On the 24th the Patricias' *"[Tactical] HQ and the mortars were in position by 0400 hrs. [Companies] dug in as rapidly as possible in preparation for heavy attacks that were expected that night. Throughout the day reports continued to come in from the forward companies of an enemy build-up all along the battalion front."*[35]

After nightfall, B and D companies bore the brunt of a series of piecemeal, frontal assaults put in by an uncertain number of Chinese – altogether perhaps as many as 3,000 men against fewer than 300. The enemy's mortar and artillery support was relatively weak, however – both problems presumably related to their logistical difficulties – but what he lacked in resources he made up in raw courage. Soon after dark *"approximately 400 Chinese troops were observed forming up in the moonlight,"* and shortly afterwards the enemy launched the first of five attacks on B Company, accompanied by the usual terrifying cacophony of yells, whistles and bugle calls, and machine-guns firing red directional tracer rounds. These unsubtle signals gave the defenders a few moments to prepare themselves for the close-quarter onslaught.

*The Company Commander called for artillery and mortar support but, despite heavy defensive fire[,] the Chinese infantry pressed home their attack.... In their initial rush the Chinese overran the position and in the confused fighting which followed the platoon was only just able to disengage itself in small groups and withdraw into the main defensive position of BAKER Company.*[36]

In several cases disengagement was made possible by the good work of a twice-wounded Bren gunner, Private Wayne Mitchell. Although wounded in the chest early in the fight, after having had his wound field-dressed he returned to the field and again and again held back the enemy to allow other hard-pressed men to break away, although by daylight *"Private Mitchell could hardly stand for loss of blood."*[37] Finally evacuated by helicopter (another Canadian "first"), he eventually collected a Distinguished Conduct Medal for his valiant efforts.

Several of the more seriously wounded Patricias were medevaced by helicopter, not only increasing their chances of survival but encouraging their comrades who remained on the hill – and, indeed, all those engaged in subsequent fighting in Korea. The prospect of quick evacuation and rapid treatment at a Mobile Army Surgical Hospital (as in M*A*S*H) did much for the morale of men in the front lines.

*During one of the night attacks [recalled Cpl. Ken Campbell] a Chinese soldier was hit by small arms fire. He had a phosphorus grenade on him, which exploded in a ball of fire. He lay out there, alive for most of the night, smoldering and screaming. I wanted to go out there and put him out of his misery, but it wasn't beyond the Chinese to have an ambush party waiting to catch anyone who might do that. We let him holler.*[38]

Reading war stories in a secure environment and a comfortable armchair, those who have never been in battle can all too easily forget or ignore the brutal, stinking reality of it. Campbell's words help to make the case, which should never be forgotten or ignored. For those in the front lines, war is hell.

The Chinese were handicapped by the very steep hillsides that they were forced to scale as they closed with the Patricias. Often, the gradients compelled them to "monkey run," with both hands and feet on the ground – not a very effective fighting posture – while Sten sub-machine guns* and hand grenades rolled downhill by the defenders took a heavy toll.[39] Another major attack hit D Company in the early hours of the 25th.

*Failing to overrun 10 Platoon positions the enemy attack...was delivered against 12 Platoon in the saddle between 10 and 11 Platoons. This attack was successful and 12 Platoon was forced to withdraw...into the 11 Platoon and Company Headquarters position.... The section of [Medium Machine Guns] located in 12 Platoon position in the saddle, was overrun and the guns captured by the enemy. With 10 Platoon cut off entirely[,] ... 12 Platoon position...occupied by the Chinese and an attack being mounted against his own position...the Company Commander called for artillery fire upon his company locality.[40]*

With their own artillery shells landing among them, the Canadians relied upon the shelter of their slit trenches and ad hoc bunkers, while the Chinese, charging about between them, were fully exposed to the blasts of shrapnel. *"We were convinced the artillery would kill us all,"* remembered Corporal Campbell, *"but there were no direct hits on any of the slit trenches."*[41]

*With artillery fire coming down on his [company commander's] troops and with 10 Platoon and 11 Platoon still holding out, the Chinese infantry found their position in the saddle untenable and withdrew to the NORTH in the darkness. Smaller attacks continued to come in on DOG [Company] throughout most of the night both from the [north-*

*west] and from the SOUTH. None of these were successful and when first light came 10 Platoon was still in its position and 11 Platoon and 12 Platoon with Company Headquarters were still holding out on Hill 677.... 12 Platoon position...was re-occupied shortly after first light and the MMGs were recovered.*[42]

Private Ken Barwise "slaughtered six men in vicious close-quarter fighting: two with grenades, two others with their own guns, one with a machine-gun he retrieved from the Chinese, and a sixth with his own rifle."[43] The two men manning one of the Vickers medium machine-guns were killed at their post and it is possible that they were killed by Canadian bullets, so confused was the fighting in the dark of night. *"Our platoon was firing into that area,"* reported one Canadian. *"They might have got it from one of our own Brens."*[44] The other Vickers was also taken by the Chinese, but its crew, although wounded, were able to escape. In both cases, Bren gunners from the neighbouring platoons were able to maintain the immediate vicinities of the two lost guns under enough "friendly fire" to keep the enemy from either using them or carrying them off, and *"when the position was retaken [the next morning] it was found that one-half of the ammunition belt still remained to be fired in one gun and about ten rounds remained in the belt of the second."*[45]

More Chinese had infiltrated between the companies and threatened, perhaps cut and certainly made unsafe the track that led to the rear. *"With the battalion surrounded and in need of supplies and ammunition Lt Col STONE called for an air drop...[which] took place at 1030 hrs,"* but *"by 1400 hrs patrols from B [Company] reported the road...clear of the enemy.... The [companies] continued to improve their positions in case of a delay of the battalion's relief and in anticipation of continued Chinese attacks."* However, *"enemy activity on the battalion front was limited to light patrolling without any penetration of the battalion perimeter,"*[46] until it was relieved by an American unit the next day. As we have noted, there really was no "battalion perimeter," but old habits (and customary terminology) die hard.

The Chinese casualties at Kap'yong are unknown, although 51 bodies were counted around B Company's position alone. Private Bordeleau, sent with his section to *"clear the area at [Battalion] HQ, which had also been overrun...could see dozens of bodies on the ground but no movement,"*[47] and Lieutenant Middleton, walking down a draw towards the main road,

---

* Early Second World War Stens, poorly machined, often jammed and were easily fired accidentally, but after 1943 they were admirable weapons with an adequate safety catch, simple to field strip and re-assemble (less than 30 seconds) and no more likely to pose problems than any other sub-machine-gun in the Korean mud. "On patrol I still preferred to carry the Sten Mark 5... It was crude but reliable under all conditions." – Robert S. Peacock, *Kim-chi, Asahi and Rum*, p. 22.

reported *"about twenty dead Chinese soldiers on the path."*[48] Perhaps the total number of Chinese killed approached 400 but the Patricias had no opportunity to count bodies before the brigade went back into reserve. Their own casualties had been amazingly light – 10 killed and 23 wounded – considering the vicious, close-quarter fighting that had occurred. Colonel Stone wrote in 1992:

> *Kapyong was not a great battle, as battles go.... Personally, I believe that Kapyong was the limit of the planned offensive of the Chinese at that time. Had that limit been five miles [eight kilometres] further south we should have been annihilated, as were the Glosters. The numbers that the Chinese were prepared to sacrifice against a position meant that eventually any unsupported battalion in defence must be over-run. The Chinese soldier is tough and brave. All that he lacked at the time of Kapyong were communications and supply.*[49]

The Australians, 2 PPCLI and the American tank company involved at Kap'yong were all awarded US Presidential Unit Citations "to recognize outstanding heroism and exceptionally meritorious conduct in the performance of outstanding services." The Citation takes the form of a blue streamer with the name of the action in white, to be attached to the regimental colour; while all members of the unit at the time it participated in the action may henceforth wear, throughout their service, a small dark-blue ribbon with gold edging (in the American case on the right breast). Additionally, all current members of the unit concerned may wear the emblem.

Unfortunately, General Van Fleet did not consult the appropriate Australian, British and Canadian authorities before awarding the Citations. Although the British and Australians speedily granted permission to the units and men concerned to display or wear the individual insignia, Ottawa was much slower to respond. Not until 21 February 1956, almost five years after Kap'yong and after immense pressure from the press and concerned individuals, were individual Canadians granted permission to wear the badge. The presentation of the streamer (by the US ambassador) followed in June of that year.[50]

In addition to the awards detailed above, Stone was decorated with a second Bar to the DSOs he had won in Italy and northwest Europe six years earlier, and Captain J. G. W. Mills, the company commander who had called down artillery fire on his own position, received a Military Cross.

Major George Flint briefing a 2 PPCLI patrol that includes Sergeant Tommy Prince (second from left)
(PPCLI Museum)

# CHAPTER V

## *25 Brigade in Action*

THE DECISION TO SEND the balance of 25 Brigade to Korea, as originally planned, rather than to Europe, was confirmed by Ottawa on 21 February 1951, and the brigade, less 2 PPCLI, sailed from Seattle on three ships between 19 and 21 April. Two of the three, carrying the fighting elements, reached Pusan on 4 May, while the third delivered the administrative "tail" and the Reinforcement Group to Kure, Japan, on the 6th.

The armoured squadron, still equipped with M-10s and unhappy about it in light of the horror stories reporting grenades being lobbed into open-topped armoured vehicles in the course of mass Chinese night assaults, had been designated C Squadron, Lord Strathcona's Horse, just before leaving Fort Lewis. Major Quinn had been assured that when he reached Korea the squadron would be re-equipped with either American Patton tanks or British Centurions, but in Pusan he learned that neither Pattons nor Centurions were available. The only alternative was the tank in use by the US Marine Corps, which *"spoke so highly of their [M4A3] Sherman tanks."*[1] Happily, it was a tank with which the Canadian Regulars (and some of the Second World War veterans) were already broadly familiar, and arrangements were promptly made to purchase 20 of them (there was financing for another

10 replacements if and when needed) and, only 24 hours behind the rest of the brigade, C Squadron set off up-country. All moved by rail as far as Seoul.

The Sherman might well have proved disastrous had it been necessary to fight Russian-designed and -built T-34s. However, there were no hostile tanks to speak of – they had mostly been destroyed by tactical airpower and those that still existed were hoarded by the enemy generals. *"It is not a modern tank as far as tank versus tank fighting is concerned but fills its role here very well. It has plenty of power with the 500 hp Ford engine, good cross-country performance and an excellent gun for our purposes."*[2] "Good cross-country performance" meant that it could reach places on the rugged Korean hillsides that Pattons and Centurions could not, and from there provide support for the infantry, simply serving as static strong points and engaging in large-calibre sniping on occasion.

Brigadier Rockingham was determined that his men would be able to reach any Korean terrain in fighting condition, and started all the infantry on Exercise CHARLEY HORSE on 11 May. *"D Company of the RCR were the first victims. Considering that the men have had very little practice in hill climbing, they performed excellently. In addition to personal weapons and large packs a section of 81 mm mortars and all platoon*

*3.5 rocket launchers were toted up the 2,000 foot [600 metre] peak."*[3]

The first unit of the brigade to meet the enemy was 2 RCHA, which arrived at the Han river on 17 May and *"immediately went into action"* supporting 28 (Commonwealth) Brigade. The others soon caught up and, as part of a general Eighth Army advance, on 25 May the Canadians began to move towards the 38th Parallel along the Uijongbu-Kumhwa road, about 45 kilometres west of Kap'yong and directly north of Seoul. The Van Doos led the way, together with the Filipino battalion substituting for the Patricias (who were still with 28 Brigade), with three Strathcona troops in direct support, while the fourth troop and the RCR formed the brigade reserve.

The infantry plodded cautiously forward, up ever-narrowing valleys and along knife-like ridges with peaks and spurs that were sometimes occupied by small, troublesome rearguards that discharged a few bursts of long-range machine-gun fire and then skipped away to a position further back as the Canadians deployed to attack them. Before dark, the leading troops scraped slit trenches out of the stony hillsides and all except the sentries snatched what sleep they could.

By the morning of 27 May the brigade had advanced about 14 kilometres and reached the 38th Parallel without meeting any serious opposition. On the 28th an armoured patrol pressed another 10 kilometres north and managed to garner four prisoners – *"dirty, ill-kempt specimens, poorly dressed, without boots and inadequately equipped, whose reaction on capture appeared to be a combination of indifference, resignation and fear."*[4]

Although they certainly all had boots and were well equipped, many of the UN's front-line troops were "dirty, ill-kempt specimens, poorly dressed" as well, since *"No mechanical laundry facilities were available for other than CANADIAN units prior to 5 February 1952 because of lack of suitable equipment and trained personnel."*[5] The men who operated 25 Brigade Ordnance Company's bath and laundry platoon were rarely in a position to distinguish themselves in any other fashion until, on 28 May, they caught two enemy soldiers in a farmhouse while setting up their equipment only a few kilometres behind the front.[6] Of course, more than one witty (or jealous) rifleman argued that the captives were not really soldiers but simply Chinese laundrymen in search of a new job...

Two days later, the brigade advance resumed, and that evening they reached a main defensive position where the Chinese had decided to make some kind of a stand. In front of the Van Doos, protruding into the valley from the east, rose a rugged twin-peaked feature known to the Koreans as Kakhul-bong and to the Canadians as Hills 464 and 467. The road north, essential to any further advance, swung around the western base of these hills, then through a village called Chail-li. The Van Doos came under mortar and machine-gun fire from the nearer Hill 464 in the early evening of the 28th, and the next morning the RCR passed through the Van Doos, preparatory to attacking Kakhul-bong.

Both peaks would have to be secured before any further major advance was possible, and the assault began just as a tempestuous wind and rainstorm soaked and chilled the troops. The violence of the storm decreased after a while but a cold drizzle continued to fall, limiting ground visibility, while an air strike scheduled for 0630 hours had to be cancelled due to the low cloud ceiling. *"Weather conditions could not have been worse and had the effect of hampering the operation in no small way."*[7]

D Company was assigned to take Hill 464 and soon discovered that the Chinese had sited their expertly camouflaged bunkers with great skill. Nevertheless, Hill 464 was cleared and the leading platoon scrambled across the gully separating it from Hill 467. This second peak proved to be better defended, however.

*From the very top of this pinnacle a well-placed enemy machine gun completely dominated the approaches. Artillery and mortar fire was brought down, and the platoon commander of No. 11 Platoon ordered his 3.5-inch rocket launcher to fire against the lone machine gun, but stubborn Chinamen could not be dislodged. The leading section worked its way to within 20 feet [six metres] of the crest, but found it impossible to dislodge the machine gun.*[8]

An air strike, using napalm, might have done the trick, but, as we have noted, the terrible weather precluded air support. Even aerial observation was impossible. The guns of 2 RCHA were using up a lot of ammunition firing by the map, but the Forward Observation Officers could not confirm where their rounds were landing and make the usual minor corrections, so that much of the shelling was to no purpose.

The other companies and two troops of C Squadron had been sent forward along the valley bottom, towards Chail-li, in an attempt to outflank the Chinese on the two hills, while, in what was to prove a wise precaution, a third troop of tanks was stationed astride the road at the foot of Hill 467 *"to form a base upon which to withdraw and to be a ready reserve of tanks."*

> *By 1030 hours A Coy had entered Chail-li and were reorganizing in and around the village.... Beginning at 1130 hours the Chinese began to react very strongly...[and]...despite the intense fire of the battalion supporting weapons and 2 RCHA, the enemy pressure continued to increase. At 1300 hrs the Chinese began to infiltrate on the right flank... At first, due to the poor visibility, this movement on the flank of the company was ignored. According to the company commander, the troops he saw were wearing ponchos and looked very much like Canadian troops. He mistakenly took them to be some men of C Company and, as he could not raise C Coy on the wireless, he could not determine otherwise. It was not until this flank erupted in a hail of small arms, mortar and machine gun fire that he realized the Chinese were circling to his rear.* [9]

More weight (and better weather) would be needed to drive the Chinese from Chail-li. The RCR fell back under the protective fire of the Strathconas, who had one tank hit on its suspension by a 57mm anti-tank gun round. It was recovered, but another that became deeply mired in mud had to be abandoned after *"stripping the weapons"* [10] from it. Easy enough to dismantle the Browning machine-gun and carry it away, but presumably stripping the main gun meant merely removing the breech-block, rendering it inoperable.

The battalion lost six other ranks killed and two officers and 23 other ranks wounded. Subsequently, it reported on the engagement for the benefit of their fellow soldiers and the training echelons in Japan and Canada. Most of the points were quite technical in nature, dealing with such matters as the effectiveness of various radios and cooperation with supporting arms, but under the heading of *"Conduct of Troops"* the enemy was assessed as *"stubborn and determined. He is skillful with respect to camouflage and siting of weapons. He is an excellent digger and appears to have good morale and discipline."* As for our own men, they

> *showed a steadiness under fire which was exemplary, they were anxious to close with the enemy, and maintained a very high morale in spite of casualties and very adverse weather conditions. They were quick to take advantage of what they had been taught in training and applied the lessons without hesitation and automatically. The*

> *sub-unit commanders exhibited fine control and leadership with a good sense of judgement.* [11]

The two hills and Chail-li itself remained in Chinese hands until 5 June, when an American regimental combat team – the equivalent of a Commonwealth brigade – succeeded in re-taking all three.

Having learned a painful but useful lesson, the next day, 1 June 1951, 25 Brigade went into I (US) Corps reserve, while the brigade commander and three battalion commanding officers met to decide just what the basic load of an infantryman, in addition to his rifle, should be over the difficult Korean terrain, and how it could best be carried.

> *It was decided that the following articles were mandatory: Water bottle, Pack...Poncho, Shaving Kit, Towel, two Pair of Socks, Sweater, 24 hours worth of rations, 100 rounds of ammunition, either a pick or shovel and 3 grenades. It was agreed that web equipment was unsatisfactory for crawling and climbing with cross straps. Experiments will be carried out to determine the best way of supporting basic pouches from the web belt alone.* [12]

On 11 June the Van Doos were sent to 28 (Commonwealth) Brigade for a week, to relieve the Patricias (whose commanding officer had briefly returned to Canada to be with a critically ill daughter) in holding a patrol base just north of the confluence of the Imjin and Hantan rivers. An unwalled fortress, heavily wired and mined, this base formed the tip of a salient protruding into enemy territory and provided a secure foundation from which company-strength patrols could probe deeply into no man's land.

Nothing worth mentioning happened to either battalion during their brief sojourns there. The Chinese had pulled back a matter of 10 to 15 kilometres beyond the UN front line, leaving a substantial no man's land into which the Eighth Army was reluctant to advance, given that it was now across the 38th Parallel and intruding, once again, into North Korean territory – a politically loaded situation in this most political of wars.

On 18 June 25 Brigade became exclusively Canadian again when the Filipino battalion left and the Van Doos rejoined their fellow-countrymen as the brigade moved forward to positions on the Chorwon end of the WYOMING Line. Once the brigade was in position, on 19 June, its front covered a little more than seven kilometres along a line running southwest from the outskirts of Chorwon; and, since the entire front was now congealing, its relatively simple task, like that of every other formation at the front, was to keep a wary eye on the enemy and monitor his actions for any signs of a forthcoming offensive. The only activities the brigade had to fear were the possibility of small patrols seeking prisoners by night, trench raids or the increasing unlikelihood of a major offensive, which would, inevitably, be revealed by air reconnaissance before it could be launched across the relatively broad no man's land that lay between the two antagonists. Nevertheless, the first two of those threats were very real.

*The battalion front is over 3500 yards [3,200 metres] long and is very badly cut up by gullies and draws, most of them reaching from front to rear of the company positions and greatly complicating the company commander's problems of securing all round defence. Each platoon, and even some of the sections, are 100 yards apart. Due to this thinness on the ground, great emphasis has been placed on the wiring and mining of the numerous gaps that exist in the battalion front.*[13]

On 21 June 1951 the RCR mounted its first reconnaissance in force, two companies strong, supported by two troops of tanks, a troop of artillery, an engineer platoon and a tactical air-control party. Mine-clearing sappers were needed to clear the route at least as far forward as the intermediate firm base established by the artillery and some of the tanks.

*The only mines encountered in any quantity were wooden, box-type, anti-tank mines.... They were generally laid in groups of three or four along trails, roads or verges, rather than in minefields. The Chinese also favoured mining by-passes and turn-offs from the major trails in terrain previously traversed by vehicles, particularly in the disturbed ground left by tanks. Among the most difficult mines to detect were those that had been laid deep under roads by burrowing in from the built up edge.*[14]

Depending on the topography, the guns would normally advance no further than was necessary to provide support at a comfortable range – that is, no more than 7,000–8,000 metres, the maximum range of a 25-pounder being 12,250 metres. In this first case, one infantry company, a troop of tanks and all the guns formed a base 4,000 metres out, and the rest of the force pushed on another 6,000 metres before encountering automatic weapons fire and withdrawing on the approach of darkness.[15] Such heavyweight patrols quickly became standard practice.[16]

There was also tactical air support available from the Americans, but although it had become a virtual benchmark of modern war six or seven years earlier, the same problems that had plagued it then were resurfacing in Korea.

*When the [PPCLI] patrol reached the top of Hill 501 it was still very hot from the napalm bombing... It is of interest to note that whenever a napalm attack has been followed up closely no enemy have been encountered on the objective [dead or alive]. The enemy apparently retires from a location that he knows is about to be attacked by aircraft and returns to the area as soon as it has cooled sufficiently to permit re-occupation. The prolonged process by which the close support aircraft are vectored to the target and given the exact target, permits the enemy to ascertain the exact impact area and evacuate it prior to the attack. Some method of directing the attack should be devised whereby the enemy would remain in doubt until the last minute and therefore be unable to move rapidly enough to avoid casualties.*[17]

Easier said than done, and no doubt the poor bloody infantry would have been the first to complain if speeding up the process had resulted in an error in targeting and brought the fearsome napalm down on the wrong people! As it was, *"the troops suffered considerably from the heat especially as most of the movement was climbing through dry and dusty bracken, in some places four feet high."*[18]

The environment was causing all kinds of aggravation besides that provided by the local flora, the climate, the Chinese and the North Koreans. During the winter it had been colds, influenza, frostbite and "trench feet." Now, in the early summer, there were other torments to keep the medical officers busy.

*Heat rashes are becoming a problem. Many of the men are covered with very painful rashes. There is also some small insect that is bothering the men. The bites become infected and then seem to spread over the body. Very small red ants are also troublesome in this area. There is a form of poison-oak growing in the area which has added to the mens' [sic] discomfort. Another ailment which owes its origins to the hot weather is the masceration [sic] of the mens' [sic] feet caused by overheated feet made tender by the cold weather and wet conditions of the first part of the year. Nothing but a*

The 25th Brigade joins the Commonwealth Division.
Front row, left to right: Major-General A. J. H. Cassels; Mr. A. R. Menzies, Head of Canadian Liaison Mission, Tokyo; Brigadier J. M. Rockingham,
Back row: Major D. H. Rochester, 57 Field Squadron RCE; Lieutenant-Colonel J. A. Dextraze, 2nd R22eR; Lieutenant-Colonel R. A. Keane, 2nd RCR; Lieutenant Colonel J. R. Stone, 2nd PPCLI (PA 128862)

Brigadier Jean-Victor Allard commanding 25 Brigade, at a Salvation Army Christmas Party. December 1953.
(SF 8682)

*complete rest and treatment of the feet for four or five days seems to cure the trouble.*[19]

It was, indeed, a very sour little war. Large-scale patrolling continued, at a small but regrettable cost. Nothing dramatic, like Kap'yong or Chail-li, but too often one or two men were killed and three or four wounded. According to the historical officer's weekly summary:

> *For most of this week [27 June to 3 July] the three battalions carried out daily patrols into the hills across the CHORWON PLAIN.... There were only two roads providing access across the plain and little could be done to vary the routes of the patrols. Little opposition was encountered on the plain itself. It was only when the troops began to ascend the ridges leading to the dominating ground [beyond the plain] that the Chinese reacted by firing cunningly-hidden automatic weapons. Enemy casualties were difficult to establish owing to the small number actually seen and encountered. However, it was believed that our own artillery and the Tactical Air Control Party were responsible for a considerable number.*[20]

The credit given to the Air Control Party suggests that not everyone was as dissatisfied as the Patricias with the close air support provided.

An unexpected problem arose with the Korean villagers inhabiting no man's land. The government of Syngman Rhee had often treated students and peasant farmers with great brutality in the past – and, indeed, it was continuing to do so, despite American efforts to restrain it.[21] But while Communist propaganda kept all North Koreans fully informed about the atrocities of Rhee and his henchmen (and even those of the Americans in the early days of the war[22]), they had heard little or nothing of the iniquities inflicted by Kim's own people on their political opponents or on captured South Koreans. Nor, perhaps, would they have cared if they had heard. After half a lifetime of Japanese exploitation and oppression (since 1910) and four years of Kim Il-sung's rule, all they wanted was to be left alone to raise their children and cultivate their rice paddies. Better the devil you know than the devil you don't. Thus, many of them saw the Communists as the lesser of two evils, and *"There is reason to believe that when the Chinese descend from the hills to the villages after dark, there are many ready informants among the villagers to give them all the information they require about our own patrols."*[23]

In an attempt to prevent that, most if not all civilians were compulsorily evacuated from the battle zone. Nevertheless, the RCR lost three men when a small, short-range "security patrol" was ambushed just outside the village of Sokang-ri on 2 July. The Patricias' war diary, taking note of the RCR's misfortune, recorded that the *"consensus of opinion is that the three men were ambushed by North Korean civilians and Brigadier J.M. Rockingham...has laid on vigorous security patrols for following day to clear all civilians from the area."*[24] It may well have been that the ambush was conducted by Chinese or North Korean troops wearing civilian dress, but it made little difference to the Canadians' response. The RCR's next patrol included flame-throwers. Sokang-ri was burned to the ground and another 200 villagers were transported to camps in the south, where they would not be subjected to pamphlets (written in English as well as Korean) that emphasized "the wickedness of Wall Street machinations and the tragedy of simple honest folk (like the Canadians) being deluded by the imperialist monsters."[25] *"The enemy leaflets found in our area by the scouts and snipers show a decided improvement over their predecessors. They are written in good English and quote statistics. They are well printed and designed intelligently."*[26]

The Chinese were also adept tacticians, as indeed they should have been after more than 15 years of nearly continuous fighting against the Japanese and Chiang Kai-shek's Chinese "nationalists." After the first week of July, the Brigade war diarist noted:

> *The Chinese practice of permitting us to closely approach their positions before opening fire has a twofold result. First, the proximity of our troops to the enemy when the fight begins nullifies to a certain extent our fire power superiority and forces us to attack without all our support or makes us draw back in order to engage the enemy position. This allows him to do either of two things: one, withdraw after inflicting maximum casualties in the first contact, or, two, reinforce his position having determined the point of our attack. The second result is of course, that we have little if any idea of his exact location, enabling the enemy to hold a great deal of ground with a small force and protecting his positions from bombardment by us.*[27]

By the middle of the month:

> *During the first week in July the enemy confined himself largely to observation from a safe distance,*

*but they are now coming further forward to meet our penetrations with gradually increasing strength. The difficult going and the restricted means of access to the line of hills now being held by the enemy has meant that each patrol must follow the same route out and in.... The only tactic that can be used to prevent a successful counter-patrol by the enemy against our extended flanks has been the alternation in the weight thrown against the enemy. First strong patrols on the right supported by a small patrol on the left and then the reverse. It is apparent from the enemy's inability to successfully engage either patrol that as yet he does not hold the ridge line in sufficient strength to take effective action against us in the valley. It is equally obvious that the day is soon going to come when he will be able to do so and the [Brigade Commander] repeatedly cautions the [battalion commanders] about this eventuality.*[28]

In fact, the first manifestation of Rockingham's prophecy came the very next day, when a small patrol provided by a PPCLI platoon came under fire from a number of enemy machine-guns. The patrol commander called for artillery fire, including smoke, on positions no more than a hundred metres from his own. Under cover of the smoke, the platoon withdrew at a cost of two killed and four wounded. *"Due to the nature of the engagement no attempt was made to recover the bodies of the dead soldiers."*[29]

The Van Doos endured a number of mishaps during the first half of July. On the 6th one of their deep patrols was met by intense artillery fire and four men were wounded before the patrol could withdraw, bringing their wounded with them. Three days later another reconnaissance was accompanied by the temporary battalion commander, Major Lionel Gosselin (Colonel Dextraze was taking a few days' local leave), when the half-track in which he was travelling ran over a mine, killing him and two men and injuring two others. Gosselin would be the most senior Canadian to be killed in action in Korea, but his successor as second-in-command, Major Yvan Dubé, died only a week later when his Korean servant accidentally discharged his pistol while cleaning it. The war diary noted that Dextraze *"is greatly affected by this continual streak of misfortune that seems to have followed the Unit for the last two months."*

On 14 July 1951 the brigade was told that it would be relieved on the 18th, in order to take over the advanced patrol bases on the west bank of the Imjin river, immediately north of the Imjin-Hantan confluence, where it had spent the last two weeks of June.

These bases monitored the natural axis of any Chinese attack aimed at cutting off the two American divisions manning the Chorwon salient. The move was made on schedule and that night the Van Doos' still incomplete defences were probed by a Chinese patrol. It was driven off with one Chinese soldier killed and no Van Doo casualties, but the next night, after a day of rain that left the Imjin in flood, the two ferries across the river became inoperable shortly before the French Canadians were subjected to their own, smaller-scale, version of Kap'yong.

*At 2315 [hours] "A" [Company] engaged enemy at about 20 feet [six metres] away from their position. For nearly three hours fierce fighting was carried out by "A" Coy and the Scouts [Platoon] against an estimated 110 enemies.... Artillery was called [for] and for what seemed like an hour shelled the forward edge of our position for 15 minutes. A few shells fell in the centre of our TAC [battalion headquarters?] but fortunately no one was injured, for all had dug their hole[s] as previously instructed by the [Commanding Officer]... It was the first fierce battle that the unit had encountered to date. The final count was two dead [and] one injured for the unit while the enemy suffered two counted dead and an estimated seven wounded.*[30]

The river became quite impassable the next day, and a footbridge, swept away by the current, took out all the telephone lines to the units and subunits on the west bank of the river, leaving the artillery radio net the only reliable method of communication at a time when there were great fears of a localized Chinese attack. Indeed, it would have been an excellent time for them to launch one from their point of view: the weather made UN air support impossible, and all the combat elements of the Van Doos, three rifle companies of the RCR and one of the Patricias, a troop of tanks and 75 assorted wheeled vehicles were trapped on the far bank in three separate enclaves. With both the ferries still out of action, re-supply was limited to what could be transported by a few inflatables powered by outboard motors. Fortunately, no attack developed, and on the 23rd and morning of the 24th the west bank was evacuated except for the RCR rifle companies, which were deployed to protect the forward terminus of the one ferry now back at work.[31]

On 28 July 1951, 25 Brigade came under command of the newly formed 1 (Commonwealth) Division,

The RCASC "ration run" is seen here moving over the Red Diamond route north from Pusan, Korea. Cliff-climbing and winding, almost every turn offers a spot for ambush by guerrilla bands that roam the hills. A single sniper on a mountaintop can delay a convoy for hours. (PA 131792)

Koreans were used for carrying rations to Canadian riflemen in contact with the enemy. The porters could take two hours to reach the front-line troops. 16–17 April 1951 (SF 1339)

A Canadian signalman checks 25 Brigade telephone lines, assisted by one of many young Koreans who attached themselves to the force as "indigenous labour." May 1951. (PA 128811)

The 2nd Regiment RCHA in support of the 2nd RCR patrol towards Hill 730 on 21 June 1953.
(SF 2019)

Lord Strathcona's Horse (Royal Canadians). (SF 1963)

According to the original caption, this is part of an attack on 3 November 1951 by the 1st PPCLI
supported by tanks. It is suspected, however, that it is only a training exercise carried out by D Company
of the 1st Patricias the day before the relief of the 2nd PPCLI, and that the feature in the background is Hill 222,
which the 2nd Royal 22e Regiment had occupied in September 1951. (PA 188796)

led by Major-General James Cassels. Together with 28 and 29 brigades, 25 Brigade comprised a formation that was 58 per cent British, 22 per cent Canadian, 14 per cent Australian, 5 per cent New Zealanders and 1 per cent Indian.[32] A Canadian, Lieutenant-Colonel E. D. Danby, was appointed the commander's senior staff officer for operational matters, to be followed, in turn, by Lieutenant-Colonels N. G. Wilson-Smith and E. A. C. Amy.

Within the Canadian brigade the impact was slight. Rockingham had other problems to worry about. Brigade and unit records are careful to avoid discussing personalities and personal relationships in any realistic way (as are most regimental histories), but there are indications that, although Rockingham had been permitted to select his own senior officers, he and the RCR's commanding officer, Lieutenant-Colonel Keane, did not always see eye to eye. On 31 July 1951 *"[the Brigade Commander] and [Intelligence Officer] left to visit the 2 RCR positions"*:

> *At 1315 hours the Brigade Commander and Lt-Col Keane left to visit D Company. The [Brigade Commander] expressed considerable concern over the poor disposition of the left forward [platoon] of D [Company] and the [Commanding Officer] 2 RCR agreed that they would have to be re-positioned immediately. The feature occupied by the platoon was a long series of small pimples all densely wooded with pine and brush. The position of the platoon as laid out by the platoon [commander] illustrated the folly of "contour chasing." Each section was out of sight of one another and completely incapable of supporting each other in any way. Each successive knoll or pimple appeared, and in most instances was, to be dominated by the next little feature. In his efforts to secure dominating ground the platoon [commander] completely removed any chance the platoon might [have] had for usefulness or mutual support.[33]*

The immediate fault was clearly that of the platoon commander, probably a young, inexperienced subaltern, and the next level of failure was on the part of the company commander, a wartime veteran who should have known better, but Rockingham clearly (and rightly) held Keane ultimately responsible. The latter most certainly had the expertise to have ensured the platoon position was better sited; it would appear that he had not been providing adequate tactical direction and supervision of his battalion.

The Communists were now unable, and the United Nations unwilling, to achieve victory in Korea. What had once been a war of manoeuvre had settled into a war of slow, set-piece attrition, which from a United Nations point of view was a more doubtful matter on two counts. The despotic Chinese, however weak their technological and industrial base, could absorb any number of casualties and were not handicapped by a need to propitiate an electorate. Their democratic opponents, on the other hand, did have to worry about casualties and the resultant pressures of public opinion. Very few voters were content with the idea of their sons or husbands risking their lives indefinitely in efforts to reunite a remote and insignificant Asian peninsula. They wanted a quick but honourable solution to the Korean imbroglio.

In Canada, Lester Pearson had argued in the House of Commons on 14 May that the only viable policy for UN forces was "to continue inflicting heavy losses on the aggressors...and at the same time to avoid any measures which are not absolutely necessary from a military point of view."[34] Three days later, however, a motion in the US Senate called for an armistice to restore the pre-war demarcation along the 38th Parallel, and a little more than a month after that, on 23 June, the Soviet delegate to the UN Security Council, Jakob Malik,* suggested that negotiations for a cease-fire might be considered. On the 29th the US chiefs of staff directed General Ridgway to initiate discussions with the enemy concerning the possibility of holding talks, and Ridgway suggested (in a radio message to P'yongyang the next day) *"that such a meeting could take place aboard a Danish hospital ship in Wonsan harbour."*[35] Wonsan was an east coast port well north of the 38th Parallel and the current front lines.

A joint response came from Kim Il-sung and General P'eng, commander-in-chief of the so-called Chinese People's Volunteer Army. They would be happy to engage in talks but Wonsan was not an acceptable site. They preferred a tea-house at Kaesong, near to the west coast and north of the Imjin – closer to the front although just as firmly in their hands. The Americans agreed and talks began on 10 July, with Vice-Admiral Turner Joy heading the UN delegation and North Korea's General Nam Il leading the communist bloc.

---

* Realizing their mistake in boycotting Security Council meetings a year earlier, the Russians had been quick to resume their seat, but because of the other permanent members' vetoes could do nothing to remedy their initial blunder.

The significance of the fact that Kaesong was firmly in communist hands became rapidly apparent: the Chinese...had come to receive the UN's capitulation, or at least to score a major propaganda triumph. It had been agreed that the UN party should fly to the talks [by helicopter] under a white flag which the Westerners regarded as an emblem of truce. They quickly discovered that the communists were presenting this symbol to the world as a token of surrender. Joy's delegation found that across the conference table, they had been seated in lower chairs than their communist counterparts.... Every procedural detail, the most basic discussion of an agenda, was dragged down into a morass of ideological rhetoric and empty irrationality... A low point in negotiations was attained on 10 August, when the two delegations stared across the table at each other in complete silence for two hours and eleven minutes.[36]

The talks were broken off on 23 August after the Americans were accused of dropping a napalm bomb within the designated neutral conference area during the night. The Chinese retaliated by marching a company of armed men through this same neutral area while the matter was being argued. Ridgway, his patience exhausted and with the backing of his superiors, called the talks off and ordered a limited offensive that had the hoped-for result. It rattled the Communists' growing confidence in the United Nations' unwillingness to continue the fight, and drove them to propose that discussions be resumed, this time at Panmunjom, a deserted hamlet in no man's land about eight kilometres east of Kaesong.

Talks resumed on 25 October 1951. Although their approach was far from straightforward and they quibbled over every little detail, the Communists were careful not to drive the United Nations away from the negotiating table again, and 21 months later, on 27 July 1953, an armistice would be signed. But that was a process in which Canada played no direct part and 21 months left time for plenty of fighting, even if it was not intense fighting.

The Commonwealth Division played only a very minor part in Ridgway's armistice-motivated offensive, the two major assaults being delivered by American and South Korean formations in the vicinity of the Hwach'on reservoir, well to the east of the Commonwealth Division's positions. The enemy was driven off "Bloody Ridge" on 5 September, after three weeks' hard fighting (and the expenditure of nearly half a million artillery rounds) that cost the winners nearly 3,000 casualties and the losers an estimated 15,000. It took another six weeks to capture "Heartbreak Ridge" at a cost of more than 3,700 casualties (among the worst hit being a French battalion under American command), while the Chinese and North Koreans lost an estimated 25,000 men in their vain attempts to retain the two ridges.[37] But if these costly advances brought the enemy back to the conference table in a slightly more cooperative frame of mind, they also confirmed in United Nations eyes the political necessity of *not* launching any more major offensives.

During September and October, as part of Ridgway's limited offensive, I (US) Corps carried out two operations to improve its positions on a new front line, code-named JAMESTOWN. Expanding from their bridgehead across the Imjin, formerly manned by the RCR and now in the hands of a British unit, the three Canadian battalions drove forward, more or less in line, on to the higher ground that formed a watershed between the Imjin and the Nabu-ri, a much smaller tributary of the Sami-chon (which, in turn, would join the Imjin further downstream). This was Operation MINDEN, and, in contrast to what was occurring further east, it was accomplished with very few casualties. The Van Doos lost one killed and five slightly wounded while winning two Military Crosses and two Military Medals.[38]

The second stage of this limited offensive saw 25 Brigade, in Operation COMMANDO, pushing down into the valley of the Nabu-ri and establishing the JAMESTOWN Line on the rising ground along its southern bank and the ridge line behind it. On the eve of COMMANDO, a 2 PPCLI reconnaissance patrol discovered an unoccupied bunker to the battalion's front, and that night a platoon-strong reconnaissance patrol went out to investigate the area immediately north of the bunker. It was a very dark night – so dark that the platoon sergeant, leading the patrol, actually stepped on a sleeping Chinese soldier! The sleeper, just as surprised as the sergeant, let out a yell before he died, and a number of his comrades poured out of nearby dugouts and trenches. A mêlée ensued, distinguished by the liberal use of grenades and bayonets and resulting in five Patricia casualties, four killed and one (the platoon commander) wounded, while the Chinese were estimated to have lost 20 killed and wounded.[39] The Patricias' ratio of killed to wounded – a reversal of the customary figures – gives some indication of the ferocity of that close-quarters skirmish.

When COMMANDO actually began, Chinese resistance was tough but not adamant, the brigade losing eight killed in action and 35 wounded between 3 and 9 October – most of them during the afternoon and evening of the 3rd, when the advance began with a costly firefight and several notable feats of courage. B Company of the RCR, and particularly its leading platoon, came under heavy fire from both flanks while scrambling through the usual maze of gullies and ridges embellished with much low scrub and often dense undergrowth. The successful withdrawal of that lead platoon was made possible by a battery of 2 RCHA, its shooting directed by Lieutenant Matthew O'Brennan, the Forward Observation Officer, who was seriously wounded in winning a Military Cross. O'Brennan's wireless operator was killed and Lance Bombardier F. M. Dorman, who had been laying a telephone line between the battery and O'Brennan's position, began to initiate fire orders and pass them back despite *"very heavy enemy mortar and machine-gun fire,"* until the platoon had been extricated from its perilous position. Meanwhile, when Lance Corporal Turgeon, the company commander's wireless operator, was wounded, Private W. D. Pugh went forward from the comparative safety of company headquarters, took over Turgeon's radio under heavy fire, and re-established the vital communication links with the supporting tanks and mortars. Dorman and Pugh each won a Military Medal.

The above acts were complemented by what were certainly the bravest deeds carried out by any Canadian in Korea, and probably the pluckiest by any member of the Commonwealth forces. Despite the relentless mortar and machine-gun fire that the Chinese were laying down, when Turgeon, O'Brennan and Riddler were wounded in turn, Corporal Ernest Poole, B Company's medical orderly, *"rushed forward to give [them] aid,"* according to eyewitness Private H. J. Roach.

*In spite of the casualties, and in spite of the heavy volume of fire, Cpl. POOLE went from one to the other of these wounded and administered first aid, applying tourniquets and giving morphine. Cpl POOLE carried each of the wounded back below the crest of the hill, out of the line of direct fire. Each time he returned for one of the men, he submitted himself to extreme danger, yet he was calm and cheerful throughout. I called to him to keep his head down, that he was going to get killed and he answered, "I can't help it, I have a job to do and I'm going to do it."*

*Cpl POOLE's courage and devotion to duty was beyond anything I have seen and his example gave all of us great encouragement.*

*Later that evening I saw Cpl POOLE improvising stretchers from blankets and branches of trees, and lashing the wounded, who now numbered ten, onto the stretchers by using heavy vine as rope. He organised a carrying party from the platoons and Korean labourers and started back with them to the [Regimental Aid Post], which was about 3000 yards away, across extremely difficult country.*[40]

Initially, an infantry NCO was detailed to lead the stretcher party back, *"but he was wounded before they had gone more than a few yards. Cpl POOLE then assumed leadership of the party and led it back to the [Regimental Aid Post]."* Colonel Keane recorded:

*The route was subjected to continuous shell fire, Enemy patrols had infiltrated along both sides, the area was heavily mined... But Corporal POOLE led his party with confidence and all the casualties were borne safely to the Regimental Aid Post. Undoubtedly his leadership and the persistence with which he carried out his duties...was vital in saving the lives of one Officer and three Other Ranks and in preventing two of the wounded from falling into the hands of the enemy.*

Finally, the battalion's medical officer, Captain H. C. Stevenson, appended his tribute: *"On examining the casualties, I found they had been exceptionally well attended. Splints, stretchers and tourniquets had been improvised in a remarkably skilful manner under extremely difficult circumstances."* Colonel Keane pulled these accounts together in a well-deserved citation for the Victoria Cross, which was countersigned by Brigadier Rockingham. The recommendation then went to General Cassels – where it was downgraded to a Distinguished Conduct Medal, categorized as "the poor man's VC" by the cynical soldiery.[41] Stories like this one provide an excellent rationale for a distinctly Canadian honours system.

With the conclusion of Operation COMMANDO and occupation of the JAMESTOWN Line, 25 Brigade had reached the positions that it would hold – give or take a few metres and punctuated by a number of vicious fire-fights – for the remainder of the Korean conflict. It had also reached that point in its history when troop rotations would begin.

Edward Zuber, 1932–
*Welcome Party*
CWM-90026

## CHAPTER VI

# *Holding the Line*

THE LENGTH OF A KOREAN TOUR had been set (by Ottawa, in July 1951) at one year, in terms of units rather than individuals, so that 2 PPCLI, the first Canadian unit to arrive in theatre, was now coming to the end of its projected tour. The first companies of the replacement battalion, commanded by Lieutenant-Colonel N. G. Wilson-Smith, arrived on 5 October 1951, followed by the remainder of the unit over the next month. Officially, 1 PPCLI was a regular force unit, and the officers were, indeed, regulars without exception, but the other ranks were quite a mixed bag in terms of service status. There were, as well as a cadre of long-service regulars and men who had enlisted since the Korean conflict had begun as part of the general expansion of the army, a considerable number who had joined the Special Force and been trained and held as replacements for the 2nd Battalion, together with a sprinkling of men who had actually joined that battalion late, as replacements, and were now transferred to the 1st.

Landing at Pusan, the first two companies of 1 PPCLI entrained on *"a conglomeration of the oldest and worst cars in the universe. No washing facilities, crude toilet facilities and three-tier bunks made of wood."*[1] Welcome to Korea! At noon on 7 October they arrived at Tokchon, a hamlet 30 kilometres northwest of Seoul, and the following day intensive training began, emphasizing hill climbing and instruction in such new weapons as the 60mm and 81mm mortars, the 3.5-inch rocket launcher, and (for the signallers) new and better radios. After four days of that, they set off on foot for the front, a distance of another 30 kilometres.

Their first experience of battle came that night, when the PPCLI, old and new, bore the brunt of a Chinese raid, losing one officer and three men killed and 12 wounded in beating back the enemy. *"Colonel Stone gave great credit to the 24-gun battery [sic] of the RCHA which had fired off some 3,000 rounds or forty truckloads of ammunition during the night."*[2]

In the early hours of 23 October, the brigade launched Operation PEPPERPOT, in which one company from each of the three infantry battalions attacked enemy lines in a fashion very similar to that of the Chinese against the Canadians 10 days earlier. This venture brought one of the artillery's Forward Observation Officers, Captain J. E. W. Berthiaume, a Military Cross when, during its withdrawal, the Patricia company headquarters found itself under fire from its own artillery as well as from the Chinese guns. *"He sat down in the midst of the mixture of Chinese and Commonwealth artillery fire and lifted the [friendly] concentration off us by wireless."*[3] The Patricias took 13 casualties – three killed, plus one died of wounds, and nine wounded, including two killed and four wounded when two stretcher parties wandered into a minefield; the RCR lost one killed and four wounded and the Van Doos one killed and six wounded.[4] They claimed, however, to have killed 37 of the enemy, with another 20–25 believed killed and 20 believed wounded, while one prisoner was taken by the RCR.[5]

Ten days later, after dark on the evening of 2 November, the Royals survived what their regimental historian has described as "Second Battalion's finest hour" when A and C companies were raided by a complete battalion of Chinese.

> It was anything but a silent attempt; flares were going up all over the place, bugles were blowing and whistles shrilling; it seemed as though the Chinese had reverted to their religious practices in dealing with the foreign devils; some of their men had come to grief on a minefield and their screams and moans added to the tumult.[6]

In the third of three attacks, the enemy burst through the wire and overran one platoon of A Company, only to be met by the platoon commander, Lieutenant E. J. Mastronardi, "in Wild West fashion, revolver in one hand, Verey pistol in the other, scoring hits with both." The platoon withdrew, taking their wounded with them. The rest of the defences held, however, and next morning the lost outpost was reoccupied without opposition. "They found everything almost as [it] had been left, bedrolls, parkas, etc, untouched along with 7 dead Chinese within the platoon wiring. By 0915 hrs another 11 dead enemy bodies were found, making the total 18 with the minefield and [the] forward slopes yet to be searched." The final count of enemy dead was 35. RCR losses totalled one killed and 14 wounded, and Mastronardi won an MC.[7]

While intermittent talks continued at Panmunjom, both sides dug deeper and deeper into the Korean hillsides. The Chinese, understandably intent on neutralizing superior UN firepower, created a wide belt of deep bunkers and tunnels – perhaps as wide as 15 kilometres – all along their 250-kilometre front. As long as the war remained static, their minimally mechanized logistics could maintain three quarters of

a million men south of the Yalu, most of them in that forward zone and nearly all of them digging, digging, digging. Since they lacked a significant counter-battery capability and an air arm that could frustrate American tactical airpower, earth was their only protection.

Between the slit trenches and bunkers of the combatants, protected by belts of barbed wire and minefields, there lay a no man's land one to three kilometres wide depending on the contours of the ground. By day, no one moved there; by night, working parties renewed or improved their foremost defences, while reconnaissance and ambush patrols crept about their dangerous business, as they had done between battles on the Western Front some 35 years earlier. In fact, increasingly the Korean War was coming to resemble that archetypal struggle, compounded by the extraordinarily hilly terrain. Under these circumstances, the only role for armour – in the Canadian case, C Squadron, Lord Strathcona's Horse – was as mechanized snipers, using their tank guns to shoot at the firing slits of Chinese bunkers, and acting as mobile bunkers in support of infantry incursions into no man's land.

The infantry were expected to dig their own trenches and bunkers. The sappers of 57 Independent Field Squadron, RCE, were kept busy building and maintaining roads (tracks would be a more accurate word – most of the forward ones were only four metres wide, with six-metre-wide passing locations spaced along them) and bridges in order to get supplies as far forward before Korean civilian porters had to take over, humping supplies of food and ammunition the last few hundred metres to battalion headquarters. There would be a period of uncertain length each spring when the thaw, combined with heavy, monsoon-type rains, would make many tracks virtually impassable despite the efforts of the engineers and everything depended upon the "rice burners."

United Nations forces, stretching back to Pusan, now mustered nearly half a million men, about half of them being Koreans. Both sides had armour – the United Nations far more than their opponents – but the enemy tanks were neither seen nor heard, while the role of UN tanks

> *appeared to be that of providing direct sniper fire support for the endless infantry night patrols. The nightly turret/radio watches were particularly nerve wracking, although one would never admit to it. The noise of patrols going out or returning*

*through the wire, the constant thumping of Vickers and .30-calibres [machine-guns] firing on fixed lines, the frequent lighting of the sky by some equally nervous infantryman firing off flares, the shadows created by the searchlights providing the artificial moonlight, and every shrub exposed by the flares appearing to move — all had the tendency to make one rather anxious.*[8]

How tanks could provide significant "direct sniper fire support" by night in the absence of night-vision equipment, a much later development in armour technology, is not clear.

On 11 November the last element of 2 PPCLI left the line, and the infantry component of the brigade now consisted of 2 RCR, 1 PPCLI and 2 R22eR. On the 17th, *"for the first time since the Brigade has been in Korea Brigade HQ received about 10 rounds of enemy shelling, which coincided with the visit of Mr. MAYHEW (Minister of Fisheries) and Mr. APPELWHAITE (MP for SKEENA)."*[9] Apparently no one was seriously hurt, but it seems likely that incident still marks — or should one say celebrates? — the last occasion when a Canadian Cabinet minister came under hostile fire in a literal sense, if not metaphorically.

As far as the Canadians were concerned, the first three weeks of November 1951 were marked by small-scale, short-range, ineffective patrolling, both by them and by the enemy, although the British battalion on their right came under relatively heavy attack on the 17th. *"At 1800 hrs the remnants of one platoon came into the lines of 1 PPCLI to report that they had been captured by the Chinese and then released."*[10] If their story was true, one can only wonder why that should have happened. No explanation is forthcoming from the records but perhaps Jacket Coates could have given us an answer!

On 22 November the Chinese delivered a rather more serious blow against the positions held by the Van Doos, even though its objectives were still strictly limited. This raid followed hard on a general re-deployment of the over-extended (19,000-metre) Commonwealth divisional front to a more acceptable 15,500 metres, in which 25 Brigade shifted slightly to the right, and D Company, at the apex of the Van Doos' new position, found that the defences it was inheriting from a British unit were "much too crowded and lacked mutual support." Worse, some of the firing points were built up (with sandbags) instead of dug down, making them "perfect targets for high-velocity weapons."[11] And worse still, the American defenders of the dominating local feature, Hill 355 — soon to be nicknamed "Little Gibraltar" — on

D Company's right, were in the process of briefly losing it to the Chinese. But there would be no time to re-site the defences; the enemy attacked that night, presumably aware of the change-over and hoping to catch the new garrison in a state of disarray.

A heavy attack came in on D Company, who manned the most exposed position and whose sand-bagged dug-outs and tin-roofed bunkers were incapable of resisting high-velocity artillery rounds in the one case and air bursts of shrapnel in the other. That evening they and the American battalion on their right came under *"intense [artillery] and rocket fire for several hours."*[12] "Intense fire" falling on a company area could be *"a hundred rounds of artillery fire every minute for up to a half-hour before the attack commenced."*[13] At 0400 hours the next morning, the war diary recorded, *"snow is falling now and it has become quite cold. D Coy is still receiving enemy artillery fire."* The bombardment lasted a full 24 hours. Now that the front was stabilizing, the Chinese logistics system was getting up to speed, such as it was, although few future bombardments would last as long and be so intense as this one.

*Wire*
*Although we had a reasonable quantity of wire (4 to 6 rows of double apron fences with tangle wire between) it was, in most cases, completely destroyed by the enemy artillery. Wire must be in great depth and where possible sited on reverse slopes or positions where it is difficult for the enemy to hit it.*

*Minefields*
*These suffered the same fate as the wire and the same lessons apply....*

*Communications*
*All wireless sets must be in strong bunkers with really thick head-cover. All [telephone] lines were invariably cut almost immediately and, in some cases, wireless sets were buried or destroyed.*[14]

By late afternoon on the 23rd the Van Doos' D Company was under attack by an estimated two companies of Chinese. *"Lt Col Dextraze, although extremely concerned over his now open right flank, expresses his resolution, in a [radio] net call to all sub-units, to hold the present positions."*[15] Supported by artillery, armour and mortars (the mortar platoon expended *"over 5100 rounds"* in 16 hours), the battalion resisted stoutly, and during the night an American unit took off some of the pressure by attacking and retaking the western slopes of Hill 355.

Attacks came in all night long and well into the morning of the 24th. At one time D Company was surrounded, just as their peers in 2 PPCLI had been at Kap'yong, but steady fire from UN artillery and mortars weakened the attacks, and the pioneer platoon laid anti-personnel and anti-tank mines in the area, hampering if not prohibiting any further Chinese penetration. In the early hours of the 25th the Americans succeeded in re-taking Hill 355, thus relieving some of the pressure, but D Company was in poor shape physically. The weather had brought snow each night that thawed in the mornings, so that men living in their fire trenches and getting no sleep were, in turn, cold and wet and both.[16] On the morning of the 26th D and B companies managed to exchange positions, but the immediate danger was over. The Chinese retired whence they had come. Seven onslaughts, over three days, had left the Van Doos with 16 killed and 44 wounded, about half of the casualties belonging to D Company. Among the seven decorations awarded, the company commander, Major Réal Liboiron, received a DSO, and the commander of the scout and sniper platoon that bore the brunt of the Chinese onslaught, Corporal (acting Sergeant) Leo Major, a Bar to his DCM.[17] (Major's original "gong" had been won with the Régiment de la Chaudière during the previous war: two DCMs form a very rare distinction indeed.)

There was another down side to all this. On the 24th three soldiers manning a forward trench, Privates J. T. Allain, Arthur Baker and J. A. Bellefueille, were taken prisoner – the first but not the last Canadians to suffer that misfortune in Korea. However, they were lucky to fall into Chinese rather than North Korean hands, as had happened to many Americans during the first six months of the war, and find themselves incarcerated in camps situated in North Korea but administered by the Chinese. Neither China nor North Korea had been signatories to the Geneva Convention of 1949 and they both took the line that all their prisoners were war criminals. But there was a great difference in the way that they treated their captives. The North Koreans looked upon theirs primarily as forced labour and had little or no regard for their welfare in any form or at any time. Many thousands of captives, mostly South Korean, died in these camps. The Chinese, on the other hand, had a "lenient policy," in which each prisoner was offered communism as a means of redemption and, provided that he did not actively resist, was furnished with minimal food and shelter. He did not have to become a communist, but he could not act in an anti-communist fashion.

*After capture, prisoners must be friends and no longer adopt a hostile attitude; they must learn repentance and the meaning of peace. They are lucky to be alive after fighting for the capitalists and they should be grateful that they are prisoners of the Chinese and have the chance to study until they go home... The Lenient Policy is unchangeable but there must be no sabotage of study. A hostile attitude to study or any attempt to spoil other students' study will be punished... If you are friendly to us you will be treated as a friend, but the Lenient Policy has its limitations as regards our enemies.*[18]

Arriving in a Chinese camp, a prisoner was required to complete an itemized autobiography, beginning with a brief description of himself including his nationality, racial origin, home town and address, education, previous employment and hobbies, as well as the usual name, rank and serial number (as stipulated in the Geneva Convention) together with his unit and type of duty. Then came a requirement for a full family outline, including finances and occupations, religious beliefs, social activities and political affiliations of himself, his parents and his siblings. Next, they sought much more detail concerning the prisoner's military career:

1. *When, where, why and how did you enter the armed forces?*
2. *Assignments (time, places, units, rank, duties and principal functions).*
3. *Your intimate colleagues (officers and men) in the past various assignments.*
4. *What kind of military training have you received (when, where and in which units?) The main courses and subjects studied?*
5. *How many times have you entered the armed forces?*
6. *Have you ever been discharged? If so list your civilian jobs and pay (time and place).*
7. *Did you fight in World War II? If so where and what duties?*
8. *Were you wounded or captured during World War II? If captured when, where and how did you get out?*
9. *How many campaigns have you participated in, when and where?*

And that was just the short form. When it was completed the prisoner might well be asked to complete a

The RCR reinforce their barbed wire defence. (PA 183961)

The shovel was an essential part of an infantryman's kit. (PA 139109)

much longer, more detailed version that entered into psychological matters: *"Thoughts and ambitions in different periods. What influenced you?" "Events or hardships. Love. Hatred and miserable this in different periods [sic]."* Finally, an *"Outline of Self-Analysis"* included such questions as *"What knowledge and understanding did you gain from your parents, grandparents, etc.? What part of this family teaching created the deepest impression?"* and *"What were feeling and ideological attitude towards army life, e/g/ [sic] salary, ranks[,] discipline, etc.?"*[19] By the time a prisoner had provided answers to those questions that had no absolutely military implications, the Chinese had a good foundation for a psychological profile of the person concerned.

From the very beginning prisoners in Korea were told that they were students: they were not prisoners, they were not to be referred to as prisoners. They were to call each other students. The men who controlled them and lived with them were called instructors. And the average soldier's first contact with an instructor came almost at the point of capture. Instead of being kicked around and slapped and spat upon and beaten [as he would have been by the North Koreans] he was simply taken to a collecting point where he met a young Chinese, usually in his late twenties or early thirties, who spoke remarkably good English...

To the man expecting the burning bamboo splinter routine, the new instructor said the following. He said, We wish to welcome you to the ranks of...the people. We are happy to have liberated you from the capitalistic, imperialistic Wall Street warmongers who sent you here...

The Chinese went on to say: ...We ask from you only one thing, and that's your physical cooperation. Don't resist us. Don't fight us. We are people like you are, and so simply cooperate, try to live with us until the senseless slaughter started by the Wall Street warmongers is allowed to end. And in return for your physical cooperation, we give you this: no work, no physical labour. There are no slave camps or road gangs or coal mines here. We have what we call the lenient policy for Americans. We will feed you and clothe you and house you and give you medical care comparable to what we give our own people, the best we possibly can. And granted these things won't be civilized like they are in the United States because we're way

behind the United States. But they'll be the best we've got.[20]

Corporals and below were held in different camps from officers and senior NCOs, thus removing the ordinary soldier from those most likely to encourage resistance. A lack of responsiveness to these attempts at indoctrination was tolerated, but any attempt to thwart the process by inspiring active opposition among other prisoners resulted in beatings, starvation, segregation in solitary confinement and denial of medical treatment. And a carefully cultivated system of informing on minor miscreants that presented doing so as a civic duty and earned the informant a small reward – perhaps a few cigarettes or candies, while bringing only a mild reprimand to the culprit – went far towards keeping prisoners in line.

The instructor would say: Now look, John, we know you have committed such and such an act. Don't deny it. We know you've committed it. You're not here to determine your guilt. We would like you to examine your own behaviour in terms of the welfare of this group. We want you to confess that it was wrong. We want you to assert your determination to be better in future.[21]

In such a poisonous environment, taxing enough to frustrate even Jacket Coates, committees supporting and coordinating escape attempts, as had been common practice in Second World War German and Italian camps (even Japanese camps had had their covens of plotters), were simply unworkable. There was little need for barbed wire or watchtowers and one man was sufficient to guard a hundred prisoners.[22] The only exception appears to have been one small camp (180 prisoners) to which intransigents were transferred.

Excluding the South Koreans, Americans were the most susceptible to this brainwashing, measured by the number that declined repatriation at the conclusion of hostilities. Of the 3,746 Americans who survived life in the camps (about the same number died in captivity, most of them in North Korean camps during the early days of the war), 23 chose not to return when the armistice was signed in 1953, although several later changed their minds. Out of nearly a thousand British officers and men, only one refused repatriation in 1953, and even he went home 12 years later. Altogether, 33 Canadians fell into enemy hands and all of them chose to return as soon as possible. However, several did sign so-called peace petitions,[23] which offered one way of letting relatives in Canada know that they were still alive.

Two Van Doos who spent many months in captivity were examined by psychiatrists after their return and reported on as follows:

> Internment has left a definite mark on their personalities. They show little emotional reaction to the stories of fear, hate and resentment they tell of camp life. This emotional "flatness" which belies their inherent Gallic temperament is attributed to a deep distrust of both the Chinese guards and their fellow prisoners.
>
> Their successful resistance to indoctrination can be attributed to the moral support they provided one another, the language barrier which restricted their company and the religious belief which caused resentment to [sic] the "self criticism" periods.[24]

Where an insurmountable language barrier existed between the "instructors" and the prisoners, the effects could be even greater, especially when it was combined with an almost tribal cohesion, as with the few Turkish prisoners. When the Chinese found a compliant Armenian who spoke Turkish and inserted him into the prison community as a "mole" to foment distrust among the Turks, he simply disappeared. Never seen or heard of again. No body, no bones, no nothing![25]

One long-term result of post-war study of these brainwashing techniques was the introduction of a prisoner's Code of Conduct, subsequently adopted (with local variations) by most Western nations.

Behind the front, support units struggled with a variety of operational and administrative problems. No. 54 Transport Company, RCASC, which on 25 July 1951 became responsible for ammunition replenishment for the Commonwealth Division (2 RCHA alone used up 70,000 rounds of 25-pounder ammunition in its first five months of operations, and more than 170,000 rounds in the next five months to 17 March 1952[26]), carried out its duties while grappling with a variety of self-inflicted medical problems.

> The incidence of [venereal disease]...has shown a sharp decrease.... There were 12 men infected during the month and successfully treated.... All men clearly understand that infection automatically earns them a slot on the bottom of the [Rest and Recreation] leave list for Japan. This is not calculated to be a penalty but rather a means of extending our appreciation to the men of the Unit

> who remain free from infection. There were 20 men treated for ear infection caused from swimming in nearby rivers...[27]

Ironically, furloughs in Japan were the leading cause of VD. "The incidence of this disease is very high, the rate being 450 per 1,000 per annum. It has been found that ½ to ⅔ of the cases are contracted whilst personnel are on leave in JAPAN." This rate was "roughly ten times as high as it was during the Second World War," but antibiotics provided a quick and easy remedy for infections. Appeals on health and moral grounds proved ineffectual and the only restraint seemed to be that anyone infected had to wait 90 days before repatriation to avoid spreading the diseases at home. The Red Cross thought that this rule led to attempts at concealment and favoured abolishing it, but Brigadier Rockingham thought otherwise and his view carried the day.[28]

The beer issue dropped to four bottles per week per man. "This is hardly enough in such a hot climate and should be increased to one bottle a day, otherwise, native brew will trickle in with the usual devastating results." Alcohol, like sex, was an ongoing threat to the efficiency of the brigade out of the line, but there was also a very different, and admirable, side to things.

> The children of our neighbouring village presented quite a problem as they ran over and under trucks in the Unit lines.... Then our [Workshop] Officer suggested a novel scheme to contain them... He was given the green light and as if by magic, in three days time, a modern playground was created in a corner of our Unit lines. The [Workshop] boys designed and manufactured 6 high and low swings, 6 teeter-totters, a may pole, sand box and slide...surrounded with a sturdy fence and ornate bridge type entrance. All the trappings were brightly painted and above the entrance hangs a sign "Harry's Happy Haven" as a tribute to Capt Harry McKenzie the first soldier to sell democracy to Koreans.
>
> The children flock to the playground daily and our men frequently are found pushing the swings or teaching the little people a group game.[29]

As for delivering ammunition, there was much hard work and some danger involved, in addition to the obvious threats imposed by heavy and sometimes fast-moving traffic on narrow, dust-obscured roads.

> Two trucks of "C" Platoon (drivers Leclair and Servell) came under enemy Mortar fire on 3rd of [October] while delivering 4.2[-inch] Mortar

*[Ammunition] to Battery sites. One of the trucks was ventilated but the drivers fortunately escaped uninjured.*

*A "B" [Platoon] truck (driver Cloutier) hit an enemy heavy anti-tank mine and the vehicle was damaged beyond repair. Pte Cloutier was blown through the canvas top and has been evacuated suffering from severe shock. Two nearby English gunners were instantly killed by the same explosion.*

*Three North Korean[s] were taken prisoner by members of the unit in the general area of our ammunition Roadhead.[30]*

Lieutenant-General Van Fleet's limited offensive appears to have encouraged the Communists to be more cooperative at Panmunjom, and on 25 October they tentatively abandoned their claim for the 38th Parallel as the demarcation line and accepted in principle the United Nations insistence on the more militarily defensible positions that the latter now held.

René Lévesque, a CBC war correspondent who would one day become premier of Quebec, visited Panmunjom, and his account gives some idea of the awkward, uneasy environment that prevailed at the talks:

*We would fly over the Chinese lines by helicopter, landing in a fortified area surrounded by barbed wire. In the middle was a small building with a pagoda roof. The press was parked near the door reserved for the UN negotiators. On the other side a bunch of Oriental soldiers with red stars on their caps kept close watch on their own territory. They spoke among themselves in low voices, but if one of us made so bold as to approach, he would be greeted by a deathly silence. Even the most pleasantly put question would be met with an enigmatic stare.[31]*

Inside the *"small building with a pagoda roof"* the atmosphere was just as unsociable. Delegates spent hours sitting and staring blankly at each other across a long table, then haggled interminably over details. When the Communists pressed for a no man's land that would require the UN forces to withdraw some 30 kilometres, thus compelling them to abandon their naturally strong positions and also making it more difficult to monitor the enemy front, the UN response was to propose a mere four-kilometre-wide "demilitarized zone" between the two protagonists. Moreover, the demarcation line had to be the "actual line of contact at the time of the signing of the armistice."[32]

Meanwhile, the UN commanders were happy to stand on the defensive. Indeed, on the night of 27 November 1951, 1 Comwel signalled all three of its brigades that, in the light of progress – very slow progress – at Panmunjom:

*All future patrols will be strictly [reconnaissance] NOT fighting. Their object will be to gain [information] only and NOT fight the enemy. [Artillery] will fire only [Defensive Fire] tasks and active [Counter Battery] tasks. The object of these instructions is to show him (the enemy) that we are willing to honour a cease fire if one is agreed.[33]*

General Cassels and his brigade commanders thought this a terrible blunder, although there seems to have been some uncertainty about the UN purpose. The original instruction, presumably as passed down from corps and army HQs, had proclaimed that the object was to *"show the enemy that we are willing to honour a cease fire,"* but in his relevant periodic report Cassels espoused a very different purpose.

*The aim was to make the enemy so curious that they would come in some strength to see what was happening and we could then kill them in large numbers and capture some prisoners.*

*My own view was that the operation would give the enemy exactly the opportunity he wanted to improve his defences on the forward slopes and to work his way forward with impunity. As we had spent the previous month using every possible means to force the enemy back and off the forward slopes and had destroyed many of his bunkers, I protested strongly against this operation. I was overruled.*

*I regret to say that the result has been exactly as I and all my commanders anticipated. The enemy is now right down the forward slopes in very deep and strong bunkers and all our previous efforts have been completely nullified. The enemy sent out a few patrols and found we were still there and then calmly proceeded with his digging. We are now trying to force him back again but it will take a long time and considerable effort.[34]*

Two nights later the divisional directive was amended to permit artillery activity to revert to normal, infantry on reconnaissance patrols could direct gunfire on observed enemy, and in general the Brigade could attack *"with everything but infantry."* Units were to maintain their positions, limit them-

War correspondent René Lévesque of the CBC interviewing Lieutenant-Colonel J. A. Dextraze, Commanding officer Royal 22e Regiment, Korea, 16 August 1951. (Left to right: Lieut.-Col. Dextraze, Mr. Lévesque, Mr. Norman Eaves.) (C 79007)

René Lévesque puts his mini-tape recorder on his head and fords a small stream as he works his way forward to RCR troops deeper in enemy territory. Korea, 14 August 1951 (C 77793)

selves to reconnaissance patrolling and, as the brigade historical officer noted, *"avoid casualties."*[35]

At strategic and operational levels (and most of all as a public relations exercise) that made perfect sense, but tactically it posed all kinds of problems. It tended to discourage commanders and troops alike from taking any kind of risk that they could reasonably avoid in the short term – although that might well lead to heavier casualties in the long run. The build-up for any major offensive could be identified by aerial reconnaissance and radio monitoring, but without frequent and aggressive patrolling by night no one could know when the Chinese might schedule a raid. Nevertheless, the RCR's Colonel Keane, obeying orders, told his companies:

*During this next 30 day period avoid casualties at all costs. Through our own actions demonstrate that we intend to honour the demarcation line as laid down. We will maintain present positions and avoid engaging the enemy except if or when the enemy threatens our positions. Undertake no offensive operations.*[36]

However, perhaps because Rockingham was not a career soldier – or had not been so before being lured into becoming one after joining the Special Force – and was willing to turn a Nelsonian eye on foolish or unnecessarily dangerous orders, neither Cassels's nor Keane's (both were expressing the intentions of higher authorities) lasted very long. It was essential for the general, long-term safety of his men that they continue to dominate no man's land, and Rockingham was apparently unwilling to see them surrender that supremacy. After 10 obedient days, 1 PPCLI and 2 R22eR sent out fighting patrols on the night of 9/10 December, which exchanged shots with the enemy before returning with no casualties and no prisoners. The next night, however, a PPCLI raid on Hill 227 *"reached its objective, destroyed several enemy bunkers and M[achine] G[un] positions,"* unfortunately incurring 25 casualties – *"one killed and 24 wounded, including the coy commander and two platoon commanders."* Enemy losses were not even estimated.

Twenty-four wounded was a substantial number by Canadian standards – it will be remembered that Kap'yong had brought the PPCLI only 23 – and though few of the wounds were life-threatening, or even severe, this gave 37 Field Ambulance's casualty clearing post a good work-out. If a severely wounded soldier was recovered, he might be lucky enough to be evacuated by helicopter (as had happened to three at Kap'yong), but most wounded were removed in the conventional way, on foot – the man's own or those of stretcher-bearers – and then by jeep and ambulance. Every infantryman had to be proficient in first aid, and soldiers wounded while in a platoon position or on patrol in daylight had often to be given a shot of morphine and made as comfortable as possible until dark unless the wound was sufficiently life-threatening to require risking a stretcher move by daylight, above ground and at the risk of further injury, to both the wounded man and his stretcher-bearers.

*On occasion, the hilly terrain and the location of company headquarters, platoons and outposts anywhere up to two miles [3.5 kilometres] beyond jeep head level necessitates the carry by stretcher of wounded that distance uphill and [down dale], through slit trenches and above ground until jeep head level is reached. Normally the greatest time loss encountered in casualty evacuation is found to be this needful long carriage of wounded back to where the ambulance is waiting. Once embarked, only a fraction of the time is required to return the wounded to [Regimental Aid Post level].*[37]

*Casualties on patrols caused real problems as there was never an option – we carried our casualties with us...*

*...A casualty on patrol took one or two other men away from being able to fire and fight. Casualties also limited the ability of the patrol to manoeuvre quickly to gain some tactical advantage. A serious casualty had to be carried by four men usually using a blanket and extra rifle slings taken along for the purpose. It was essential, in my mind anyway, that those who risked their lives should expect that everyone else would give his best effort to get them back if they became casualties. The morale effect of this was very strong and quietly understood by all ranks.*[38]

The next step back was to the Advanced Dressing Station operated by the Field Ambulance staff.

*Due to the poor road conditions and often times the forward routes being under enemy observation and within range of enemy mortars and shelling, the ambulance team must run the gauntlet of enemy fire during daylight hours or travel without lights after dark... They must return via the same route at low speeds (5 mph) [8 kph] depending on the severity of injuries sustained by the casualty.*[39]

Slowly the number of fighting patrols increased again. Although no formal instruction seems to have been issued, the divisional diary began to record how *"normal patrol activity continued, with the emphasis on trying to capture [Prisoners of War],"*[40] and "ambush" patrols – in which platoon-sized groups simply went out into no man's land, established themselves on ground that Chinese patrols might well choose to use and waited hopefully – increased in frequency but were usually fruitless. Over the next three weeks, however, including the Christmas celebration, all three battalions sent out several more fighting patrols (Keane's specific order having apparently been quietly relegated to obscurity), with those from the Van Doos incurring eight men wounded and the RCR losing two killed before the tempo of fighting patrols began to once again slow down.

The term "fighting patrol" speaks for itself – 15 to 40 men creeping up to the enemy line in search of the enemy to be killed or taken prisoner – but small reconnaissance patrols could be even more nerve-racking. A fine example occurred on the night of 6/7 December.

*A game of cat and mouse was played with enemy patrols by our own during the night. "D" [Company's reconnaissance] patrol [one NCO and three men] first encountered an enemy patrol of five men at [Map Reference] 131149. Our patrol didn't fire but went to ground and later followed the enemy. Fifteen minutes later a second patrol of 3 enemy were encountered at MR 130151 who fired 3 bursts of burp gun fire and threw one grenade. Our patrol didn't return fire. This last patrol of 3 went to hill 166 MR 122156. Our patrol proceeded and at MR 127148 heard the first enemy patrol following. Again "D" Coy men went to ground and the enemy went to hill 166. Our patrol after a wait of 20 minutes went to 123147 and climbed up along the feature and then [northeast]. In the valley they heard nothing at all. No sight nor sound of movement at [Hill] 166. Patrol was ordered back at 0100 hrs so didn't proceed further. With no further enemy contact the patrol arrived back at 0130 hrs.*[41]

The Chinese, with an impressive faith in the power of propaganda (and Christian charity), were now trying other ways of winning the war. A week later:

"B" Company [1 PPCLI] awakened to be confronted by two large and neatly-lettered signs which had been erected during the night beyond its outposts, with arrows pointing to nearby piles of Christmas stockings containing handkerchiefs printed with appropriate Communist slogans,

Peace Dove pins, cigarette holders and plastic finger rings. On the same night "C" Company apprehended a Korean boy approaching the Patricia lines laden with similar gifts; he carried as well a "Signatory Book for Demanding Peace and Stopping War" which the recipients were invited to sign and to return; he also bore a letter of invitation to a joint Christmas party between the lines. The invitations were ignored, the presents accepted. They had a high souvenir value but unfeeling Intelligence Officers impounded most of them.[42]

In mid-January 1952, the brigade moved into divisional reserve after a period of four and a half months in the line. While the brigade was "resting," the Chief of the General Staff, Lieutenant-General Guy Simonds, visited it – which meant little rest and much "smartening up" – and pinned decorations on a number of officers and men. Not among them, however, were Lieutenant-Colonels Keane and Dextraze, both of whom had been posted back to Canada during December, the former to a staff post and the latter (who had followed Rockingham's example and enlisted in the Regular Force) to Staff College.

Keane and Dextraze were replaced by Lieutenant-Colonels G. C. Corbould and J. A. A. G. Vallée. Vallée had little previous experience of battle, having only briefly seen action as a company commander with the Van Doos in Sicily, before being posted back to Canada. Like Keane, Corbould had once commanded a motorized infantry regiment but, like Rockingham, Stone and Dextraze, after the war he had returned to civilian life prior to joining the Special Force. Given Rockingham's apparent predilection for his own kind, one wonders why he had not selected Corbould for 2 RCR in the first place, instead of Keane. But in the absence of a Rockingham memoir we shall likely never know the answer.

After six weeks in reserve, the Canadians returned to relieve 29 (British) Brigade in positions astride the Sami-chon tributary of the Imjin river, with two battalions positioned on the west bank of the river and one on the east bank. The stalemate held while talks at Panmunjom continued, although there was one notable raid against a C Company platoon of 1 PPCLI commanded by Sergeant R. G. Buxton on the night of 25/26 March. The platoon, holding a position 400 metres in advance of the main company positions, was surrounded but held on, supported by a ring of fire (including illumination rounds) from the battalion mortars. A second platoon was ordered forward to replenish the defenders' ammunition and bring out casualties, and after three hours of intermittent attacks in the now traditional Chinese fashion the enemy retreated, leaving behind 25 dead and one prisoner. The Patricias lost five men killed and Sergeant Buxton won a DCM.

Both sides were strengthening their defences, making them almost impregnable. The UN forces relied on minefields, wire and firepower; the Chinese, while not neglecting those aspects, had fewer resources, and thus relied more on Mother Earth.

*The amount of digging accomplished by the enemy in the preparation of his defensive positions has reached fantastic proportions. Enemy Forward Defence Lines are a maze of fire trenches, bays, bunkers and dug outs connected by deep communication trenches. These latter trenches extend down the forward slopes of some positions and of all positions rearwards for as many as three to four miles [five to seven kilometres], thus providing concealment from view and protection from our artillery fire when moving to and fro. The greater part of this digging, especially in forward areas, was carried out under the cover of darkness.*[43]

Winter was ending and a new style of fighting was becoming the rule, one that emphasized, on the one hand, UN artillery dominance and deeply dug enemy defences, and, on the other, patrols and raids by night in which Chinese skill and patience in the dark – they excelled at night work – their willingness to take casualties and their abundant supply of automatic small arms gave them a countervailing edge.

Casualty Clearing Post operated by 37 Canadian Field Ambulance serving front-line battalions. Korea was the first war in which helicopters were used to evacuate the wounded. (MR 168146)

Not an ink-blot test but a night-time image of a Vickers machine-gun position.

(PPCLI Museum)

## CHAPTER VII

# *Stalemate*

A UNIT TOUR IN KOREA having been set at one year, it was now time for the balance of the original volunteer force to follow 2 PPCLI back to Canada and be replaced by units of the regular force. However, under the threat of the Cold War the army had been substantially expanded during the previous year, so that many of the newcomers, including the junior officers, although professionals were also relative rookies.

The first major unit to be relieved was 54 Transport Company, RCASC, which completed its official handover to 23 Company on 11 April 1952. No. 2 R22eR was replaced by 1 R22eR (Lieutenant-Colonel L.-F. Trudeau) by 24 April and 2 RCR by 1 RCR (Lieutenant-Colonel P. R. Bingham) on the 25th. Both Trudeau and Bingham had first enlisted in the pre-Second World War Permanent Force, but the former had never commanded more than a company in combat and the latter had no combat command experience at all – he had held staff and training appointments throughout the war.

Rockingham was succeeded by Brigadier M. P. Bogert, DSO, on 27 April. Bogert, whose DSO had been won in Italy, was noted for his sense of humour and his "booming laugh," traits that would serve him well in his new post, for "maintaining morale in that dispiriting war was a greater challenge than its tactical problems."[1] No. 23 Field Squadron, RCE (Major E. T. Galway), was replaced on 3 May, and 2 RCHA gave way to 1 RCHA (Lieutenant-Colonel E. M. D. McNaughton*) on 6 May. The last of the original 25 Brigade units, C Squadron, LdSH, was replaced by B Squadron (Major J. S. Roxborough) on 8 June.

Among the newcomers, Colonel Bingham got an early taste of the hazards facing them. On 14 April 1952 he was inspecting a platoon position when someone stumbled over a tripwire and a booby trap laid for the Chinese exploded, spraying him and the platoon commander with shrapnel. Their wounds were superficial and, despite being evacuated to Japan, Bingham was back with the battalion two weeks later, just as General Ridgway was replaced as the United Nations commander-in-chief by General Mark W. Clark: the regimental history does not bother to discuss the wounds inflicted on the unfortunate subaltern, but they were clearly no more serious than those of his commanding officer since he

---

* Who would subsequently change his surname to Leslie on 20 March 1953.

was out leading a patrol the night before Bingham returned.

A re-adjustment of boundaries gave the line west of the Sami-ch'on river to a US Marine division and added frontage to the east that once again made Hill 355 ("Little Gibraltar") a Commonwealth responsibility.

*10 Platoon [of 1 RCR] found itself at the foremost part of the battle line, with nothing between us and the enemy except some unimpressive real estate, a small stream and a certain amount of barbed wire. The battered but still dangerous features, known by their spot heights as Point 116 and Point 113, glowered at us, with their faces scarred by United Nations high explosives and Chinese digging. In front of these hummocks was a great amphitheatre of Point 113, the ridge of Point 72 and the hump of Point 75. On the left was the Sunggok Ridge with its gnarled tree, an invaluable landmark to patrols. We were isolated but all our needs were filled, strong Korean legs being the means of transportation.*[2]

The Canadians' style of patrolling was changing. Now, "Fighting and ambush patrols were directed by radio from behind the lines of the Royal 22e, usually by an officer who was privy to the details of the mission"[3] – a kind of micro-management not likely to endear him to a man creeping about no man's land in the dark. On 6 May a Van Doos fighting patrol in search of a prisoner was ambushed by the Chinese and three men were killed and the platoon commander wounded. The terse, unornamented account reproduced in the brigade war diary gives the flavour of three terrifying hours.

*Proceeded on course to NICK (126119) where wireless broke down. Patrol commander ordered patrol to take defensive positions while set was being repaired and while he went forward with Cpl LeBlanc to reconnoitre. Reached river [the Sami-ch'on] without seeing or hearing anything. Left the Cpl at the river and returned halfway to patrol. Signalled to patrol to come forward. As patrol Officer signalled, burp gun and mortar fire opened, [by an] estimated one platoon [in strength]. Lieutenant wounded, 2 rounds right arm, one left arm (fractured). Pte Dubois put the Lieutenant on his shoulder and began withdrawal. Burp guns opened on right (south) and Pte Gendron was shot in the face. Patrol opened fire and withdrew. Wireless operator fired into set*

*and left it. As the patrol reached JOKER Pte Dupuis stated that enemy were on left (north). Enemy fired burp gun, killing Dupuis (2 bullets in the heart). Friendly outpost engaged enemy to assist the patrol. Patrol states that Cpl LeBlanc almost certainly killed by fire that hit him at the river.*[4]

Corporal LeBlanc's body was recovered a month later.

Throughout May, all three battalions were sending out patrols bent on capturing a prisoner but none had any success, while themselves suffering casualties. To put it bluntly, the Chinese were better in the dark than the Canadians. Searching for a new way to gather tactical information about the enemy, in early June the RCR devised a new, apparently less risky, way to obtain information about Chinese tactical dispositions.

*A patrol of usually one officer and twelve men in strength move towards the enemy lines after last light. When they are sufficiently near to the enemy to arouse his suspicion, they get down in a firing [position] and open up with every weapon at their disposal. By doing this, they give the impression to the enemy that an attack or raid is pending and invariably cause the enemy to disclose his position by opening fire. Once the so-called Jitter patrol has caused the [enemy] to reveal his [position] they withdraw some three or four hundred yards and take up [an] ambush [position] in the hope that the Chinese will follow them and be caught in their trap.... The Brigadier is keen for the other [battalions] to try this form of patrol.*[5]

However, none seem to have succeeded in catching the Chinese in a trap.

"Jitter" patrols or not, according to the R22eR's most recent history, "it was quite evident that in the summer of 1952 the Commonwealth Division's sector of no man's land was under very tight Sino-Korean control."[6] The Van Doos' history makes the point that the personnel of this second rotation were not comparable with their predecessors, with their cadres of Second World War veterans. "Arriving in the month of April, the battalion was largely made up of young men with little experience in the Army: it was simply not up to the task on the front lines."[7]

Nevertheless, General Cassels continued to emphasize the need for prisoners, and in their effort to oblige the RCR paid a heavy price on the night of 21 June: a fighting patrol incurred three killed and 21 wounded (without managing to secure a prisoner) when it was caught in a mortar barrage on the approaches to Hill 113. On 22/23 June it was the Van Doos' turn; three killed and eight wounded, again with no prisoner to show for it.[8]

On this last occasion the members of the patrol were wearing what the soldiers called "flak jackets." At this time the Americans were experimenting with different versions of body armour and the Canadians were equipped with the one favoured by the US Marine Corps, constructed of *"overlapping plates of moulded fibreglass and nylon."*[9] This "Vest, Armored, M-1951" weighed 3½ kilograms and was officially described as:

A zippered, vest-type sleeveless jacket constructed of water-resistant nylon incorporating two types of armor. One, a flexible pad of basket-weave nylon, covers the upper chest and shoulder girdle; the other, overlapping curved Doron plates, covers the lower chest, back and abdomen... Although the ballistic properties of the flexible pads of basket-weave nylon and the Doron plates are virtually the same, by using the rigid plates where flexibility is not mandatory the problem of protrusion [blunt impact trauma] and the resultant wounds under the armor is reduced.[10]

It reduced battle casualties by as much as 30 per cent, with the greatest reduction in the Killed In Action category, preventing 60 to 70 per cent of chest and abdominal wounds, while from 25 to 30 per cent of wounds occurring through the vest were reduced in severity.[11] This "Bullet Proof Vest," or BPV, was far from bulletproof, however. A PPCLI officer tested one *"by firing two rounds from my 9mm pistol from a distance of twenty feet. One bullet was deflected from entering where the torso would have been, while the second went cleanly through the vest. It all depended on the angle of contact."*[12] A rifle or machine-gun bullet was likely to have a much greater velocity, with the appropriate result. Another down side to it was that fibreglass splinters from the Doron plates "have unpleasant properties if introduced into a wound."[13] The US Army firmly rejected the idea of Doron and produced the T-52-1, relying entirely on nylon, but by the spring of 1953 the M-1951 would be on issue to each infantry battalion of 1 Comwel.

At the end of June the brigade went into reserve, taking the opportunity to try and improve the training standard of the infantry. More than better training was required, however, for innovative tactical thought was sadly lacking. Defences were based on all-around defensive perimeters sited on hilltops, but although these defended localities were scattered across the countryside in depth, there was no depth within the individual perimeter: *"We occupied too many hills and in consequence did not develop the defences on any one hill to their natural conclusion,"* wrote Major W. H. Pope (a veteran of the Italian campaign who arrived in Korea with 1 R22eR and subsequently volunteered to stay on with 3 R22eR) in a post-armistice analysis.

*We never stood back to look at our hills and ask ourselves what they were in the essence. They were, of course, fortresses or castles. [But] By simply developing our hills on the all around defence techniques of 1940–45 and on the dug-in techniques of 1914–18 we had made the mistake of not extracting all the lessons of the Great War, in particular the one of the mutually supporting lines. As a matter of fact we could have gone back to the Middle Ages to find this technique revealed, for a castle did not base its defence on having another castle on the next hill behind but rather on having several lines of defence – each mutually supporting – within the castle, starting with battlements behind the moat and ending with the keep.*[14]

What did the enemy, advancing under cover of artillery and mortar fire, have to overcome?

*... a single circle of fire trenches joined by a communication trench around the top of a hill. And were the men of the platoon manning their weapons? No! They were taking cover from the enemy artillery and mortar fire in their Chinese [sic] holes or, worse still, in their bunkers.... And so the enemy bombardiers approached our trenches and threw their grenades.... The enemy machine carbine assault teams then passed through, entered the single line of trenches, and practically unopposed, went about their work of execution and securing of prisoners....*

*I am well aware that in our defensive planning we laid much stress on the enfilade fire support available from flanking companies. The [light machine-gun] and Browning [medium machine-gun] tasks of the companies in front and on the flanks of each other looked very impressive – on [map] traces. But they did not work out in practice. The flanking companies were being neutralized [by mortar and shell fire] and their commanders, strongly imbued with the idea of "not revealing their positions," were usually quite willing to remain quiet and under cover.*[15]

Back in 1944, the Royal Canadian Artillery had established its own small air component in the form of Air Observation Post flights – the airborne eyes of the guns. The one regiment of artillery in 25 Brigade was not enough to justify the employment of a flight, but the divisional artillery included one with aircrew drawn from all the participating contingents in 1 Comwel. The first Canadian in the flight was Captain Joseph Liston, who joined it at the end of July 1952, but on his 13th mission, flown on his 13th day in Korea, his Auster aircraft was hit by enemy ground fire. He baled out and became a prisoner of war – the only Canadian officer to fall into enemy hands until Squadron Leader Andy Mackenzie, RCAF, joined him on 5 December 1952.

Liston was followed by Captain Peter Tees, who had rather better luck. During his tour, Tees flew 185 sorties and conducted 453 artillery "shoots" on enemy troop concentrations, guns, bunkers and vehicles, frequently directing not only the divisional artillery but that of the whole X (US) Corps. His Auster was often hit by small arms fire. Once he had to crash-land and on two occasions he glided back to base following engine failures. Tees's efforts were rewarded with a Distinguished Flying Cross. He was the first Canadian soldier so honoured since the First World War, when all Canadian airmen were soldiers seconded to the British flying services.[16]

American DFCs were probably rather easier to come by. The US Air Force had several AOP-type units equipped with T-6 two-seater North American Harvards, also known as Texans. Sometimes they conducted artillery shoots; sometimes they marked targets for tactical air attacks. They were flown by Air Force pilots but usually carried army officers as observers, and the first Canadian of nine so employed in Korea was Lieutenant D. G. MacLeod, 2 PPCLI, from May to August 1951. He was followed by Captain L. R. Drapeau in September and October (both of them were awarded the usual Air Medals, the Americans being inordinately generous with their decorations), but it was the summer and fall of 1952 before Canadians really distinguished themselves in this role, winning three American DFCs between May and October.

On 24 May Captain O. J. Plouffe and his pilot marked a series of targets for fighter-bombers near P'yongyang, their efforts resulting in the destruction of four bunkers, two mortar positions and an artillery emplacement. Then Captain R. J. Yelle directed an air attack near Kosong on 15 August:

*Despite low clouds over the target area, partial failure of his radio equipment, and battle damage to his aircraft, he directed his pilot in marking the targets with his smoke rockets. He then directed the fighters onto the marked targets. As a result of these actions, there were seven supply houses destroyed with two secondary explosions, plus four artillery positions, four mortar positions, and one automatic weapons position destroyed. Four artillery positions were damaged.*[17]

The third American DFC would be won by Lieutenant Arthur Magee after he vectored three flights of fighter-bombers on to enemy positions, knocking out an enemy command post and a variety of weapons and accounting for *"at least 20 enemy troops...counted killed."* That was the score for 1952, but a fourth such decoration would go to Lieutenant W. E. Ward of Lord Strathcona's Horse for work done on 13 March 1953.[18]

Another prisoner-of-war imbroglio now raised its ugly head, but this time the problem involved UN prisoners and guards. Some 120,000 North Koreans and 20,000 Chinese had been captured by the United Nations, the vast majority of them in the drive to the Yalu that took place before any Canadian soldiers arrived in theatre. They were held in a number of neighbouring compounds on the island of Koje-do, off the south coast of the peninsula, under a 4,000-man guard composed of corrupt South Korean military police and inept, "second line" American infantry.

The situation had slithered out of control, aided by a lax camp regime which had allowed the prisoners to set up unsupervised metal-working shops in the compounds, ostensibly to develop vocational and technical skills which would help them after release, where all manner of lethal weapons – hatchets, spears, knives and flails tipped with barbed wire – were being mass-produced. A generous ration of petrol, issued to fuel the prisoners' stoves, went to manufacture Molotov cocktails.[19]

Commissars, in touch with P'yongyang by clandestine radio, had set up their own internal governments and kangaroo courts that punished prisoners who failed to take a sufficiently uncooperative approach towards their captors. Some were merely beaten, others were killed. Riots were commonplace and employed by the commissars to win further conces-

Engineers' Camp Imjin. (PPCLI Museum)

Crossing the Imjin. (PPCLI Museum)

sions from the camp authorities. Guards could enter the compounds only in large, well-armed bodies, and from time to time they were compelled to open fire in self-defence. The worst such case came in February 1951 when a battalion of US infantry killed 77 and wounded 140 for the loss of one of their own men (speared to death) and the wounding of 38. The commissars quickly passed that information to P'yong-yang, where it was embellished with such loaded language as "butchery" and "massacre" before it was re-transmitted (by left-wing British and Australian journalists in league with the North Koreans) to the uncommitted world and such UN bastions of liberal values as London, Ottawa and Delhi.

At Panmunjom discussions had turned to the matter of repatriating prisoners of war and the UN delegates were determined that no prisoners should be returned against their will. But what was their will? In order to ascertain it, prisoners needed to be questioned individually. In 10 of the more accessible compounds it quickly turned out that many prisoners had no desire to return to their homelands, but in seven "hard line" compounds all attempts at screening were frustrated. On 7 May 1952 the Koje commandant, Brigadier-General F. T. Dodd, while negotiating entry with the commissars at the gate of one of the compounds, was seized by them, dragged into the compound and held hostage. In order to secure his release, his successor, Brigadier-General C. F. Colson, foolishly agreed to a number of conditions that virtually accepted that the guards had been mistreating and unjustifiably killing prisoners.[20]

Dodd and Colson were fired and demoted, and command of Koje was handed over to a "no nonsense" infantryman, Brigadier-General H. L. Boatner, who set about restoring order with alacrity.* Because he wanted other contingents to share the responsibility for any further mishaps, General Mark W. Clark, now commander-in-chief of UN forces, decided to make the provision of camp guards a United Nations rather than American and South Korean commitment. He assigned a Dutch battalion (because it was there and uncommitted) and companies of Greek, British and Canadian infantry.

Ottawa's response was predictable. The Cabinet quickly worked itself into a tizzy over this tenuously political employment of Canadian troops. Terrified at

---

* Boatner, as chief of staff to General "Vinegar Joe" Stilwell, deputy "supremo" to Lord Louis Mountbatten in the China-Burma-India theatre, had worked with Commonwealth troops in northern Burma during the Second World War.

the public relations risk if something went wrong, and ignoring their original position that Canadians had gone to Korea to participate in a "police action" – what was this if not a police action? – they howled with apprehension, using the argument that the Canadian "entity" – 25 CIBG – was being broken up. They even attempted a little discreet blackmail, instructing the Canadian ambassador in Washington:

> You should inform Mr. Acheson that in the Prime Minister's opinion it would be more difficult to have our people agree to any additional contribution that may be required of them in Korea if a Canadian Company were to be sent to help guard the Koje Island prison camp. It was, therefore, in his opinion, in the general interests of the United Nations that the Canadians should not be asked to do this. The Prime Minister was thinking, for example, of the possibility of a renewed offensive and a request for more Canadian forces.[21]

Clark might have chosen to restore Canadian unity by dispatching the whole of 25 Brigade to Koje-do! In fact, B Company, 1 RCR, was selected and Ottawa's indignation quickly dwindled when the British did not seem nearly so upset about their contribution. In the end:

> The Canadian Government...views with concern the despatch of a Company...without prior consultation.... Meanwhile, the Canadian forces concerned will, of course, carry out loyally the orders of the Unified Command... The Canadian Government also wishes to be reassured that, if it is proposed in the future to detach any Canadian forces from Canadian command and control...this will be done only after consultation....[22]

B Company arrived on the island on 25 May and, together with their British peers from the King's Shropshire Light Infantry – the KSLI company commander had overall command of this Commonwealth detachment – took over the hardest of the hard-line compounds. Sticking to the letter of the Geneva Convention, the two companies brought the prisoners into line with little difficulty while working alternate 24-hour shifts.

> *We occupied seven towers, placed at intervals about the Compound, with a Bren gunner on each of the towers' two platforms. Between these towers, there were sandbagged ground positions, seven in all, each containing a Bren gunner. There were*

*three high barbed wire fences about [Compound] 66 and in between the outer two we had an 8-man perimeter guard, constantly patrolling and watching the PsOW for unusual occurrences or disturbances. There were approximately 3200 prisoners in the Compound, chiefly North Korean Officers. Our job was to keep them inside the Compound and to apprehend prisoners who might try to escape.[23]*

General Boatner ordered the 7,000 inmates of Compound 76 to be moved to a new compound, and assigned well-disciplined American paratroopers to supervise the process. The prisoners fought the paras tooth and nail. Over a hundred of them were killed or wounded, and the commissars slaughtered an uncertain but substantial number of their own comrades who seemed willing to conform to American orders. Next in line to shift to more manageable quarters were the occupants of Compound 66, who moved at the behest of the RCR and KSLI without giving any trouble (although the body of one murdered dissident was found in an empty hut after the change-over had been completed). On 8 July the British and Canadians handed over to an American unit and left the island. This particular tempest in an Ottawa teapot was happily over.

More genuinely serious from an Ottawa perspective were Russian and Chinese allegations of bacteriological warfare by the United States that had first surfaced in January 1952. Under physical torture and psychological manipulation, a captured American airman subsequently "confessed" over Peking radio to having dropped germ-filled bombs, and American denials were simply met by more confessions, while United Nations efforts to have the charges investigated by the International Red Cross were rejected.

Of course, all those governments with contingents in Korea were tarred by the same brush, but Canada became more deeply involved when a former Canadian missionary in China, Dr. J. G. Endicott, visiting his old stamping grounds, claimed that his "personal investigations" had revealed that the charges were valid. Although he later denied it, he was also reported to have said that some of the germs were being produced at the Canadian Army's chemical and biological warfare centre at Suffield, Alberta. The secretary of state for External Affairs, Lester Pearson, was quick to respond in the House of Commons.

It is, of course, a slanderous falsehood to say that Canada has participated in any way in any form of germ warfare. It is equally false and equally slanderous, but more cowardly and despicable, to imply without stating it in so many words that Canada is making any preparations in this field except for defence against such warfare. ...some of our best qualified scientists, though they would not of course be permitted to make on-the-spot examinations, have already examined the so-called evidence of Korean germ warfare that has been made public by the communists and have pronounced it...to be a transparent and clumsy hoax.[24]

There was some discussion in the Commons as to whether Endicott should be charged under the Criminal Code – everything from slander to high treason was suggested – but MPs finally agreed that the less publicity he was given, and the less his prospect of communist martyrdom, the better. Endicott's charges were reiterated by left-wing fanatics, and are still occasionally raised to this day, but the persistent refusal of the Chinese and North Koreans to permit any neutral investigation of the matter seriously weakens their case.

Soon after 25 Brigade's return to the front line, on 10 August 1952, torrential rains, the result of a typhoon raging over the Yellow Sea 80 kilometres away, left both UN and enemy forces struggling to maintain their defences and left little time (or opportunity) for any kind of aggression. In one week more than 150 Canadian bunkers collapsed or were otherwise rendered uninhabitable and the troops were kept busy restoring them. *"On one position, which 6 Platoon [1 PPCLI] occupied...we lost eleven of fourteen bunkers in a single day.... Some estimates were that a minimum of ten inches [25.4 centimetres] of rain fell in a twelve hour period driven by winds of eighty to one hundred mph [130 to 160 kph]."[25]*

The PINTAIL and TEAL bridges thrown across the Imjin by British sappers, and essential to Canadian re-supply, were in continual danger of being swept away as the river rose 12 metres above its normal summer level. Indeed, TEAL's piers gave way on the last day of July and the bridge collapsed; following a similar rise on 24 August, PINTAIL's centre pier was "displaced" by the pressure of water, but happily it held up and that crossing continued in use for essential traffic – minimal ammunition and rations.[26] However, the Chinese probably faced even worse problems in maintaining their enormously complex, deep-dug defences, and were in no position to take advantage of 25 Brigade's predicament.

Land mines were used extensively to deny ground
to the enemy and slow down their attacks.
(PPCLI Museum)

Both sides employed mortars for indirect fire. (PPCLI Museum)

3 PPCLI moving up. (PPCLI Museum)

Korean labourers working as stretcher-bearers carry a wounded member of the "Van Doos," Private Sam Cyr of Montreal, across a stream. (PA 185022)

One platoon of Dog Coy of "Van Doos" advance uphill to establish a firm base from which to operate. 13 June 1951. (PA 213643)

On 13 August, three days after the Canadians had returned to the line and in the midst of the rains, Major Roxborough instructed his tank crews *"to dig their tanks in deeper"* – not an easy job at the best of times, tanks being as big as they were. But digging them in was no protection against high-angled mortar bombs.

*Sgt Colwill's and Sgt Falconer's tanks on Hill 159 were both hit by mortars up to 105mm in size. Although no other tanks were hit across the front there were several near misses, one hitting Cpl MacDonald's bunker on [Hill] 210 but he emerged unscratched and unshaken. At approximately 1900 [hours] 3rd troop received 18 shell[s] in a matter of ½ hour... At 2300 [hours] Lt Burch asked to have Sgt Falconer's tank on [Hill] 159 replaced as its traversing mechanism wouldn't work. Sgt R J Camponi took out a replacement before first light and brought back the damaged tank.[27]*

A week later, there was more of the same to report with rather more serious results.

*We suffered our first fatal casualty today. At 1245 [hours] Tpr L G Neufeld, [radio] operator in [tank] 3B, was killed by a mortar as he crawled under his tank. 15 minutes previously, Tpr Gilmour, the gunner of 2A, was seriously wounded by a mortar believed to be of 81mm calibre. To add to our troubles, two of third troop tanks were hit and damaged but the extent of the damage will not be known until Lt Leonard examines the tanks at last light.[28]*

On 6 September the Patricias' war diary noted, *"All [our patrols] have reached their objective and returned without encountering or sighting the enemy."* One wonders if some of these patrols were, in fact, going where they were supposed to go and subsequently claimed to have gone. Certainly they were not going about their business in a professional manner.

*Members of a fighting patrol were seen to go out wearing trousers which due to regular scrubbing and washing, were bleached almost white. Ambush [patrol] members were seen to light cigarettes and smoke them out in No Man's Land. Another night, members of the patrol were boisterous and jocular whilst proceeding to a position at the foot of a suspected enemy position. With no stretch of the imagination can we expect patrols conducted in this manner to succeed. To continue on this same trend, patrol leaders (on more than one occasion) took it on themselves to change their routes without first notifying the patrol master. Some patrol Commanders have failed to report by wireless or telephone when they have crossed or arrived at a report line. To relate one incident a patrol reported it was returning. Prior to this we had no report of its progress after it had left the [Forward Defence Lines]. Neither the firm base nor the patrol master had any idea of the patrol situation until after the objective had been reached, exploited, and the patrol assembled for the return trip.[29]*

A rare success in capturing a live, unwounded prisoner came on the night of 24 September when a reconnaissance patrol consisting of Lieutenant H. R. Gardner and five men of B Company, 1 RCR, crept up on an enemy position. Finding no one there – or if they were, all were asleep in their deep bunkers – Gardner and Corporal K. E. Fowler sneaked a little further forward, cut a telephone wire and waited to see what would happen. Very shortly a Chinese signaller came looking for the break and they overpowered him, but not without rousing the enemy. Their three-man "firm base" group held them off while Gardner and Fowler brought the prisoner back, and then the entire patrol returned safely with their captive. Gardner got a Military Cross and Fowler a Military Medal.

At the end of the month 1 RCR's war diary noted, *"The front is continually being probed by small numbers of enemy with no damage being done."* No immediate physical damage perhaps, but there seems little doubt that the Chinese had now come to dominate no man's land, while the Royals, for one, were concentrating on their reputation as Canada's "spit and polish" regiment. The day before that entry, *"while visiting E [Company]\* under the shadows of hill 227, the Brigadier was pleased to note in one of their fighting trenches, grenades with highly polished base plugs, a can of Brasso and a polishing rag. He remarked between chuckles, 'It is no more than is to be expected'."[30]* The other battalions may not have been so addicted to spit and polish but they were also relinquishing the initiative.

The enemy was thus encouraged to try something more, and there was no need for any sophisticated

---

\* An additional company had been created and the battalion was now one thousand strong, an adjustment made necessary because 1 R22eR was understrength.

analysis of his probes to tell when and where the next significant attack was coming. Chinese mortars and guns made it perfectly clear well in advance that they intended to recover Hill 355 – "Little Gibraltar," currently defended by the RCR – which was the dominating feature of Commonwealth Division's front.* The bombardment began with three days of heavy mortaring and shellfire that caused few casualties since the Royals' bunkers and dug-outs had been thoroughly restored after the rains. Nevertheless, *"bunkers were caved in, reserve ammunition was buried, and telephone cable cut to pieces."* On 16 October:

> *The enemy continued to shell forward positions of the R22eR and the RCR comparatively heavily. It is interesting to note that neither the first battalion of the RCR nor the first battalion of the R22eR have previously been subjected to shelling on this scale... They appear to be standing up to it extremely well and the spirit among the troops is remarkably high.*[31]

All telephone communications with B Company, RCR, which was dug in about a kilometre west of the peak, were cut, leaving only a radio link to battalion HQ, and in the early evening of 23 October the Chinese launched a battalion-strength attack on the company from three sides. Despite 1 RCHA's enthusiastic support, the remnants of B Company were forced out of their positions with a loss of 18 killed, 35 wounded and 14 taken prisoner. But the Chinese could do no more. An unnamed officer in the RCR command post recalled *"the South Korean who was monitoring the Chinese radio net reporting that the Chinese commander gave a Situation Report to his Headquarters something along the lines of 'I am boxed in by artillery fire. I can't get reinforcements forward'."*[32] As for the lost B Company position, a counter-attack by D Company, heavily supported by artillery, restored the situation in the early hours of the 24th.

The other unit most directly involved, 1 RCHA, "almost miraculously" took no casualties. Indeed, when the unit concluded its tour in Korea it had suffered only five dead and eight wounded. But, recollecting its experience in Korea a year later, the gunners noted that:

> *The guns of the regiment were never subjected to enemy counter attery fire. In this we were for-*

---

*General Cassels had now been succeeded by Major-General M. M. Alston-Roberts-West, who, for the convenience of his "colonial" troops, chose to be called simply General West while in command of the division.

*tunate because gun positions of the other two regiments in the Divisional Artillery were engaged by the enemy causing heavy casualties. Nearly all 1 RCHA casualties occurred to men serving with the O[bservation] P[ost] Parties. The fact that there were so few casualties is a tribute to the strength and durability of the very excellent OPs constructed by the regiment, as the intensity of shelling of the F[orward] D[efended] L[ocalities] was, if anything, worse than that encountered in World War II.*[33]

Among the prisoners taken by the Chinese was Private George Griffiths, who took some shrapnel in his foot during the artillery bombardment and found himself unable to keep up with his fellow Royals as they moved along a trench.

> *Just as I came around a corner in the trench, a Chinese soldier jumped down from the parapet and stood in front of me, his rifle pointed towards me.... I ducked back to the corner, trying to figure out what to do next... The next thing I knew, the guy threw a grenade and it blew up and hit me in the face and chest. The wounds were rather superficial but I realised right away that my face was bleeding and I was getting mad. I rammed [sic] back around the corner and blasted the guy from about four feet. I imagine he died, because I shot him in the gut....*
>
> *I was trying to figure out how I was going to get myself up the trench. I knew the Chinese were just above me, so I threw a couple of grenades and stumbled along until I came to a dead end, a bunker with a blanket across [the entrance]. As I half turned to try to escape, another grenade came over the top and hit me in the left knee and left shoulder. By this time I hurt like hell, I'm trapped, and I figure it's all over. There's all this flashing, explosions, just like lightning, and I'm scared – no, terrified.*

Griffiths climbed down into the bunker and found four dead men there.

> *...then the blanket was pulled back and two Chinese soldiers filled the doorway. One was carrying a flashlight and the other a burp gun. I was back to one side and I didn't even breathe. I was hoping they would see the dead and perhaps not see me – and for a minute I thought I was okay. The guy with the gun went to each body and pushed his bayonet through the corpse. But when they came to me I turned and they realized I was*

Korean children dressed in Western clothing. (PPCLI Museum)

Canadians were always amazed by the heavy loads Koreans carried on their A-frames. (PPCLI Museum)

The Canadian army, like all the UN forces, augmented its fighting strength with "Katcoms"— Korean soldiers permanently attached to its infantry companies. (PPCLI Museum)

*alive.... They motioned for me to drop my rifle, get my hands up, and get out of the bunker.*[34]

Subsequently his uncooperative attitude led Griffiths to a small prison camp reserved for intransigent prisoners – *"180 misfits who wouldn't believe in communism."* When seriously sick or wounded prisoners, including two Canadians, were exchanged in Operation LITTLE SWITCH during May 1953, Griffiths might have been a third, but he had been given no medical treatment for his injured foot during the seven months he had been a prisoner and the Chinese were not anxious to let the world know that.

*They called me in right after "Little Switch"... and told me they had decided to attend to my wounds... They froze my foot, gave me a few opium seeds to chew, and put a pillow-case over my head so I couldn't see. I nearly smothered under the pillow-case, so I took it off and watched them digging away at me. They took six hunks of steel out – but I wouldn't want to have them do a heart operation...*

*As I was recuperating, they kept supplying me with opium seeds and half the time I was higher than a kite. I would walk along a pathway and a little stone would look like a boulder and I would take a huge step over it....*

*Because I was wearing glasses when I was in prison, they decided to give me an eye test. One day this guy showed up, and all he had was a little case in his hip pocket. He had no other instruments. He sat me down, looked at my eyes, and said I didn't need to wear glasses unless I wanted to do so. I didn't know whether to believe him or not. Later on, after I got out, they examined my eyes in a million-dollar building in Kure, Japan. They told me the same thing but it took twice as long and was a hell of a lot more expensive. It was too bad the dental guy in the compound was not as good as the eye doctor. While I was in prison, all my teeth rotted out. They ached and ached. After a while the ache stopped.*[35]

At the end of the month 25 Brigade went into divisional reserve once more. "Thus ended one of the brigade's most trying periods of the war, and certainly its most costly – in less than three months the RCR had suffered 191 casualties, the Patricias 18, and the Vingt-deux 74."[36] It is impossible to say what proportions of these losses were the result of inefficient or inadequate patrolling and the increasing failure to dominate no man's land, but it is virtually certain that

some, perhaps most, were due to that understandable but self-inflicted weakness.

Rotation time was coming around again for the Patricias and the commanding officer of 3 PPCLI, Lieutenant-Colonel H. F. Wood, and a few key officers had flown to Korea in the middle of October, each member of his group familiarizing himself with the Korean environment by living and working with his 1st Battalion counterpart. The rest of the battalion arrived by sea and on 3 November the two battalions exchanged positions. However, 3 PPCLI'S fitness for battle was questionable. Its training had been beset by too much coming and going, with drafts to replace 1 PPCLI losses going out and other, untrained, drafts coming in. An appendix to the war diary for July 1951 had detailed the problem from Colonel Wood's point of view.

*It has been observed that far from being encouraged to learn his trade by watching the complexities of collective [training] the new soldier who participates is discouraged by the assurance displayed by his seniors and the "new boy" feeling is only partially dissipated by the appearance on the next exercise of even greener new arrivals.*

*...When the problem is complicated by the [reinforcement] of two other [battalions] at the rate of about 100 men per month, with a corresponding intake of green men, the method must be altered. The criterion in such a case, is not that a man be fitted into a team in the 3rd PPCLI and be prepared to fight as well as his [training] permits, but that the 3rd PPCLI turn out an acceptably trained soldier to take his place in one of two other [battalions], whose men expect that a new teammate be thoroughly versed in his trade.*[37]

Nevertheless, 3 PPCLI continued to gain and lose men with startling frequency almost until the day it sailed for Korea, thus making a mockery of collective training. The same problems would beset the other 3rd Battalions in due course, and it was probably their good fortune that they served on a static front, limited to patrolling activities and defensive fighting, in which the lack of collective training was not as serious as it would have been had they been required to participate in major attacks.

Arriving in Korea, Wood and his medical officer were *"having their days rounded out by [disciplinary] orders and sick parades."*

*Lately there have been quite a number present on both. It appears that the brief sojourn in Japan has* disrupted both discipline and moral[e] of some members of the unit. The 1 PPCLI personnel who stayed on with 3 [Battalion] also were strongly represented though mostly on the delinquent side. They probably suffered from the neglect due to their leaders and buddies preparing for rotation.[38]

Although the brigade was now in reserve, shortage of men in the other brigades of the division meant that from time to time some of the Canadians were employed to reinforce the front. Thus when the Chinese launched a battalion-strength attack against the Black Watch holding the ridge known (because of its shape) as "the Hook" on the night of 18/19 November, 3 PPCLI was brought up to the line. The enemy had established a foothold on the dominating ground of Hill 146 and, while the Black Watch mounted a counter-attack, one company of neophyte Patricias took over the defence of the remainder of the highlanders' position, while a second stood ready to reinforce the Black Watch counter-attackers if necessary. Their assistance was not required, however, and Canadian participation in their introduction to the Hook was limited to occupying the re-conquered positions and helping to clear the casualties. Both PPCLI companies stayed forward, one for three days and the other for five.

Throughout the hours of darkness 3 men standing patrols were despatched from C [Company]... At intervals they would report enemy movement. They would return to our [Forward Defence Lines] while artillery and mortar fire was laid down. They would then return to their positions. This activity continued throughout the nights of 19/20, 20/21 November with obvious success. On three occasions the screams of enemy wounded were heard, and each morning more enemy bodies were seen...

The enemy was found to be fast and efficient in his evacuation of dead and wounded by night. He did not hesitate to risk new casualties in order to evacuate others, and did so with a rapidity that [foiled] two attempts to secure a wounded prisoner. Our patrols did not move with the speed necessary to forestall his evacuation of casualties caused by our [artillery] and mortar fire.[39]

The Patricias' losses were four killed, five wounded and two "battle accidents" – one soldier wounding himself in the hand by an accidental discharge of his own Sten gun, and one being hit in the leg by a rifle bullet fired by a comrade who was cleaning his weapon.

At the end of November the Commonwealth brigades were re-deployed so that instead of two being forward and one in reserve, all three were up in line and each had one battalion in reserve. Given the unlikelihood of a really major enemy attack, requiring a strong reserve, this arrangement gave each brigade commander the advantages of a narrower front and defence in more depth, together with an adequate counter-attack force already under his own command. No. 28 (British) Brigade held the right sector, 29 (Commonwealth) Brigade side-stepped to take over the centre of the divisional front and the Canadians of 25 Brigade came into the line on the left. Aside from the dominating Hill 355, now the responsibility of 29 Brigade, the most vital ground held by the Commonwealth Division was the so-called Hook position that closely covered a probable invasion route to Seoul, down the valleys of the Sami-ch'on and Imjin rivers – a route that the Chinese and North Koreans had already used once in this war. The Hook consisted of high ground that lay on the west bank of the Sami-ch'on, with the sharp bend in it that gave it its nickname turning southward, roughly parallel with the river and less than 800 metres from it. On the other side of the Sami-ch'on, and no further away from it, was the hump of higher ground known as Yong-dong. Brigadier Bogert assigned 3 PPCLI, plus one company of the RCR, to the vital Hook position, with the Van Doos on Yong-dong, across the Sami-ch'on, and the remainder of 1 RCR in reserve behind the Patricias.

The newcomers spent much time training for, and practising, patrolling, to no great avail. Their first fighting patrol, on 22 November, "did not go well at all," although there were no casualties. Mostly the battalion engaged in standing patrols – a euphemism for listening posts – and "artillery and mortar fire were directed so as not to encourage the enemy to become too bold."[40]

Once in a while, too, there was an entirely unofficial "patrol."

At 1645 [hours] the F[orward] O[bservation] O[fficer] with B company reported seeing two Canadian soldiers on PHEASANT [codename for a position close to the Chinese lines]. When the full story was unfolded it was found that four soldiers from B Company had left their platoon positions without permission. They had all been under the influence of alcohol. One fell asleep at [Map Reference] 110106 and was apprehended and returned to his position with no trouble. One *returned to his position after searching out WARSAW. The other two, one a corporal, went to PHEASANT, became involved in a fire fight during which they claimed to have killed five enemy. They returned through B company [positions] unharmed. They reported seeing the bodies of three US Marines near [Map Reference] 118108. All four soldiers were sent to A Echelon under close arrest.*[41]

Shades of Jacket Coates! The war diary does not report the result of the disciplinary action taken against the four men, but one likes to think that they dodged the metaphorical disciplinary bullets just as well as they had the real Chinese ones.

Just before the end of the year, the Royals exchanged positions with the Patricias on the Hook, with the latter leaving one company under RCR command.

Patrolling continued, but with no great enthusiasm, the emphasis being on improving defences, particularly on the Hook, where first the British and now the Canadians were rivalling the Chinese in their devotion to digging. As soon as the brigade returned to the front, a troop of 23 Field Squadron carried on with a tunnelling programme their British predecessors had started, and later the entire Squadron, supplemented by Korean labourers, joined in. In January 1953 they dug out 20,000 cubic metres of tunnel[42]

– a mere bagatelle compared with their Chinese opponents. Meanwhile the infantry, with sapper and Korean assistance, reinforced command posts and bunkers and deepened and extended their trenches. The gunners of 1 RCHA designed, and the sappers built, a roof for the former's forward observation post calculated to protect them from the heaviest artillery. Nearly three metres thick, it consisted of alternating layers of crushed rock and sandbags resting on a framework of angle irons, and the OP was set so deep into the ground that the top of the roof was level with the surrounding ground.[43] If and when it became necessary to call down fire on their own position, the gunners would certainly be safe. Though the infantry never quite matched the artillery in digging, their efforts (and the general reduction in patrolling activity) also made life safer for them. Canadian casualties in December 1952 and January 1953 totalled 57 – 12 killed and 45 wounded – as compared with 131 in May and June 1952 and 232 in September and October.[44]

On the last day of January 1953 nearly all of the Commonwealth Division was withdrawn into Corps reserve, for the first time in the 18 months since its inception. Only the divisional artillery remained in the line, its new role being to support the relieving force, 2 (US) Division, which included a number of non-American units and was sometimes unofficially described as 2 (UN) Division – 1 Comwel being the 1st.

Canadian units often employed young Koreans to do odd jobs in return for food and clothing.
(PPCLI Museum)

Edward Zuber, 1932–
*Daybreak, Gulf of Korea*
CWM-90025

## CHAPTER VIII

# *Islands and Packages*

THE ROYAL CANADIAN NAVY devoted more of its resources to the Korean War than the other two services. In all, eight of Canada's 11 destroyers served in Korea from the outbreak of hostilities to the armistice in July 1953; *Athabaskan* completed three tours, *Cayuga, Huron, Iroquois, Nootka* and *Sioux* two, and *Crusader* and *Haida* one each.[1] This effort, which involved some 3,621 personnel, many of whom did more than one tour, exacted a heavy toll on the navy.

Keeping three destroyers on station in the Far East actually required five ships: three in Korean waters and two "relief" ships preparing to go. The reader will recall that Pacific command had to "borrow" personnel from other duties in order to get the three ships in the first deployment up to wartime establishment in July 1950. This policy of robbing Peter to pay Paul to keep the ships destined for Korea at wartime complements continued throughout the conflict, straining the navy to the limit. In February 1952 the director of naval plans and operations warned that *"the training of personnel has been seriously affected,"* and that *"the planned expansion of RCN forces with which to meet our NATO obligation is also being seriously affected as unless the manpower situation can be improved... an adequate number of trained men will not be avail-*able to man additional new construction and modernized ships as they become available.*"[2] In addition, the continual need to rotate destroyers to Korea caused an 11-month delay in the programme to convert the ships into anti-submarine destroyer escorts (DDEs), and at one point even forced the navy to ask the RN to provide a plane guard destroyer for the aircraft carrier HMCS *Magnificent* on a European cruise.[3] In short, Korea was in danger of bankrupting the service.

Despite this, senior officers never flagged in their determination to maintain the commitment, nor can they really have been expected to. As Rear-Admiral Harry DeWolf, vice-chief of the naval staff for much of the Korean period, recalled, *"The Navy saw it as more important to have destroyers in Korea than it was that they [actually] be there."[4]* The reason for this is not hard to see. As naval analyst Peter Haydon has argued, Korea enabled the navy to raise its political profile.[5] It demonstrated that the RCN had a role in the post-war world, and one that could bring international prestige to Canada. There was little risk involved – something attractive to politicians – and the ongoing presence of three ships in Korean waters demonstrated Canada's strong backing of the United Nations to both domestic and international audiences. It also gave Canada clout at the proverbial bargaining table, and, as Denis Stairs pointed out, a means to constrain the United States.[6] In short, there was little that was not attractive from a political point of view, thus if Korea caused some internal upset, naval leaders were willing to accept that price, and the three-ship commitment continued until after the armistice.

At the end of Chapter 2 we left the naval war in December 1950, with the Chinese driving UN ground forces back from the Yalu. As we have seen in the intervening chapters, the front eventually stabilized in the vicinity of the 38th Parallel, transforming a contest that had heretofore been characterized by dramatic advances and retreats into a virtually static campaign. For the sailors, however, not all that much changed. Their primary task remained coastal blockade, with the screening of carrier forces – the Corpen Club – a secondary, and still unpopular, duty. On the west coast, operations focused on defending what became known as the "friendly islands"; on the east, they centred on the interdiction of rail transport, or "trainbusting." Rather than tediously outlining the operations of each individual ship in these activities, this chapter will take *Cayuga*'s role in the island campaign and *Crusader*'s trainbusting operations as representative, and more or less typical, of all.

*Cayuga* arrived in Japan for her second Korean tour on 17 July 1951. Much had changed on board the ship since she had left Korean waters four months earlier. Commander James Plomer, who had replaced Brock as captain (and CANCOMDESFE, or flotilla commander), was another veteran of the Battle of the Atlantic. However, the fact that Plomer was one rank lower than Brock meant that he would rarely be the senior officer of UN naval formations. About three quarters of his crew was new to *Cayuga* and, according to Plomer, many of the personnel changes *"were moves of desparation [sic] to bring the ship's company up to complement before sailing."*[7] Only two officers and fewer than 10 per cent of the petty officers were veterans of earlier Korean operations.

Before leaving Canada, *Cayuga* had been fitted with a new piece of kit that would prove key to her success on this second tour. The reader may recall from Chapter 2 how *Athabaskan* had made excellent use of her high-definition navigational (HDWS) radar during the evacuation of Chinnamp'o. Later arrivals were fitted with the even better Sperry variant of HDWS.[8] No other UN ships had radar nearly as

accurate and precise, and the Sperrys became so highly valued by task force commanders that Canadian destroyers were often specifically selected for operations in shallow water because of it. That, and the fact that they usually succeeded in their missions, made them the undisputed stars of west coast inshore operations.

*Cayuga*'s first task was with the Corpen Club in the Yellow Sea, screening the aircraft carriers USS *Sicily* and HMS *Glory* as they launched a series of air strikes into North Korea that, like General Ridgway's limited offensive, were designed to coax the enemy into picking up the pace of the cease-fire talks. Escorting carriers would occupy about half of *Cayuga*'s time during this second deployment, but, as Plomer explained, the Canadian destroyers spent less time on that frustrating duty than the destroyers of other UN navies *"because of their good fortune in having H.D.W.S. Radar, which has been invaluable for inshore patrols."*[9] Thus *Cayuga* was thrust into the island campaign, the origin and significance of which can best be outlined through a briefing given the US secretary of the navy during a Korean tour in March 1952:

> After our troops were driven back from their thrust to the Yalu River, a handfull of islands off both coasts of Korea were retained as bases, from which intelligence teams were launched, from which guerrillas could operate behind the enemy lines, and on which the Fifth Air Force erected Shoran [SHOrt RAnge Navigation] and Radio Stations to guide and direct their B-29 [bomber] and fighter missions.
>
> …[Subsequently] The Far East Air Force brought out the tremendous importance of these islands to their operations – that in addition to the Shoran stations, their whole concept of interception and direction of fighters in MIG Alley [discussed in the next chapter] depended on their radio and radar network, and that it was essential to the successful conduct of the air war to retain those islands having air force equipment.[10]

On 9 August *Cayuga* moved into the waters around the islands of Ch'o-do and Sok-to, which lay seaward of Chinnamp'o and south of the mouth of the Taedong estuary. The islands were eight nautical miles (14.8 kilometres) apart, the southern extremity of Sok-to being just a mile and a half offshore where a point of land known as Pip'a Got jutted out into the sea between the two islands. To the northeast, a small peninsula, Am Gak, extended into the estuary to a point four miles due east of Sok-to. There were many islets, shallow water was the rule and mud flats abounded, while the nearby mainland was studded with shore batteries. Commodore J. C. Hibbard, RCN, an experienced destroyer officer, commented during a May 1952 inspection tour, *"I am amazed at the confined waters in which our tribals are operating. There is the ever present knowledge that if they run aground they would, with daylight, be under fire from up to eight enemy batteries – sometimes at point blank range."*[11]

After shelling a small troop concentration, a machine-gun post and two observation posts on Pip'a Got, *Cayuga* anchored off Sok-to where she was boarded by Master Sergeant Hubert Frost, an American operating with an amphibious guerrilla group based on the island. He supplied intelligence about targets on Am Gak and that evening the destroyer fired some 200 4-inch rounds at an artillery bunker, a gun emplacement and a former mining plant believed to be in use for the construction of concrete fortifications. Then *Cayuga* moved out beyond Ch'o-do for the night.

Shortly after it had anchored:

*...five junks came alongside with some ninety South Korean geurrillas [sic] who were proceeding on a raiding party to the mainland in the vicinity of P'ungchon. They required information from maps which was given them as well as a small map. Their leader seemed a most energetic and enterprising person.*

*At 0700 [hours] on the following morning some explosions and smoke were heard and seen in the direction of the geurillas. At 0810 considerable rifle and machine gun fire came from the beach in that sector. At 0830 a motor fishing boat with more geurrillas from [Chodo] came alongside. From the officer that came onboard and remained throughout the operation it appeared that with no wind the geurrilla force was trapped on the beach and was unable to withdraw in junks. CAYUGA closed to within 2500 yards of the beach and the firing ceased. The junks came out from shore... One junk was towing a "liberated" cow – still alive. The cow did not seem to appreciate its new political freedom.*[12]

*Cayuga* continued to bombard P'ungch'on and then fired on a party of enemy soldiers before heading out to sea. That afternoon, acting on more information from Sergeant Frost, the destroyer followed two ROK minesweepers into a channel south of Sok-to

where she anchored and fired at gun positions, barracks and a crossroads. Some return fire was experienced but it fell well short, and before withdrawing from the area Plomer made contact with Frost, who *"was well pleased with the day's work although Sokuto [Sok-to] Island was by now being shelled [by the enemy] for the first time."*[13]

Plomer thought the level of enemy activity on the mainland to be ominous. *"There is no doubt that a fair build up is underway and it is the enemy's intention either to recapture Sokuto or at least make it untenable, and with [Chodo] to follow,"* and suggested that *"shelling by naval forces could improve the situation."*[14] Not everyone shared that viewpoint. There was considerable disagreement among senior UN naval officers about the nature of operations on the west coast and how aggressive their forces should be during the peace talks. Royal Navy officers did not share his enthusiasm for maintaining a rigorous bombardment regime and Plomer became aware of what he termed a "go easy" policy:

*The first clear impression we had of this "go easy" policy was after particularly successful results in supporting a Guerrilla raid on the enemy mainland [on 8 September 1951], with no losses to the friendly Guerrillas but approximately 170 killed among the enemy forces[.] I was received on the return to harbour in an atmosphere of strong disapproval. No encouragement was given in any way and no messages were made. It so happened that the Flag Officer, Second in Command [Rear-Admiral A. K. Scott-Moncrieff] was having lunch onboard CAYUGA the following noon. He said to me in front of my officers after mentioning feuds against mothers-in-law and money-lenders and generally throwing cold water on the event, "we do not want to upset these people," however, there had never been any written orders or instructions stating a definite policy in such operations.*[15]

In contrast, Plomer found Rear-Admiral G. C. Dyer, USN, the commander of Task Force 95, to be much more pessimistic about the results of the peace talks, with the result that he *"has consistently followed an aggressive war-like policy."*[16]

This difference of opinion between the RCN's main allies continued to fester, and was also noticed by Commodore Hibbard during his visit in May 1952.

*Admiral Dyer is of the opinion that we do not yet use sea power to the best advantage. He feels that we must press close inshore with our blockade....*

A ROK naval vessel comes alongside *Cayuga*. Such craft were typical of the rag-tag shipping that plied Korea's coastal waters. (DND CA-61)

*Crusader* in the Sasebo dry dock in November 1952 for repairs to the sonar dome. UN destroyer crews emblazoned the dock with murals of their service and it was natural for *Crusader* to advertise her train-busting prowess. (DND CU-1092 and CU-1095)

Liaison with forces ashore was a regular feature of the island campaign. Here, Commander J. Plomer (centre), Lieutenant-Commander P. G. Chance (left) and Lieutenant J. G. Waters from *Cayuga* discuss matters with American and South Korean personnel. (DND O-2248)

A happy ship is an effective ship. *Cruisader*'s overall success in Korea certainly proved her effectiveness, while theses photos of a tug of war on the upper deck and her cook's blasting away at a target seem to demonstrate the happiness. (DND CU-10 and CU-1141)

*Admiral Scott-Moncrieff on the other hand, is of the opinion that our operations [on the west coast] are a great waste of effort and a drain on [the] British economy. He is greatly concerned with the risks we are taking with our ships from the navigating point of view and cannot believe they are justified.*[17]

Such policy disagreements are not uncommon in coalition warfare, but in this case the sniping apparently became quite poisonous and Plomer deprecated the constant criticism directed by certain British staff officers at their American allies, some of it quite openly. The solution, he thought, was to establish an integrated UN naval staff in the theatre.[18] That was never done, but the actions of the commanding officers of Canadian ships in Korea demonstrate that they agreed with Dyer's strategy; they were at war and wanted to keep the pressure on the enemy.

The situation in the islands remained much the same throughout the autumn of 1951, with *Cayuga* maintaining her aggressive posture. On 29 October, however, she nearly got as good as she gave. Plomer let his navigator, Lieutenant-Commander Peter Chance, do much of the ship-handling so that he could focus on the tactical situation, and on that day *Cayuga* went close inshore where she anchored preparatory to engaging newly reported artillery positions on the Am Gak peninsula. Chance recalls:

*We had what was known as the CC-BC which was the Cayuga camera and binocular club. Every Stoker, Cook and God knows who else was staring around having a lovely time, when suddenly to our horror there was an enormous sort of d d d d and wheeeee!!! We were straddled from the shore with mobile weaponry and [from] a long way, about [18,000] yards.*

*...Well this was about enough and I said "excuse me Sir, but it's time to go." "Slip" [the anchor]. And so they whacked and let the cable go and I did something that I learned and I practised on that occasion. You put your hands up in front of you and [designate them] starboard and port and turn around and you've still got starboard and port and I took her out full astern.*[19]

Giving wheel orders and maintaining course is a difficult matter when going full astern at 16 knots — especially under fire — but Chance pulled it off. Still, it was not for some 19 minutes, and after an estimated 100 shells had been fired at her, with several straddles, that the destroyer disappeared — stern first —

around Sok-to and the barrage ceased. The only casualties were the lost anchor, some cable and the motor cutter, which was towed under during the withdrawal.

It was during this period that one of the most embarrassing incidents in Canadian naval history came to light. *Cayuga*'s doctor and morale officer, Surgeon-Lieutenant Joseph Cyr, was a popular member of the ship's company, taking genuine interest in their welfare and performing his medical duties quite competently. Indeed, when South Korean guerrillas sought medical help during the island campaign, Cyr "performed several operations during a two-month period, ranging from the amputation of a gangrenous foot to the removal of bullets from arms and elsewhere. He operated quickly and efficiently, and gave no one any reason to question his talents as a surgeon."[20] But Cyr was a fake — *The Great Imposter* according to a Hollywood movie of his life. He was actually an American named Ferdinand Waldo Demara who had spent his adult life passing himself off as somebody else, working in a variety of professional jobs, none of which he was actually qualified for. The Canadian navy was short of qualified surgeons during the Korean War, so when Demara presented himself at a recruiting office he was greeted with open arms. His credentials, stolen from the real Joseph Cyr, a New Brunswick doctor, seemed real enough, so his induction was expedited and he found himself joining *Cayuga* days before she left for Korea.

Demara might well got away with the charade for the entire commission had not the real Dr. Joseph Cyr read about "himself" in his local newspaper and contacted the authorities. The jig was up and a signal went out to the ship on 23 October ordering Plomer to relieve the doctor of his duties. Stunned, Demara took a drug overdose, *"either as a sedative or to commit suicide,"* Plomer reported, but Petty Officer Robert Hotchin, the sick bay attendant, pulled him through, and on 26 October he was transferred to a British ship for passage back to Japan.[21] The navy had no desire to add to its embarrassment by court-martialling him, so Demara was quietly handed over to American authorities, who turned him loose. This bizarre affair came to a happy end when Demara attended a *Cayuga* reunion in 1979. "He was greeted with warmth by those who had known him as a friend and shipmate twenty-eight years before," historian Edward Meyers has written. "The welcome made it obvious that Demara had made no enemies aboard *Cayuga*. By all accounts he enjoyed the party."[22]

Commander Plomer had consistently warned that the enemy was likely to make a move against the friendly islands, and on 29 November 1952 the Chinese did so by seizing Taewha-do, the outermost of a chain of islands in the northern Yalu Gulf. That area had often been patrolled by *Cayuga* and *Athabaskan*, who, through their HDWS radar, were usually able to frustrate the movements of small enemy vessels in the area. On this occasion, however, the British destroyer *Cockade* was responsible and, lacking high-definition radar, she was unable to detect the invasion force of junks and rubber rafts until it was too late.

The loss of Taewha-do set off alarm bells in the corridors of power, with the result that the defence of the remaining islands became the number one naval priority on the west coast and Rear-Admiral Scott-Moncrieff ordered that a Canadian destroyer should be on patrol in the Ch'o-do/Sokto area whenever possible.[23] That kept *Cayuga*, *Athabaskan* and *Sioux* busy throughout December, maintaining a nightly anti-invasion watch, illuminating invasion routes with star-shell, bombarding enemy positions and providing boarding parties for ROK vessels. Nevertheless, the enemy succeeded in taking two islets south of Sok-to, and at the end of December they repulsed a counter-attack by South Korean guerrillas that was supported by *Cayuga*.[24] The enemy never succeeded in taking Ch'o-do or Sok-to but, like all the friendly islands north of the 38th Parallel, they were turned back to North Korean control after the armistice.

The operations throughout the fall of 1951 marked the height of activity by Canadian destroyers in the island campaign. The increased prominence given to defence of the remaining islands and the immobility that prevailed ashore meant that there was little excitement, although the naval presence kept alive the threat of another amphibious flanking attack along the lines of the Inch'on operation. *"That this threat has been appreciated,"* wrote the commander of Commonwealth naval forces reporting on the period July 1952 to April 1953, *"is shown by the large numbers of troops the enemy has had to disperse in a purely defensive role over the past year. On the West Coast alone these forces have been increased from about 40,000 to approximately 80,000 – forces which otherwise could have been employed in the battleline, or in immediate reserve."*[25]

However, mention might be made here of two achievements. First, on the recommendation of Commander Plomer, Lieutenant Donald Saxon, RCN, was appointed naval liaison officer between the UN command and the South Korean guerrillas operating out of the friendly islands, and he performed that duty so capably that he was awarded the Distinguished Service Cross.[26] Second, on the night of 22 September 1952, in what the USN official history called a "signal honour," HMCS *Nootka* captured a North Korean minelayer off Ch'o-do, one of few enemy vessels captured at sea during the war.[27]

The United Nations' overwhelming advantage in airpower forced the Chinese and North Koreans to move most of their supplies at night, and rail was the most effective way for them to do that. But at certain points along the east coast the rail lines lay within easy range of destroyers, which could sail close inshore because of the depth of the water on that side of the peninsula. In July 1952, after the American destroyer USS *Orleck* destroyed two trains in a 12-day period, an operations officer on the staff of CTF-95 organized the Trainbusters Club as a way to boost morale. By the time the competition ended, at the armistice, 28 trains had been destroyed by 18 different UN destroyers, and with four "kills" HMCS *Crusader* was recognized as the undisputed champion of the club.[28]

After arriving in theatre in June 1952, *Crusader* had spent three months on the west coast, steaming with the Corpen Club or carrying out the usual blockade activities among the friendly islands.[29] In October she received her first east coast assignment, which was preceded by the RCN's greatest misfortune of the war, an event that must have caused some trepidation among all destroyer crews.[30] On the morning of 2 October, HMCS *Iroquois* and USS *Marsh* were close inshore, bombarding the rail line on the east coast, south of Songjin, when a shell from an enemy battery struck the starboard side of the Canadian ship, abreast of "B" gun. In the only battle casualties suffered by the RCN in Korea, Lieutenant-Commander John L. Quinn and Able Seaman Elburne A. Baikie were killed instantly, while Able Seaman Wallis M. Burden succumbed to his wounds that night, and 10 more sailors were wounded.[31]

Eleven days later, *Crusader* joined the four USN destroyers comprising TE 95.22, the Songjin component of the east coast blockade force. It operated north of the cease-fire line exclusively and a Canadian destroyer was undoubtedly included to maintain the UN integrity of the force by providing a non-American component. The duty was as unvaried as that on the opposite coast but not nearly as hazardous; *Crusader*'s CO, Lieutenant-Commander John Bovey, noted with relief, *"After the somewhat treacher-*

The champion train-buster; *Crusader* steams off the Korean coast. (DND CU-908)

A USN intelligence photo of PACKAGE 2 that clearly shows the damage wrought by *Crusader*'s shoot on 23 October 1952. (DND E-22363)

Altogether, eight Canadian destroyers served in Korea. Above, *Nootka* pounds a railway bridge at Songin in May 1951 (DND NK-667). Below, *Huron* returns to Halifax on 17 March 1954, having been away for 11 months, eight of which were spent under the UN flag in Korean waters. (DND PIX-4100)

ous coast of western Korea it was a pleasure to be able to operate so close in and yet still be in deep water."[32]

During the day the destroyers would carry out either a NORTHERN patrol from Yang-do to Ch'ongjin or a WINDSHIELD patrol between Yang-do and Cha'ho. At night the ships would lie off one of five PACKAGE areas (a PACKAGE being a shoreline target suitable for both ships and airplanes). Radar reflection buoys were planted off each one to assist in navigation and shooting accuracy. If these targets – three of the five included bridges – could be interdicted, the flow of enemy supplies from the USSR would be impeded.[33]

PACKAGE tasks were twofold: to engage trains attempting to run the gauntlet and, because the North Koreans were adept at repairing damaged rail lines, to carry out harassment shoots to frustrate their efforts.[34] On 13 October *Crusader* took position 2,750 metres off PACKAGE 4, a section of track lying at the foot of a mountain where work crews were maintaining or repairing track. No trains were sighted but Bovey reported, *"The target was illuminated continually and any lights or movements on shore were promptly shot at."*[35] Three nights later he returned to the same area with the same intent but a slightly different approach.

*As before, the ship was stopped about 3000 yards [2,750 metres] from the railway embankment and the engines manoeuvred to keep the ship in position. The almost complete absence of any tidal effect made this easily handled. The cutter was sent inshore at 2210 [hours] as a reporting and listening post but this did not prove to be very successful and so the boat was recalled and hoisted. Other ships have employed this method of train detection but further experience [of] CRUSADER proved that it was unnecessary to have boat inshore as a reporting position.*[36]

Despite the fact that destroyers lay so close inshore, PACKAGES usually developed into a cunning game of "cat and mouse" as the railwaymen, working at night, became proficient at masking their movements and hid their trains in the many tunnels. Then again, sometimes they just barrelled down the line at high speed, hoping to beat the odds.[37] That is what confronted *Crusader* on the night of 23 October off PACKAGE 2, a 200-metre stretch of track between two tunnels. A train was sighted but the main armament was under local control – the guns laid and trained separately at each turret – and although "B" and "X" turrets both fired rounds, the gun crews failed to hit

the target before it disappeared. As a result, Bovey decided to keep all four turrets and the gunnery director closed up when lying off a PACKAGE at night. That way, the superior optical equipment in the gunnery director would be able to quickly concentrate accurate fire onto a target. This procedure, which probably should have been carried out from the start, paid dividends off PACKAGE 2 on 26 October.

*Sub-Lieutenant F. J. Copas, RCN, the Gunnery Officer, who was in the director, and his crew reported a train at 0124 [hours].... Fire was opened and the director crew were convinced that they had seen rounds strike the two end boxcars and knock them off [the track]. The train was not seen at any time by officers or men on the bridge and there was some cause for doubt despite Sub-Lieutenant Copas' repeated affirmation that he saw the train and hit it. His claim was confirmed at a later date for our two boxcars were found on the side of the track by aircraft. There was no sign of the rest of the train.*[38]

The next night, again off PACKAGE 2, Bovey ordered the director and guns trained on the northern tunnel as a southbound train *"would be a more valuable target than one going north, as it would probably have food, stores, equipment and even troops for the front line, whereas a north-bound train might contain nothing."* At 2020 hours both bridge and director personnel observed white smoke emerging from the tunnel.

*There was no doubt this time and, using ranges from Sperry radar, which has proved better then [Type] 275 for this particular type of operation, fire was opened. The train was hit and stopped with the first salvo [which hit] along the whole length of the embankment.*

*The locomotive was observed disappearing into the south tunnel. Fire was held until it emerged again to the south of Package Two and immediately re-opened as it left the tunnel. However, it was thought that it had escaped. There was no mistaking the remainder of the train. With starshell illumination the train was worked over completely with 4.5[-inch], causing fires and explosions. The ship was brought in to a range of 1800 yards [1,650 metres] at 2035 [hours] and fire opened with 40 mm to give the close range guns' crews a chance to join in the kill and to work over the battery area. [USS] DeHAVEN, who was on*

*"Windshield Patrol,"* was called in to give support and he [sic] joined in the destruction at 2130, proceeding inshore of CRUSADER and using his 40 mm and 5[-inch] guns....

*With daylight the wreck of the train could be clearly seen extending over the whole length of the cutting. The rails were hanging down the embankment to the south and the boxcars, 13 in number, appeared reduced to broken flat cars.*[39]

The next morning Corsair and Skyraider aircraft from TF 77, arriving to finish off the job, sighted the locomotive on its side down the far side of the embankment. *Crusader* and *DeHaven* had killed the entire train.[40]

After spending November and December in the Yellow Sea, *Crusader* returned to the east coast in late January. This time, her two-week patrol was uneventful for the most part, and the only transportation target taken under fire was a truck, which *"was very effectively sniped with one 4.5" gun, causing consternation and confusion to the enemy who disgorged from the back and who were then dispersed by a few quick air bursts."*[41] Although such shoots were inconsequential in the larger scheme of things, they were good for morale. With that in mind, on a harassment shoot off PACKAGE 2, Bovey *"decided to give the non-gunnery departments, including Supply, Engineroom, et cetera, a chance to fire the guns at the enemy and to the best shooting gun's crew was to go a case of beer. This provided some amusement and some quite excellent results."*[42]

*Crusader* returned to complete her final and most successful stint off the east coast in April 1953. After spending four days on the NORTHERN Patrol, supporting ROK amphibious raiding parties, on 14 April she headed to PACKAGE 3, a stretch of railway track on an embankment featuring a small, two-span bridge crossing over a drainage canal. There she would enjoy the most successful trainbusting mission of the war. On board the ship that night, *"supposedly for a rest, bath and a change,"* was a US Marine Corps officer from one of the South Korean guerrilla raiding parties who begged to participate. Bovey decided to send him inshore in the motor cutter to listen for trains, and sure enough at 2230 hours he reported a train inside a tunnel. Nothing was seen for two hours, but then the director crew sighted a northbound train emerging from the tunnel. Salvoes from all four guns quickly smothered the area, leading the locomotive crew to slip the coupling and escape into a tunnel, but in doing so they abandoned 15 freight cars that were subsequently shot up by *Crusader* and TF 77 aircraft.[43]

Early the next afternoon *Crusader* scared off the North Koreans when their engine poked its nose out of the tunnel in daylight. Then at 1745 hours, while it was carrying out harassing fire, another train was sighted, well inland towards the town of Tanch'on. The swept channel allowed *Crusader* to close to only 12,800 metres, but even at that relatively long range her fire was effective. *"No sooner had the train been hit and stopped than another train appeared. Fire was shifted to the third train which we were fortunate enough to hit and stop as well."* This was outstanding gunnery. Yet another train was sighted near Tanch'on, but it proved to be out of range so the destroyer spent the rest of the evening sniping at the three trains she had forced to a halt over the previous 24 hours. *Crusader* now had four trains to her credit, making her the top scorer in the Trainbusters Club.

When she sailed away to join the screen of TF 77, Crusader qualified for yet another informal club: "The Windchasers." Since the beginning of the war, a force of three to five USN fleet carriers had been launching air strikes into North Korea from the Sea of Japan. This duty was an eye-opener for the Canadians as the big *Essex* and *Midway*-class carriers steamed at a much higher rate of knots than the slower light carriers of the Corpen Club, making station-keeping and replenishment operations a greater challenge.[44] But the job had the side benefit of allowing the Canadians the opportunity to witness jet operations first hand and it is quite likely that they saw Lieutenant J. J. MacBrien, RCN, fly off USS *Oriskany*, which was attached to TF 77 at the time.

MacBrien became the first Canadian naval aviator to carry out an operational tour in jet aircraft when, as an exchange pilot in March 1952, he joined USN fighter squadron VF-781 flying Grumman Panthers. In a six-month Korean deployment, he flew 66 sorties, mostly ground attack missions against troop concentrations, industrial targets and rail installations. On 1 February 1953 he led a flight of Panthers in a strike on a supply depot near Pukchong. Flying under marginal conditions and in the face of intense flak, MacBrien pressed home the attack and the Americans awarded him their Distinguished Flying Cross for his *"courageous leadership and outstanding demonstration of pilot skill."*[45] MacBrien was the only Canadian naval aviator to experience combat flying in Korea, but he might have been one of 20 or so had the fighting not come to a conclusion when it did. In May 1953 Ottawa approved the loan of the RCN's VF-871 for service off a British carrier in Korean waters and the squadron started to work up their Hawker Sea Fury fighter-bombers for a ground attack role, but the armistice intervened before it was ready to be deployed overseas.[46] One other naval aviator, Commander D. H. P. Ryan, was sent to Korea as an observer, but although he witnessed fighting ashore he was never engaged in combat flight operations.

As *Crusader* shaped course for Canada in May 1953, her captain noted that the destroyer had *"covered the enemy coast from the Yalu River to the Soviet border and, at various times, had been attached to all the different inshore patrol units, as well as the West coast carrier element – 'The Corpen Club' – and Task Force 77 – 'The Windchaser Club'."*[47] Taking up this theme, the RCN's magazine, *The Crowsnest*, reported that during her deployment *Crusader* had steamed 70,980 miles on 14 operational patrols, replenished at sea 68 times, screened 10 different UN carriers and worked in close partnership with 109 different UN ships from seven countries.[48]

The seven other Canadian destroyers that served in the Korean War generally racked up experiences and statistics as impressive as those of *Crusader*. Overall, Korea was an extremely valuable phenomenon for the RCN, marred only by *Iroquois*'s casualties from shellfire and *Huron*'s running aground on the east coast – the *east* coast, no less – two weeks short of the armistice.[49] Although seldom involved in fighting in the traditional naval sense, the Canadian destroyers played an important role in maintaining the United Nations' indisputable command of the sea and in supporting operations ashore. In a wider sense, Korea gave the RCN a much-needed jolt of positive experience after the "sickly season" of the post-Second World War years, when the navy had been cut to the bone and suffered serious morale problems.

A. B. Jerry Devigne, Winnipeg, Manitoba, in *Athabaskan*. (CA 21)

North Star in flight.

# CHAPTER IX

# *Air Operations*

ONLY ONE ROYAL CANADIAN Air Force squadron participated directly in the Korean War, and it was never engaged in combat. No. 426 Squadron flew long-range transport aircraft and only four of them ever actually reached Korea. Most missions ended in Japan. However, the unit played an important part in the logistic aspect of the war, flying between McChord Air Force Base, near Tacoma (and Fort Lewis), Washington, and Haneda airfield, outside Tokyo, via Anchorage, Alaska, and Shemya in the Aleutian Islands chain. A few return trips, mostly medical evacuations, were flown across the central Pacific, via Wake Island, Honolulu and Travis Air Force Base, near San Francisco; but the Honolulu–Travis AFB leg "was slightly beyond our safe range."[1]

The northern, Great Circle, route was no easy option, however, even in a four-engined aircraft. With a five-man crew – pilot, co-pilot, navigator, radio operator and flight engineer – the military version of the Canadair North Star had a maximum speed of 536 kph, cruised at 386 kph and could lift some 5,670 kilograms of useful load. That meant, in human terms, up to 45 fully equipped troops or 36 litter patients. It had a service ceiling of nearly 11,000 metres but was unpressurized, so that when carrying passengers (as it usually was) it could not hope to fly above the weather. Its maximum range was 3,200 kilometres when fully loaded, or 5,200 kilometres with a load of 3,200 kilograms. What most passengers remember best about the North Star is the incredibly noisy cabin as the exhaust gases from the inboard cylinder banks of the two inner engines beat upon the uninsulated aluminium fuselage[2]; but in the three-year life of Operation HAWK the squadron logged 34,000 hours in the air, and carried 13,000 personnel and 3 million kilograms of freight and mail,[3] without losing a life or incurring a serious injury, despite many harrowing instrument landings and some minor accidents, particularly on the *"grim Aleutian strip at Shemya with its ferocious crosswinds."*[4]

In a simpler, less electronic age, navigation was as much an art as a science. There were three electronic navigation aids that came together in the unreliable LORAN, an acronym for LOng RAnge Navigation. LORAN determined the aircraft's position from the intervals between signal pulses received from widely spaced radio transmitters, a radio compass and a radio altimeter, but the problem was that in remote areas, particularly the western Aleutian–Japan leg where transmitter signals were weak, they were often obscured by static or Russian jamming. Then, navigators such as Flying Officer Don Connolly had to rely upon astro-navigation by sextant if they were very lucky and the sky was clear, or, more often, "pressure pattern" flying, an arcane form of dead reckoning, when it was not.

> *An aircraft flying at a constant [air] pressure height traces an undulating vertical path across the sky. As it approaches a high pressure area it gradually climbs and similarly it slides downhill towards low pressure zones. During all of this, the pressure altimeter reading remains constant, but measurements taken with a radar altimeter will show that the true or absolute height is varying, often at a rate of several hundred feet an hour. Now because the winds in the northern hemisphere blow clockwise around high pressure areas and the reverse around lows, aircraft approaching highs will be blown (i.e., drift) to the left. Entering lows they are forced right. The stronger or deeper the pressure zone, the steeper will be the slope the aircraft traces, indicating stronger winds and greater drift. By periodically comparing pressure height and absolute height, a navigator can peg the steepness of the slope quite accurately. Then, by applying some simple math, he can calculate the degree of drift or displacement right or left.*
>
> *Unlike the traditional system of drift measurement through an optical sight, this pressure pattern method works in cloud; and it averages out the drift over a period of time.... I was always fascinated with the zen-like qualities of pressure pattern navigation and used it with confidence.... There were some of my contemporaries who did not share this zeal and treated it with some suspicion.[5]*

The Korean airlift was an early Canadian contribution to the UN effort. Towards the end of June 1950, when Ottawa made three destroyers available to the United Nations, Cabinet had also tentatively approved the contribution of an air transport squadron, "should these prove to be of potential assistance."[6] The chief of air staff, Air Marshal W. A. Curtis, ordered No. 426 to begin preparations for what was dubbed Operation HAWK, and on 25 July 1950 six of the squadron's 20 aircraft left Dorval, Montreal, bound for McChord. En route, the aircraft flew over Parliament Hill, dipping their wings in salute to former prime minister Mackenzie King, who

had died three days earlier and whose body now lay in state beneath the Peace Tower.[7] It seems unlikely that King would have approved of their mission. This, he would have argued, was the unfortunate result of J. A. Bradette's support for Korean elections back in 1947: "This United Nations is going to destroy us yet. Just imagine, *Bradette* making speeches about Korea!"

At McChord, the squadron, commanded by Wing Commander C. H. Mussels, was formally attached to the USAF's Material Air Transport Service (MATS). Much of HAWK would prove to be routine – laborious routine for those on the ground and nerve-racking routine for aircrew.

Every morning Canadian ground crews applied the final tune-up to one of the North Stars. The pilots, navigator and radio officer received their briefing. The olive-clad troops heading for the Korean battle front smoked their last cigarette before gathering up their rifles and bulky army equipment and climbing into the big plane. Soon they were airborne, heading across desolate mountain terrain for Anchorage in Alaska, where a fresh crew was waiting to take over without delay for the next leg of the flight to Shemya in the Aleutians. This was the worst part of the whole flight as far as weather was concerned. Even in summer, flying conditions over the Aleutians were bad and in winter they were much worse. Shemya was perpetually blanketed in pea-soup fog and ground control approach was used on nearly every landing....

At Shemya the crew and passengers stretched their legs, breathed in the fish-foul air and walked to the dimly-lit Quonset-hut mess for a quick meal. After the big transport plane had been fuelled and serviced, a fresh crew took over to fly the 2,100-mile [3,360-kilometre] haul to Tokyo. For the navigator this was the busiest part of the flight, for continuous fixes were sent out to let the ground stations know the aircraft position along the route. Depending on wind and load conditions the planes went either to Misawa in northern Japan and then to Haneda Airfield, or else directly to Haneda.[8]

One of those four trips to Korea involved flying A. R. Menzies of External Affairs, then head of the Canadian Liaison Mission in Japan, to Kimpo in order to visit 25 Brigade in October 1951. Menzies's account of his visit stresses the differences between the airfield from which he took off and the one on which he landed.

*The crews that fly the North Stars over the Pacific Airlift know only the settled base life of the great airports at Dorval, McChord Field, Anchorage, Shemya and Haneda. They see nothing of war for Japan today largely has returned to a settled and modestly comfortable peace-time existence, despite the continuation of the Occupation.*

*By contrast, Kimpo, the airport of Seoul, symbolizes the turmoil, destruction and impermanence of existence in war-torn Korea. As your plane comes in for a landing, you see wrecks of buildings, aircraft and vehicles on the edges of the field. Gangs of Korean workmen are chipping at the red earth with picks and shovels, levelling out areas for new runways to handle the volume of air traffic that now comes in and goes out of Kimpo. We were told it was the busiest airport in the world today and we got some impression of this from the constant string of transports that were landing and taking off and the flights of fighters and fighter bombers that streaked overhead, waiting for the signal to land... Rows of olive brown tents house evacuation hospitals, process troops coming from or going to Japan and protect great piles of urgent war materials lifted from Japan by air. As soon as we had clambered down the service ladder from our North Star, we knew we were in the war zone.*[9]

A war correspondent's perspective on the trip was provided by René Lévesque in his memoirs published 35 years later. He began by making some most unlikely allegations about the condition of the crew. *"I came close to scramming right out of there when I saw our pilot weaving up to the plane after a binge that had lasted until the small hours of the morning. The navigator didn't seem to be in much better shape, but luckily the co-pilot just looked tired."* The task that these men were preparing to embark upon was dangerous enough for well-rested, stone-cold-sober crews; and since it is unlikely that this particular crew was suicidal, perhaps it is best to assume that Lévesque was writing for effect.

*The passengers included a sergeant coming back from leave, myself, and a huge spare engine that sat in the middle of the stripped-down cabin area and took up all the space. Squeezed into our seats on either side of this bulky travelling companion, the sergeant and I dozed off while gazing at the infinite monotony of the ocean. After several hours there was nothing to see but a thick fog into which the plane began to make its interminably slow descent, seeking out Attu or Kiska, one of those minuscule rocks we were supposed to land on. Lower, and still lower, then suddenly the plane picked up altitude with the roar of an angry beast. The same scenario was repeated twice over.... At last, a crack in the fog revealed an inch of airstrip, the plane dove down on it, and when it finally consented to come to a stop, we could make out the sound of waves breaking a few feet away.*[10]

There was one narrow escape from disaster early in the three-year airlift, on 2 October 1950, when a North Star captained by Flying Officer Donald M. Payne, DFC (his decoration had been won when he was wounded by anti-aircraft fire while bombing Kiel in April 1945 and being forced down in the sea, spending 11 days in a dinghy before it drifted ashore – on German territory![11]), was on the leg from Shemya to Tokyo.

When approximately 700 miles [11,200 kilometres] Southwest of Shemya the number three engine of the aircraft he was flying suddenly went out of control; attempts to feather it proved useless and the only means of reducing the R[evolutions] P[er] M[inute] was by decreasing speed. When it became apparent that either the propeller or complete engine assembly might break loose at any moment Flying Officer Payne sent out a distress signal and prepared his crew for ditching. However, as a result of his outstanding ability, he was able to keep the aircraft airborne without further damage allowing him to return to Shemya.[12]

Payne must have recalled his earlier ditching as he struggled to keep his aircraft aloft. This time he was unhurt, but his prospects of surviving another would have been far poorer in the vast chilly expanses of the North Pacific in October than in the relatively benign North Sea in April. In the event, Payne was able to add the ribbon of an Air Force Cross to the array of decorations already on his tunic.

Perhaps the narrowest escape at Shemya occurred on the night of 27 December 1953 when a North Star captained by Flight Lieutenant C. E. L. Hare landed in snow and a 50-knot cross wind on an ice-covered runway, slid off it and toppled, nose first, into a ravine. Ground crewmen rarely get the recognition they deserve for their devoted, untiring efforts, except perhaps by the men who fly the aircraft they maintain. The recovery of this particular North Star provides an opportunity to acknowledge their part in every major operation. Flight Sergeant Arthur Engelbert was responsible for retrieving the ditched aircraft.

> The successful execution of this salvage operation enabled the aircraft to continue to its destination in Japan with a load of troops and vital supplies. Had it not been for the outstanding skill and determination shown by Flight Sergeant Engelbert a valuable aircraft might have been lost and an essential load delayed.[13]

Engelbert received a British Empire Medal in Queen Elizabeth's first Birthday Honours list, and that same list brought his commanding officer, Wing Commander C. H. Mussels, the rank of Officer in the Order of the British Empire.

Another non-commissioned officer who performed extraordinarily well in solving a different kind of problem was Corporal G. R. Reed, a toolmaker turned flight engineer.

> Due to a mechanical failure, the nose wheel became damaged on landing at Misawa and the flight was unable to proceed to Tokyo as scheduled. Unable to obtain the necessary replacement parts...Corporal Reed proceeded to manufacture the replacement brackets required, carried out retraction tests [in the air, one hopes] and finished off the remaining necessary adjustments practically single-handed. The aircraft was then able to proceed to Tokyo where permanent repairs were effected.[14]

A former fighter ace distinguished himself in a different fashion at Vancouver on 30 December 1953 when an outbound flight found one engine overheating shortly after take-off. Turning back, the aircraft began to ice up and finally crash-landed, turning upside down in the process and leaving everyone on board hanging in their harnesses or seat belts. There was an obvious danger of fire. Flying as a supernumerary crewman (the record does not tell us why, but perhaps in connection with his earlier posting as RCAF liaison officer to the United States' Far East Air Forces from June 1951 to July 1953), Wing Commander Robert W. "Buck" McNair, DSO, DFC and two Bars, who had accounted for 16 German aircraft during the Second World War, stepped into the breach.

> Self preservation was uppermost in the minds of practically everyone because of the imminent danger of fire or explosion but Wing Commander McNair, cognizant of the large number of passengers being carried and the state of turmoil that must be existing, threw caution to the winds, remained in the aircraft and fought his way to the passenger compartment. Here, he set to work, restored calm and through prodigious effort assisted all passengers in evacuating the aircraft as quickly as possible.... It is to be remembered that this officer was soaked in gasoline at the time...from an overturned Herman Nelson heater, a condition which would immediately bring to mind the fact that he had been badly burned by fire in his aircraft during the war and therefore should have been acutely aware of his precarious position.[15]

McNair was originally recommended for a George Medal, second only to the George Cross for displaying exceptional courage other than in the face of the enemy, but the recommendation was downgraded to a Queen's Commendation for Brave Conduct when a mealy-mouthed Inter-Service Awards Committee in Ottawa decided that McNair, as part of the crew, "had a special responsibility with respect to passengers and thus was doing little more than his duty"![16]

Although only one Canadian squadron was directly involved in the Korean War, 22 RCAF fighter pilots attached to USAF squadrons on exchange postings played individual roles. The first of them was Flight Lieutenant Omer Levesque, who had spent most of the Second World War in a German prison camp. In June 1950 he had just begun an exchange posting with the USAF at Langley AFB in Virginia. After a conversion course on North American F-86 Sabres, Levesque was assigned to the 334th Squadron of 4 Fighter-Interceptor Wing, and he arrived in Korea with a composite unit of the wing on 1 December 1950.

This was the first Sabre formation to be deployed to the Far East, sent there to counter the sudden appearance of MiG-15s in the hands of Chinese pilots. The only airfield in South Korean hands from which Sabres could safely operate at that time was Kimpo, just northwest of Seoul, but it was already crowded with other aircraft – tactical fighter-bombers and the like. There was not enough room for the entire wing, so Detachment A was formed from elements of each of the wing's three squadrons, while the rest remained in Japan for the time being. Omer Levesque was one of those assigned to the Korean detachment, which flew its first operational sorties on 17 December 1950, and one of them was flown by

Sabre in Korea. (RE 22037-5)

Interior of North Star. (PL 54100)

Levesque, making him the first Canadian ever to engage in jet-versus-jet combat. Although both British and Germans (but not the Americans) had flown jet fighters operationally during the last year of the Second World War, they were sufficiently rare birds never to have encountered each other.

When the Korean conflict began, US air power, relying on Lockheed F-80 Shooting Star and Grumman F9F Panther jet fighters, had made short work of the North Korean Air Force, equipped with a mixture of propeller-driven, Second World War-vintage machines.[17] But the entry of the Chinese into the arena changed the equation when MiG-15 jets based behind the Yalu, in Manchuria, began to appear in ever-increasing numbers – estimated at 300 by July 1951.[18] The MiGs were short-range machines, however, and for that reason, and perhaps also because their Chinese pilots could rarely match their opponents in combat skills (most of the latter had Second World War experience, while the Chinese, of course, did not), they stuck close to their Manchurian bases and preferred to stay high when they stayed at all. That meant a rectangular block of airspace stretching along the Yalu from its mouth in the Yellow Sea and south to the Ch'ongeh'on river, at heights mostly above 8,000 metres – an area that became famous as "Mig Alley."

The F-86 and MiG-15 were technically quite different but well matched. The lightweight MiG could fly higher and climb faster, but it had a low roll rate and a relatively low rate of fire from its one 37mm cannon and two 23mm machine-guns. Moreover, there was some loss of control at high speeds. The heavier F-86 enjoyed a very slight speed advantage in level flight, could dive faster, and had better stability (especially in high-speed turns) and a higher rate of fire from its six 50-calibre machine-guns.[19] "*Air gunnery technique was perhaps the most noticeable enemy deficiency,*" wrote Levesque.

*Deflection shooting was particularly bad. This may be due to insufficient training, wrong type of sights, inefficient guns or a combination of any of these factors... Enemy air-firing prowess can be judged from the fact that only one Sabre was shot down from 15 December, 1950 until 15 May, 1951. During this period the F-86 claimed 19 MiG-15's destroyed.*

*Self-destroying ammunition was used by the MiGs and the cannons appeared to have a slow rate of fire. The general opinion amongst F-86 pilots was that the barrels were too short, which*

*resulted in the shells toppling shortly after leaving the barrel, especially when the guns were fired in a tight turn.*[20]

The Sabre's guns gave it a distinct edge, but the difference in Korea would lie primarily in combat flying skills.

*Generally speaking, we did not find our opponents as aggressive as we expected and they gave the impression of lacking somewhat in initiative. When first encountered they could be roughly compared in skill with our pilots in World War II after they had logged 250 training hours, but as time went on they improved considerably as they gained experience. Some, usually the leaders, were better than others and the tentative opinion was expressed that these were Russians.*[21]

However, the enemy's growing skills were largely offset by technical improvements to the Sabre.[22] The F-86F, in Korean service from the fall of 1952, was a distinctly superior machine to the MiG, with an improved wing, a higher ceiling and a much improved electronic gun sight.

By the end of the war, the USAF would admit having lost 78 Sabres (and 61 other types) in air-to-air combat, while claiming 792 MiGs (and 18 other) North Korean and Chinese aircraft.[23] A high proportion of enemy losses were validated by camera guns, but since all the fighting took place over North Korean airspace and camera guns sometimes failed or ran out of film, not every claim could be confirmed. Other experience, before and after Korea, suggests that the true figure for enemy losses was more probably in the 600–700 range.

Early in January 1951, Kimpo airfield fell to the Chinese advance and Detachment A returned to Japan, but by 10 February the airfield was re-taken by the United Nations and on the 22nd 4 Wing was ordered back to Korea.[24] Kimpo was again very busy, however, and could be used by the Sabres only in an emergency. Levesque's 334th Squadron was based initially at Taegu and then at Suwon, south of Seoul, from 10 March.

On 30 March 51 a force of B-29s was sent to bomb the bridges over the Yalu at Sinuiju, under the very noses of the MIGs based in Manchuria. The 334th Sqn. was included in the escort, and Levesque was flying as wingman to Major Edward Fletcher, one of the flight leaders.

The MIG response that day was feeble, and only a few brushed with the *Sabres*. Fletcher and

Levesque attacked two, which split up, each with a *Sabre* in hot pursuit. Levesque's MIG made a few evasive manoeuvres and then levelled off, as if the pilot thought he had shaken [off] the *Sabre*.[25]

He was mistaken. *"I caught a MiG at about 17,000 feet [6,000 metres] and hit him with a good long burst. He went into a series of violent rolls and kept on rolling until he hit the ground and exploded,"* was Levesque's laconic description of what happened next.[26] In the citation for his American DFC this was designated "an act of heroic and extraordinary achievement." Additionally, "through aggressive and skillful manoeuvring he made repeated daring attacks upon the enemy which resulted in his personal destruction of one enemy aircraft. His brilliant evasion of other enemy aircraft added immeasurably to the success of his mission."[27]

Levesque remained in Korea until May 1951, when his tour expired. The Americans would have been happy to take a replacement at once, but back in Canada the RCAF was expanding, and converting to Sabres, and thought for the moment that it needed all its trained pilots at home. As pilots became available they were assigned to fly the Sabres of 1 Air Division in NATO, where there seemed an ever-present and growing danger of the Cold War heating up. However, in the early spring of 1952 it was decided that up-to-date combat experience was important too, and arrangements were made for RCAF pilots with at least 50 hours on Sabres to be attached to the US Far East Air Force for a tour of 50 missions or six months, whichever came first. Two pilots would be sent initially, and one a month thereafter.

The first two pilots sent were Flying Officers Sanford B. Fleming and G. W. Nixon, and they went before all the details had been worked out. While in Korea, Fleming was apparently given verbal instructions to complete his 50 missions and return, but no one put it in writing, nor were the Americans informed. Using his initiative, he went on to fly 82 sorties before being recalled.[28]

By the summer of 1952 both sides were catching on to the other's tactics and trying to devise counter-measures. Patrolling at speeds of Mach 0.85 or higher, the Sabre pilots could afford to spend no more than 20 minutes in Mig Alley, and, getting low on fuel as they turned to leave, were at their most vulnerable. The enemy, making the most of the MiGs' superior climbing ability and higher operational ceiling, would wait for that moment and then dive across the Yalu to launch their attacks. The Americans countered by mounting patrols operating in multiple flights of four or eight machines, scheduled to arrive in the patrol area at irregular intervals averaging five minutes. Thus the withdrawal of all but the last Sabre flight could be covered by a later flight – and it was impossible for the Chinese to know in advance exactly which would be the last one.

There were two kinds of enemy pilots, good ones – usually Chinese – and poor ones – mostly North Koreans. Monitoring of enemy radio frequencies enabled the Americans to know whether the foe was linguistically Chinese or Korean, and Flying Officer Fleming's official report explained how that information was used.

> *When he called "Jackpot Flight over Anju" [the ground controller] implied that the Anju-bound MIGs were manned by North Koreans of low pilot ability and would provide a field day for the [F-]86s that could track them down. When the 86s descended like vultures on the rarely-seen North Korean formations, the latter would break up and scatter, becoming easy meat for the well-disciplined pilots of the USAF. These "Jackpot Flight" members would demonstrate seat ejection at the slightest excuse, often before a shot was fired. It was nothing for a North Korean wingman to bail out simply because he had seen his leader set the example, or for another pilot to do likewise because he had broken too hard and his MIG had flicked into a spin.[29]*

It was never Fleming's good fortune to encounter a "Jackpot Flight," but on 13 May

> in the course of escorting an *RF-80* [photo-reconnaissance aircraft], he spotted sixteen *MIGs* preparing to attack. He led his element into the first four *MIGs*, scattering the enemy and sending a few running for Manchuria. He then attacked two *MIGs* which were firing on the *RF-80* and its close escort of two *Sabres*. One *MIG* went down and was later assessed as "probably destroyed." Fleming kept up the fight until the *RF-80* had withdrawn safely, and then returned to base, low on fuel and out of ammunition.[30]

On other occasions he damaged two other MiGs, and he was subsequently awarded an American DFC, while his colleague, Flying Officer Nixon, flew the prescribed 50 sorties and participated in a number of fights but made no claims. At the expiration of his

J. A. Omer Levesque. (PL 61154)

E. A. Glover. (PL 57511)

tour, Nixon received an Air Medal; everybody who flew 20 missions got an Air Medal.

Indeed, the Americans were a good deal more generous with decorations than Canadians were accustomed to. After Omer Levesque picked up both his American DFC and an Air Medal, the RCAF forbade its representatives to accept more than one American decoration, presumably because too much "fruit salad" on the chest was likely to arouse the envy of those not fortunate enough to win a Korean posting. Nearly all of them went to veterans of the earlier war, and as a result several pilots found themselves with both an Anglo-Canadian DFC and an American one to keep it company by the time their brief tours ended.

One who was not a Second World War flyer was 22-year-old Flight Lieutenant Claude A. Lafrance, who had been instructing in an Operational Training Unit at Chatham, Ontario. He complained to his commanding officer that he was the only instructor there without operational experience and begged for a Korean posting. In May 1952 he got his wish. On his 22nd sortie on 5 August 1952, his first as an element leader, he engaged a MiG and scored hits on it, compelling the pilot to eject, then chased another one back to the Yalu. He was awarded an American DFC and was able to walk taller when he returned to instructing in Canada. Indeed, Lafrance ended his service career in June 1981 as a major-general in Canada's unified Armed Forces, at which time he was the last serving pilot to have been in combat.*[31]

The formation tactics employed by the Americans were based on a two-plane element of leader and wingman, in which the leader initiated attacks and the wingman's duty was to guard his leader's tail. Naturally, most victories went to element leaders. Normally, a pilot flew about 20 sorties as a wingman before being promoted to leader. Two elements usually flew together as a "finger-four" – in which each aircraft occupied a position relative to the others similar to the fingertips of one hand, and leadership of such a flight usually went to a man with 50 or more sorties under his belt.

Because of their short tours, few Canadians ever reached that level of leadership, but there were exceptions and one of them was 38-year-old Group Captain Edward B. Hale, DFC, together with Claude Lafrance respectively the oldest and youngest of the

Canadians who flew in Korea. As commanding officer of the RCAF's No. 1 Fighter Wing, at North Luffenham, in England, Hale was sent to Korea to *"investigate the Tactics and procedures used in employing F-86 fighters in combat against MIG-15's. My orders were personally worded by the CAS (A/M Curtis) to allow me complete freedom to go and come as I wished and employ any means to achieve my purpose."*[32] Hale was well qualified to fly Sabres, but his only earlier operational experience had been "many sorties on anti-submarine operations in the North Atlantic," which had brought him his DFC in December 1944.[33]

He reported to 51 Fighter-Interceptor Wing on 29 April 1952, and on 1 May flew his first sortie – a commendable approach to the study of current tactics! His rank and obvious enthusiasm, not to mention the friendship he soon established with Colonel Francis Gabreski, the wing commander (who had been the top USAAF European ace of the Second World War, with 31 victories, and who would add 6½ MiGs to that total during two tours in Korea), no doubt helped him to become a flight leader, and then a wing leader.

*I was fortunate to be able to live in the same quarters with Col. Gabreski...and did my first combat missions with him on 1 May 52. On that day my roommate, Col[.] Al Schintz was shot down, and we did several missions in search of him, with the hope of effecting a rescue. He was rescued 29 days later from an island at the mouth of the Yalu.*

*On four occasions I fired on enemy aircraft, and twice saw them crash, but we were having camera troubles with the Sabres at that time, and I lacked confirmation for my claims. On the 25th of May I was leading the wing in support of a bombing mission by F 84's on Sonch'on, but the weather was very poor at the rendezvous, and the bomber force were [sic] late arriving. The mission called for close escort for the low level run from the rendezvous to the target, some 50 miles [80 kilometres], and in the resultant confusion, most of my wing ran low on fuel as we searched for the bombers at low level, and had to return to base, while my wing man and I made "one more sweep" and picked up our bombers (17 F 84's) and attempted to escort them to the target. We found them at the exact same time that the MIG's did and had a very short fight (this was one of the times when I saw my MIG hit the trees) and got*

---

* A situation that changed with the onset of the Persian Gulf war in 1991. More recently (1999–2000), Canadian airmen have seen combat in the Balkans.

*home without losing any of the bombers, although I can't say how many of them hit the target!*[34]

Hale's DFC citation spoke of "his personal courage, outstanding leadership, and devotion to duty."[35]

Only one of the exchange pilots won both a Canadian and an American DFC in the course of Korean operations. Flight Lieutenant Ernest A. Glover was another pilot with Second World War service, one who, after completing 98 sorties, had the misfortune to be shot down over France in May 1943. He served in Korea with Levesque's old unit from June to October 1952, flying his first sortie on 4 July, but saw no enemy aircraft until 26 August, after which "he saw them almost every day." He claimed to have damaged two in a fight four days later, and then was credited with his first kill on 8 September.

*He was flying as number four man in a flight of Sabres when a two ship element of MIGs was intercepted. The F-86 flight closed, but in the evasive action the MIGs made a hard right turn which the number one and two men were unable to follow. Flight Lieutenant Glover, being in a more advantageous position, fired, observing immediate hits. The MIGs dived from 40,000 to 15,000 feet [approximately 13,000 to 3,000 metres] and during one violent pull-up, the number two MIG went out of control and plunged into the ground. The lead MIG, with Flight Lieutenant Glover still firing, reached the sanctuary of the Yalu River.*[36]

The next day, while escorting fighter-bombers attacking the North Korean Military Academy at Sakehun, a large number of MiGs endeavoured to thwart the attack. Six were shot down, Glover claiming one of them. Promoted to flight leader, on 16 September Glover participated in an attack on 20 MiGs, one of which he destroyed for his third victory, before ending his tour on 18 October. His Canadian DFC citation referred to his "most commendable aggressive spirit coupled with excellent fighting ability," while his American DFC citation pointed to "his valor, proficiency and devotion to duty" and the "great credit [reflected] upon himself, his comrades in arms of the United Nations and the Royal Canadian Air Force."[37]

Only one other Canadian claimed more than one MiG. Squadron Leader J. Douglas Lindsay, DFC, had been credited with 6½ enemy machines destroyed in 1944 and 1945 (including three in one day on 2 July 1944), with another five damaged. In Korea he was made an element leader after only four sorties, and was quickly nicknamed "Mig-magnet" – by the time he had completed 20 sorties he had participated in five engagements with MiGs, a most unusual ratio, and had been credited with damaging two. Made a flight leader, on 11 October 1952 he spotted 12 MiGs *crossing the Yalu River at a very high altitude.*

*Squadron Leader Lindsay immediately started climbing to intercept the enemy aircraft. The enemy flight started a turn which enabled Squadron Leader Lindsay's flight to cut them off and close with them. Picking out the last flight of four MIG-15 aircraft Squadron Leader Lindsay began his attack on the number four man of the enemy flight and scored decisive hits on the enemy aircraft. This enemy aircraft then began a steep spiralling dive and was observed to crash and explode.*[38]

On 25 October he damaged another.

A month later Lindsay was flying his penultimate sortie with Lieutenant Harold E. Fischer as his wingman. At 15,000 metres, a height at which the enemy could be expected to have the advantage, they attacked a formation of 21 MiGs. Two of the Chinese pilots broke right in a climbing turn, and Lindsay shot one down, while Fischer got the other – the first of 10 that the latter would eventually be credited with, before he was shot down himself and taken prisoner by the Chinese.

The 13th pilot sent to Korea by the RCAF was another Second World War veteran, Squadron Leader Andrew R. Mackenzie, who had been taught deflection shooting by that incomparable marksman, George "Screwball" Beurling,* and had 8½ victories to his credit in the Second World War. On his first four sorties Mackenzie saw no enemy aircraft, but the fifth was different. He was flying as wingman to the flight leader of the top flight of one of three squadrons patrolling the Yalu on 5 December 1952 when they encountered some 20 MiGs. Some misunderstanding had his partner turning one way and he the other, and then the Canadian's Sabre was hit by a burst of cannon fire.

*I tried to break to the left to evade more fire, but found that my aircraft had gone out of control....*

---

* Credited with 32 victories during the Second World War, 28 of them in a four-month span in 1942. He joined the nascent Israeli air force in 1948 and died when the aircraft he was ferrying to Palestine crashed near Rome.

James D. Lindsay in earlier days. (PL 26643)

A. R. Mackenzie. (PL 62530 and PL 62534)

*Since there was no point in staying in the aircraft any longer, I bailed out.*

*I was at about 40,000 feet [13,000 metres] when I hit the air. Luckily my ejection seat had worked like a charm and I found myself tumbling through space at about 500 miles an hour [800 kph], my arms and legs thrashing about. At this speed, the air tore at my body, pulling off my wrist watch, my helmet, gloves, oxygen mask, and an escape kit which had been tightly tied to the seat of my parachute. As quickly as possible I released my seat (to which I was till strapped) and kicked it away. I had not yet pulled my chute. This being my first bailout, the thought passed through my mind, I wonder if this damn thing will work. Normally, if you bail out at that altitude and lose your oxygen supply, it is advisable to free drop to about 15,000 feet [5,000 metres]. But I decided not to wait and pulled my chute immediately.*

*It was wonderful to feel the jerk of the straps and see that beautiful white expanse of silk blossoming out in the sky above. Everything seemed strangely quiet. Gone were the noises of battle, the exploding shells, and the din of radio chatter in my ears.... It was cold as hell. Except for this I found the drop not unpleasant.*

He landed in North Korea, not far south of the Yalu, and was quickly captured by Chinese troops who took him across the river. An apparently endless series of interrogations then began, which, together with some occasional surreptitious contact with three American airmen who were also prisoners (one of them was Harold Fischer, who had been Doug Lindsay's wingman), provided the only diversion in his solitary confinement. The fighting ended and an armistice went into effect, but Mackenzie was still a prisoner. He was never subjected to torture in the tra-ditional sense of the word, but a favourite punishment was to order him to sit, motionless, on the edge of his bed for 16 hours a day, with nothing to do or read.

The Communists demanded that he admit to being shot down over China rather than North Korea.

*"We know that you flew over China. We have absolute proof of this. We also know that you would not do this of your own free will, that you have been used as a tool of the American Imperialists, that you were instructed or ordered to fly into our sacred air, that you were shot down, in China, and that the sooner you realize that you must confess to this truth, the better it will be for you," he [the interrogator] said.*

*For the first time I really lost my head. Banging my fist into the open palm of my hand, I shouted:*

*"I never did fly over China. I was never instructed to fly over China. I was not shot down over China and you know that. I came to China in a jeep, handcuffed and covered over with a tarpaulin, and I demand my release."*[39]

However, after *"about 465 days"* of mostly solitary confinement, a physically weakened and emotionally drained Mackenzie gave his jailers what they wanted, writing and signing a paper stating that he had indeed been over Chinese territory. Even then, it took time to arrange his release. On 5 December 1954, two years to the day after he had been shot down and 17 months after the Korean armistice had been signed at Panmunjon, Andy Mackenzie was turned over to British authorities in Hong Kong.

Twenty-five years later, Mackenzie revealed that he had been shot down by an American pilot. While trying to re-formate on his flight leader, he had flown into the path of an oncoming Sabre flight and apparently a startled young pilot had fired his guns almost by reflex.[40] Mackenzie bore him no ill will.

(SF-4141)

Final game of the 25 Brigade hockey championship "Imjin garden," February 1953.

## CHAPTER X

# *The End of the Affair*

ON THE GROUND, the Commonwealth Division remained in Corps reserve until early April 1953, spending its time *"installing a great belt of barbed wire in the third line of defence, called the Kansas Line, across the front of what had been the site of the great Kapyong battle."*[1] The Chinese were doing much the same on their side of the line, digging and wiring, and since the terrain precluded the use of massed armour the battlefield now bore a startling resemblance to the Western Front of 1916–17 during the lulls between major (and fruitless) offensives. Artillery might hammer away, and infantrymen – boasting far more firepower than their predecessors – snipe at each other, but the prospect of a successful offensive by either protagonist was now virtually non-existent, short of the introduction of nuclear weapons.

In the early spring, 1 Commonwealth Division was reinforced by 1,000 Korean soldiers, known as KATCOMS (Korean Augmentation to Commonwealth troops), who were mostly then assigned to the various infantry battalions, which received approximately 100 each. In 25 Brigade two or three went to each infantry section and each one was paired with a Canadian. *"They were young South Korean conscripts with less than*

*six months' service and only rudimentary training,"* remembered a platoon commander with 3 PPCLI.

*The major problem for them was their lack of understanding of the English language. Eight Platoon received eleven KATCOMS and only one was able to understand even the most basic English. We decided to pair off these KATCOMS with Canadian soldiers as it was the only way we could envisage getting them to understand what was happening and to establish a means of control. These bewildered individuals, who had never been exposed to much outside their previous village life, suddenly were thrust into a completely new culture. They had to conform to orders issued in a language they didn't understand and eat food they had never seen before. The first few days saw some very amazed Canadians watch the new arrivals dump sugar and milk and ketchup and whatever else was on the table on top of whatever had been dished out by the cooks, and then shovel that directly by fingers into their mouths. Fortunately, they learned very quickly to emulate the Canadian style of eating. I often wondered how they managed some twelve months later when most*

*143*

*were returned to Korean units and had to revert to their former ways.*[2]

"Despite language difficulties the scheme proved successful; for the Korean makes a good soldier, especially in night operations."[3]

Before the division went back into the line the rest of the second troop rotation began as 1 RCR was replaced by 3 RCR (Lieutenant-Colonel K. L. Campbell) in mid-March. After returning to the front, 1 R22eR was replaced by 3 R22eR (Lieutenant-Colonel J. L. G. Poulin) and 1 RCHA by 81 Field Regiment RCA (Lieutenant-Colonel H. W. Sterne) in mid-April. On 21 April, Brigadier Bogert turned over command of the brigade to Brigadier J.-V. Allard, and, lastly, A Squadron, LdSH, by B Squadron (Major W. H. Ellis) on 24 May. The Signals Squadron rotated individuals rather than units, but the various supporting services also rotated during this time.

The new brigade commander, Jean-Victor Allard, was almost 40 years old, with a distinguished Second World War record that included *three* DSOs and had culminated with command of an infantry brigade in northwest Europe. In 1961, at the height of the Cold War, he would become the first and only Canadian ever to be given command of a British division (in the British Army of the Rhine), and in 1966 he would be the first French Canadian to become chief of the defence staff. His introduction to the peculiarities of the Korean War must have come as something of a shock.

*Our orders were to wage a strictly defensive war. Thus, a brigade commander could not, on his own initiative, mount an offensive that would involve more than a platoon. To attack with a company, we had to obtain permission from the army corps commander – the divisional commander did not have that power of decision – and the corps commander had to have the blessing of the army commander to involve more than one company... If our enemy happened to dominate our positions, we had to let him snipe at us, with the ensuing loss of life which might have been avoided by capturing certain peaks from our adversary.*[4]

Of course, the nature of the ground – this freakish tangle of peaks, steep-sided ridges and narrow valleys – made it almost inevitable that if the United Nations had attacked and captured the dominating heights in question, then the enemy would still have been able to snipe at them, from other heights just a little further back or off to a flank. And although there was,

inevitably, a small but steady stream of casualties from the sniping, any significant offensive, such as those that had resulted in the capture of "Bloody" and "Heartbreak" ridges, would have led to vastly greater casualties.

Allard preferred to arrange his brigade in the traditional style, with two battalions forward and one in reserve on his front of 4,500 metres. Whether he was right or wrong in this is impossible to say with certainty, but given the circumstances – armistice talks in progress, total command of the air (with associated good intelligence), a likelihood of minor raids but no chance of a serious offensive – it might be argued that he was wrong. "Two up and one back" gave him a relatively powerful reserve, but his front line was manned more thinly than desirable on such incredibly complex terrain, making it difficult to site defensive perimeters with sufficient fields of fire to provide mutual support. A couple of sections or a platoon with inadequate or non-existent mutual support had little prospect of surviving an attack by two or more Chinese companies without relying on artillery support. However, fire from 81 Field Regiment was readily (and quickly) available. The same factors applied to a company or two attacked by a battalion or more, and nothing larger than that was in the least likely.

Such an attack did develop against the RCR on the night of 2/3 May 1953. The 2nd had been a fairly quiet day with the usual shelling and mortaring resulting in one man killed and three wounded – a more severe result than usual. An A Company ambush patrol, 16 strong, left the lines at 2030 hours, bound for a position from which it might intercept any enemy patrols attempting to penetrate between the Royals and the Patricias, and a platoon of C Company stood by to reinforce it should the need arise. It did. About two hours later, the patrol was attacked by an estimated 60 Chinese, the patrol leader was killed and half his men either killed or captured, leaving Corporal J. C. McNeil in command. A section of the supporting platoon, led by the platoon commander, went forward to help and was also roughly handled. McNeil, who won a Military Medal for his efforts,

*directed the withdrawal of the patrol, beating off successive attacks and collecting his wounded as he retired. When a second patrol which had been sent to his assistance was also attacked and the patrol leader killed he picked up some of the survivors of*

Wounded Chinese soldier captured by The Royal Canadian Regiment is bandaged by 25 year-old stretcher-bearer Private Johnny Decarie of St. Catharines, Ontario. (SF-3131)

The day everyone waited for. (PPCLI Museum)

*this patrol and made good his retreat...bringing with him four uninjured and seven injured men.*[5]

The remnants of these two groups were still in no man's land at midnight when the Chinese artillery opened a heavy fire on C Company's position, the most advanced of the four company localities. Then the Chinese infantry advanced, over-running one of the forward platoons, so that the platoon commander, 2nd Lieutenant E. H. Hollyer, was compelled to call down artillery fire on his own position. When he left his bunker on one occasion *"to observe and report the results,"* he was *"blown back into his bunker"* by an explosion, according to the citation for his Military Cross. Lieutenant L. G. Côté, the RC Signals officer serving with the battalion, who happened to have been supervising communications with the patrol still in no man's land when the attack began, *"was twice blown from the trench into bunkers,"* but still got only one MC!

The glut of natural leadership in the ranks was demonstrated by Private G. P. Julien, who had been appointed a section commander only a few days prior to the attack.

*Driven to cover by the intensity of the bombardment he nevertheless continued to encourage and inspire his men so that they were prepared to meet the actual assault with vigorous and sustained fire. When the bombardment lifted, Private JULIEN left the cover of his own positions to seek out survivors whom he rallied at his own section post, placing them skillfully, and continued to fight resourcefully although his group appeared to be the sole survivors in the position.*

*He remained in the position without communication to his platoon commander [Hollyer] and under intense enemy fire until it became evident to him that he could no longer affect the outcome of the fighting. He then collected as many wounded as he could find and withdrew in good order with his wounded and weapons to No. 8 Platoon position.*[6]

Julien was awarded a Military Medal.

The other platoon bearing the brunt of the assault was commanded by Corporal W. D. Pero in the absence of the platoon commander, who had gone forward into no man's land to take command of the remnants of the original ambush patrol. Pero also won an MM, holding off his attackers without needing artillery fire on his own position, although it was falling all around it.

After some 90 minutes the enemy withdrew. The weight of shells delivered by artillery from both sides on to this relatively minute sliver of ground was astonishing, and gives some indication of the difficulties any major attack would have posed. The Chinese were estimated to have fired some 2,000 rounds, and the divisional artillery responded with 8,000, with more than half coming from the guns of 81 Canadian Field Regiment. This engagement cost the Chinese more than 80 fatal casualties — there is no way of knowing how many bodies they took away, or how many wounded — while the Royals lost 26 killed, 27 wounded and seven taken prisoner, with four KATCOMs killed, 14 wounded and four missing. Again, the ratio of killed to wounded among the Canadians testifies to the severity and close-quarter nature of the fighting. The Patricias, catching the edge of the enemy artillery fire, lost two killed and seven wounded, and 81 Field Artillery had two gunners killed.

Since casualties meant very little to the Chinese commanders and a great deal to Brigadier Allard, he found much to concern him about this night's work. In fact, he had been concerned before the raid, and on 1 May had signed *"a long memo revising all the arrangements which would have to be made concerning the companies in a defensive war."*

*Our positions were defended by minefields and barbed wire. Through these defences, paths were marked out for the use of our patrols. Moreover, our automatic weapons, mortars and barrage artillery had precise targets to strike in case of an alert. Since these objectives did not often change, the enemy had been able to approach our static defences, probe here and there, await our response and then mark on his maps the places that were well covered by our fire and those that were less so, or not at all. Because of the width of the front, it was impossible for us to give our line complete coverage. Thus, every night, as had been the case before the attack against the RCR, numerous enemy patrols along a particular section of our front gave the Chinese a clear idea of our strong and weak points which they could subsequently avoid or use at the right moment.*

*All that had to be changed. First of all, the lines of fire of our defence would have to be changed frequently. In particular, our fighting patrols (ten men or more) that had gone out at night to occupy a few outposts would be disbanded and replaced by many more small groups of two men each...and a dog specially trained to signal unwarranted presences noiselessly; these dogs also gave confidence to these isolated, unprotected men. These small outposts would be dotted here and there in no man's land, out of reach of our defensive fire and off the beaten tracks, though staying close to them. Thus, equipped with a radio, the patrols could inform us of Chinese penetrations [of no man's land].... It would then be up to our guns to fire at the right moment and at the right place, with the advantage of knowing fairly accurately where the enemy was....*

*To achieve these results, I had to set up a patrol school under the masterly direction of [Major W. H.] Harry Pope. Other measures were also taken. Thus, I changed our defence system and added four tanks, which were placed below our positions, ready to give their support when needed. We hid them by day, and at night they patrolled the land near the former rice fields [in the valley bottoms]. I had frequent checks made of the positions of all our automatic weapons to make sure they were at maximum effectiveness. Moreover, I had our static positions redone...reinforcing the roofs of our shelters, adding wire mesh lateral support to our trenches, digging nine-foot-deep communication trenches and covering them with barbed wire (a Chinese became stuck there, once, to his great discomfiture).*[7]

In his memoir, Allard wrote that *"in the midst of these changes, the Chinese mounted a second attack, which failed, since they did not even reach our lines."* Indeed, it seems to have been so notably unsuccessful that it is now impossible to discern, from the paper evidence, just when and where this second attack occurred. There were the usual trickle of casualties and frequent but irregular "stonks" by the divisional artillery, but nothing to remark upon half a century later. On 10 July the brigade shifted position, moving from the centre to the right of the divisional front and once again taking over responsibility for Hill 355, with the Patricias on the hill and the Royals on their left and the Van Doos in reserve. Between 12 and 20 July, two companies of the Van Doos moved into the line on the right of the Patricias, relieving two companies of ROK soldiers who were needed elsewhere.

The talks at Panmunjom were moving very slowly, the greatest stumbling block being the fate of prisoners of war. United Nations forces were holding more than 120,000 of them, mostly North Koreans, and the Communists about 12,000, mostly South Koreans. While many of the former sought to stay in the South, only a relative few dedicated communists or committed family men were anxious to be returned. But freedom of choice was an arrangement unacceptable to Peking and P'yongyang. They sought compulsory repatriation of all captives.

Between December 1951 and October 1952 this was the subject of bitter and fruitless debate, interspersed with long periods of sullen silence, until, on 8 October 1952, the UN high command called an indefinite recess in negotiations. Two months later the matter was raised in the UN General Assembly, which passed an Indian resolution providing for a neutral Repatriation Commission which would take over responsibility for all prisoners, repatriating those who wanted to be repatriated but then handing over to the United Nations all those who were reluctant. Needless to say, these proposals were rejected by the communists – as we shall see very shortly, not on any point of principle but for essentially political and propaganda reasons.

On 22 February 1953 the UN high command announced that it was prepared to repatriate at once those sick and wounded prisoners who wished to be returned, and five weeks later the Chinese responded in an unusually conciliatory fashion. While still arguing that *all* prisoners should be repatriated, the Chinese premier, Chou En-lai, announced:

The Government of the People's Republic of China and the Government of the Democratic People's Republic of Korea propose that both parties to the negotiations should undertake to repatriate immediately after the cessation of hostilities all those POW's in their custody who insist upon repatriation and to hand over the remaining POW's to a neutral state so as to insure [sic] a just solution to the question of their repatriation.[8]

This was, in effect, the arrangement proposed by the Indians in the United Nations, the only difference being that those prisoners who did not wish to be repatriated would be handed over to "a neutral state" rather than the United Nations, but from a communist perspective it had the great advantage of appearing as their initiative.

A plan for the repatriation of sick and wounded prisoners, codenamed LITTLE SWITCH, was agreed on 11 April and was put into effect over the next three weeks (bringing two Canadians among those repatriated). Armistice negotiations at Panmunjom were resumed two weeks later, only to be encumbered by

President Syngman Rhee's unilateral decision to release into the South Korean community some 25,000 North Koreans who objected to being repatriated. Despite that, negotiations moved along rather more smartly as spring turned into summer, perhaps because the long-time Soviet premier and dominating figure of the Comintern hierarchy, Josef Stalin, had died on 5 March. His exit threw the entire Communist world into confusion as he was succeeded by a triumvirate dominated by the impulsive, unpredictable bureaucrat Nikita Khrushchev, whose aims and intentions were still obscure. If Stalin had not instigated Kim Il-sung's attack on South Korea and the Chinese intervention, neither had he opposed those moves. Indeed, he had given them some after-the-fact support by way of diplomatic manoeuvring and logistical assistance, and without it their position would certainly have been more difficult. Now, until Khrushchev's designs, particularly vis-à-vis the United States, became clear, the future course of the Korean conflict was necessarily in doubt and Mao and Kim had much to worry about.

On 27 July 1953 an armistice agreement between the United Nations and the North Koreans and Chinese was signed at Panmunjom. The "cease-fire line" would follow the line currently held by the respective parties to the agreement, with a demilitarized zone of 1,800 metres on each side. All those prisoners who wished to be repatriated were to be handed back and those who objected were to be assigned to the custody of a Neutral Nation Repatriations Commission. This Commission was chaired by an Indian officer, India having contributed a medical unit to the UN forces but always being something of a thorn in the Americans' side, professing an independent view and an enthusiastic desire to see the dispute settled. The other members were Czechoslovakia, Poland, Sweden and Switzerland.

While in Commission custody, prisoners might be persuaded to return to their respective homelands by visiting compatriots, and after 120 days they would be set free to do as they then wished. In September the UN command turned over 22,604 prisoners to the Commission, and the North Koreans and Chinese added 359 to the total. Of the 22,604 turned over by the UN command, 628 eventually decided to return to their homelands, 86 decided to go to India, 38 died in custody, 13 escaped and 21,839 were released into South Korea, this last figure including 14,235 Chinese, most of whom chose to go to Formosa, as it then was. Of the 359 UN doubters, 23 were Americans, one was British and 335 were South Koreans.

One of the Americans and eight South Koreans were persuaded to return to their own societies, two of the ROK prisoners opted to go to India, and the remainder preferred to stay with the Communists (although the Briton and at least three of the Americans later changed their minds).[9] Sixteen airmen held by the Chinese in China rather than North Korea remained in Communist hands. The first of these, Canadian Squadron Leader A. R. Mackenzie, would be returned early in December 1954, the other 15, all Americans, some months later.[10]

The armistice was supposed to go into effect at 2200 hours on the 27th, although Brigadier Allard records that between 2000 hours and midnight *the communists fired a record number (44,000) of shells at the 8th Army."*[11] But at first light on the 28th the Canadians faced an astonishing scene, recorded by a 3 PPCLI officer.

> *In the valley immediately below us the Chinese had set up a platform, with loudspeakers and banners announcing "the peace." On the platform men and women were dancing and singing. But what impressed the troops was what looked like millions of Chinese opposing them. No one [who was there] will ever forget the psychological impact of seeing for the first time "the human sea."*[12]

This was an armistice – a temporary cessation of hostilities – not a peace treaty, and that is the situation that still prevails. North Korean and South Korean armies still face each other across the demilitarized zone, and there is still an American military presence in South Korea. But in 1953 no one knew whether the armistice would hold, or if it did for how long. The new line along the edge of the demilitarized zone had to be built up, ready to face a new onslaught, and various training exercises were held as Brigadier Allard – along with the other UN commanders – was faced with the problem of maintaining readiness and morale among his men.

The immediate enemy was boredom, to be defeated only by giving the troops another focus besides the obvious one of preparing for a breakdown of the armistice. Training, made as interesting as possible, at every level from the individual to the division, was one answer. Another was to improve the lifestyles of peasant farmers gradually returning to the land they had been torn away from by the fighting. The final answer was to improve the lifestyles of the soldiers themselves, by winterizing their tents – wooden floors – building huts to house kitchens and

Heading home.

stores, which made for better meals, and providing many of the facilities that were part of an army base in Canada, such as a radio station, brigade cinema, library, gymnasium, recreation centre and a field for several sports and various leagues. *"When this programme was completed, we realized that the number of our delinquents had dropped by 50 per cent. In any army, this is a sure sign of improved morale."*[13]

In October 1953 a third rotation began and this time new infantry regiments, consisting exclusively of professional soldiers, were involved – the 2nd Battalions of the Black Watch of Canada and the Queen's Own Rifles, and the 4th Battalion of the recently created Canadian Guards. D Squadron of the Royal Canadian Dragoons replaced A Squadron, Lord Strathcona's Horse, 81 Field Regiment RCA was renamed 3 RCHA with a substantial turnover of personnel, and a number of other units followed the gunners' lead. In June 1954, Brigadier Allard relinquished command of the brigade, his place taken by Brigadier F. A. Clift, but before Allard left, the prime minister, Louis St. Laurent, visited the brigade in the course of a world tour. On his return to Canada, he told the House of Commons:

> *The morale of all our men is splendid. I was very happy to find that since the actual fighting has ceased they have been able to overcome by their own efforts many of the inconvenient features that interfered with their physical comfort in the surroundings in which they find themselves. But there again, one has the vivid impression that it is the human touch of the officers that contributes largely to this family spirit that you feel between the men and the officers, and this conviction of each and every one of them that he is a Canadian doing a Canadian job...in the joint effort to prove aggression to be unprofitable.*[14]

As the months rolled by and the armistice held with only minor infractions by the Chinese and North Koreans, the threat was assessed as slight and receding. In September 1954 the minister of national defence, Ralph Campney, announced that "the Canadian forces will be reduced by approximately two-thirds and that the remaining Canadian element...will consist of one infantry battalion, one field ambulance, and the necessary elements for their administrative support." The rest of the brigade would be returned to Canada "as rapidly as suitable hand-over and shipping arrangements can be made." The Commonwealth Division was gradually reduced to a brigade and, finally, to a battalion. This last, 2 Queen's Own Rifles, left Korea in April 1955, leaving only 3 Field Ambulance, an administrative section at 1 Commonwealth Division headquarters and RCOC, RCEME and Provost details in theatre – a total of some 500 officers and men. The last Canadian unit, a medical detachment, officially ceased to exist on 25 June 1957 and sailed from Inch'on three days later.[15]

"From the time the first Canadian soldier set foot in Japan until the armistice was signed 21,940 members of the Canadian Army served in Korea and Japan."[16] That figure includes only once those 484 members who served more than one tour. The peak Canadian Army strength was 8,123 all ranks, reached in January 1952, and at the time of the armistice there were 7,134 serving there. This is a small, even insignificant, figure compared with the US Army's 1,153,000 (and even more insignificant in light of the South Korean and Communist totals), but the Canadians did their duty and, by and large, did it well.

Even so, their losses were relatively low in this "sour little war" – a total of 1,543 battle casualties, all but 7 per cent of them being in the infantry. Eleven officers and 298 other ranks were killed in action or died of wounds, 59 officers and 1,143 other ranks were wounded, and two officers and 30 other ranks survived as prisoners of war. By way of comparison, 2,289 people in Canada were killed in traffic accidents during 1950.[17]

# NOTES

## CHAPTER I

[1] Quoted in K. J. Holmes, *The History of the Canadian Military Engineers,* Vol. 3 (Toronto: Military Engineering Institute of Canada, 1997), p. 216.

[2] Directorate of History and Heritage, NDHQ, Ottawa (hereafter DHH), 497.013 (D 4), "Notes on Fighting in Korea," Bulletin No. 9, Appendix A, p. 1.

[3] DHH, 410B25.033 (D 1).

[4] DHH, 145.2P7.013 (D 6).

[5] G. R. Stevens, *Princess Patricia's Canadian Light Infantry, 1919–1957,* Vol. 3 (Griesbach, AB: Historical Committee of the Regiment, 1957), p. 319.

[6] Max Hastings, *The Korean War* (London: Simon & Schuster, 1987), pp. 34 and 38.

[7] James I. Matray, ed., *Historical Dictionary of the Korean War* (New York: Greenwood Press, 1991), p. 381.

[8] Hastings, *Korean War,* p. 58.

[9] Joseph C. Goulden, *Korea: The Untold Story of the War* (New York: Times Books, 1982), p. xv.

[10] Canada, House of Commons, *Debates, 30 June 1950,* 4459.

[11] National Archives of Canada (hereafter NAC), RG 24, Acc. 83-84/167, box 465, file 1650-40, Vol. 1.

[12] A.L. Grey, "The Thirty-Eighth Parallel" in *Foreign Affairs,* Vol. 29, No. 3 (April 1951), p. 483.

[13] Michael Hickey, *The Korean War: The West Confronts Communism 1950–1953* (London: John Murray, 1999), p. 10.

[14] Goulden, *Korea,* p. 25.

[15] Hastings, *Korean War,* p. 33.

[16] Denis Stairs, *The Diplomacy of Constraint: Canada, the Korean War, and the United States* (Toronto: University of Toronto Press, 1974), p. 25.

[17] Anthony Farrar-Hockley, *The British Part in the Korean War. Vol. I: A Distant Obligation* [British Official History] (London: Her Majesty's Stationery Office, 1990), p. 26; Hickey, *Korean War,* p. 19.

[18] Goulden, *Korea,* p. 30.

[19] Stairs, *Diplomacy of Constraint,* p. 7.

[20] Ibid., pp. 17–18.

[21] Glenn D. Paige, *The Korean Decision: June 24–30, 1950* (New York: Free Press, 1968), p. 81.

[22] Hickey, *Korean War,* p. 20.

[23] Security Council Official Records, Fifth Year, 473rd Meeting, cited in H.F. Wood, *Strange Battleground: The Operations in Korea and their Effects on the Defence Policy of Canada* [Canadian Official History], (Ottawa: Queen's Printer, 1966), p. 8.

[24] Denis Stairs, 'Canada and the Korean War: Fifty Years On,' in *Canadian Military History,* Vol. 9, No. 3 (Summer 2000), pp. 49–50.

[25] Stairs, *The Diplomacy of Constraint,* p. 40.

[26] Security Council Official Records, Fifth Year, 474th Meeting, cited in Wood, *Strange Battleground,* p. 10.

[27] Robert Bothwell, 'Eyes West: Canada and the Cold War in Asia,' in Greg Donaghy, ed., *Canada and the Early Cold War, 1943–1957* (Ottawa: Canadian Government Publishing, 1998), p. 67.

[28] Canada, Department of External Affairs, *Documents on Canadian External Relations* [hereafter DCER], Vol. 16, 1950 (Ottawa: Canadian Communications Group – Publishing, 1996), p. 63.

[29] Ibid., p. 963.

## CHAPTER II

[1] Quoted DHH, NHS 1650-239/187, CNS to TF 214.4, 5 July 1950.

[2] HMCS *Cayuga, Athabaskan* and *Sioux,* Reports of Proceedings (hereafter RoPs), June–July 1950.

[3] HMCS *Athabaskan,* RoP, July 1950.

[4] W.G.D. Lund, PhD dissertation, *The Rise and Fall of the RCN, 1945–1964: A Critical Study of the Senior Leadership, Policy and Manpower Management* (Victoria, BC: University of Victoria, 1999), p. 237.

[5] DHH, 81/520, HMCS *Sioux* 8000 v. 1, "A History of HMCS *Sioux,*" p. 24.

[6] Information provided by Michael Whitby from conversations with Admiral DeWolf.

[7] Robert O'Neill, *Australia in the Korean War 1950–1953.* Vol. 2: *Combat Operations* (Canberra: Australian War Memorial and Australian Government Publishing Service, 1985), p. 413.

[8] RoPs, HMCS *Cayuga,* and *Athabaskan,* July 1950.

[9] Commander, Canadian Destroyer Division Pacific (COMCAN-DESDIVPAC), "Korean War Report," 4 April 1951, App. I, Gunnery, p. 2, DHH, NHS 1650-239/187.

[10] O'Neill, *Australia in the Korean War 1950–1953. Vol. 2, Combat Operations,* pp. 418–19.

[11] DHH, NHS 1650-239/187, COMCANDESDIVPAC, "Korean War Report," p. 5; App. I, pp. 1–2.

[12] COMCANDESDIVPAC, "Korean War Report," App. I.

[13] Ibid., Appx. 1, p. 7; HMCS *Cayuga,* RoP, August 1950, p. 1; Thor Thorgrimsson and E. C. Russell, *Canadian Naval Operations in Korean Waters, 1950–1955* (Ottawa: Queen's Printer, 1965), p. 13.

[14] PRO, ADM 116/5794, Flag Officer Second in Command Far East Station, "Korean War - RoP - No. 15 - At Sasebo," 30 Aug. 1950.

[15] Ibid., "Eleventh Report of Proceedings–6th to 12th August, 1950–At Sasebo," 16 Aug. 1950.

[16] Ibid., "Korean War Report of Proceedings No. 12–West Coast Patrol and Activities at Sasebo. 11th–16th August, 1950," 21 Aug. 1950.

[17] DHH interview with Vice-Admiral A. L. Collier, 37-38.

[18] Farrar-Hockley, *The British Part in the Korean War. Vol. 1: A Distant Obligation,* p. 70.

[19] HMCS *Sioux,* RoP, August 1950.

[20] Thorgrimsson and Russell, *Canadian Naval Operations in Korean Waters,* pp. 15–17.

[21] For more on the Inch'on operation see Curtis A. Utz, *Assault from the Sea: The Amphibious Landing at Inchon* (Washington: Naval Historical Center, Department of the Navy, 1994).

[22] Lieut-Commander A. G. Capps in "MacArthur Sells Inchon," ibid., p. 16.

[23] Ibid., pp. 16–17.

[24] DHH, 81/520, *Cayuga,* RoP, 21 Nov. 1950, pp. 1–2.

[25] DHH 81/520, *Athabaskan,* ROP, 1 Oct. 1950, p. 2.

[26] PRO, ADM 116/5794, Flag Officer Second in Command Far East Station, "Korean War - RoP - No. 19 - At Sasebo. 21-27 Sep, 1950," 19 Oct. 1950, pp. 3–4.

[27] DHH biog. file, interview with Rear-Admiral R. P. Welland, p. 10.

[28] DHH 81/520, COMCANDESDIVPAC, RoP, 28 Nov. 1950, p. 1.

[29] Thorgrimsson and Russell, *Canadian Naval Operations in Korean Waters,* p. 23.

30 DHH, 81/520, COMCANDESDIVPAC, RoP, 28 Nov. 1950, p. 1.

31 Farrar-Hockley, *The British Part in the Korean War*, Vol. 1, p. 156.

32 DHH, 81/520, COMCANDESDIVPAC, "Korean War Report," p. 1.

33 HMCS *Sioux*, RoP, 18 Oct. 1950; *Athabaskan* RoP, 8 Dec. 1950, p. 3.

34 DHH, 81/520, COMCANDESDIVPAC, "Korean War Report," p. 7.

35 Ibid., p. 8.

36 PRO, ADM 116/5794, Flag Officer Second in Command Far East Station, "Korean War - Reports of Proceedings No. 24 - Implementing Plans for Reduction of British Commonwealth and Allied Naval Forces in Japanese/Korean Waters, And Move of Flag Officer Second-in-Command, Far East Station, with Staff to Hong Kong, 11–28 Nov 1950," p. 1.

37 CNS to MND, 21 Nov 1950, cited in Thorgrimsson and Russell, *Canadian Naval Operations in Korean Waters*, p. 28, note 49.

38 PRO, ADM 116/5794, Flag Officer Second in Command Far East Station, "Korean War - Reports of Proceedings No. 24."

39 PRO, ADM 116/5794, Flag Officer Second in Command Far East Station, "Korean War - Reports of Proceedings No. 26 - Concentration of all British Commonwealth and Allied Ships Off West Coast of Korea, 4–15 Dec 1950," 28 Dec. 1950, p. 1.

40 DHH, 81/520, HMCS ATHABASKAN 8000, CTE 95.12 to CTG 99.2, 4 Dec. 1950.

41 Athabaskan, RoP, 5 Jan. 1951, p. 1.

42 Ibid.

43 DHH biog. file, interview with Vice-Admiral A. L. Collier, pp. 40, 42. See also "The Chinnampo Affair" by A.J.P., in *The Crowsnest*, Vol. 3, No. 4, Feb. 1951, pp. 4–6.

44 DHH biog. file, interview with Rear-Admiral R. H. Leir, pp. 109–112; *Athabaskan* RoP, 5 Jan. 1951, p. 1.

45 DHH biog. file, interview with Vice-Admiral A. L. Collier, p. 42.

46 O'Neill, *Australia in the Korean War*, Vol. 2, p. 434.

47 *Athabaskan*, RoP, 5 Jan. 1951, p. 2.

48 *Cayuga*, RoP, quoted in Thorgrimsson and Russell, *Canadian Naval Operations in Korean Waters*, pp. 34–35.

49 NAC, RG 24, Acc 83-84/167, Box 695, File NSS1926-DDE-218 v. 2, Flag Officer Second-in-Command Far East Station to Commander-in-Chief, 22 Jan. 1951.

## CHAPTER III

1 House of Commons, *Debates*, 7 July 1950, 2nd Session, p. 94.

2 *DCER* Vol. 16, 1950, pp. 115–117.

3 Wood, *Strange Battleground*, p. 25.

4 Ibid., p. 28.

5 Ibid., p. 29.

6 Arnold Warren, *Wait for the Waggon: The Story of the Royal Canadian Army Service Corps* (Toronto: McClelland, 1961), pp. 327–28.

7 Ted Barris, *Deadlock in Korea: Canadians at War, 1950–1953* (Toronto: Macmillan, 1999), p. 27. Canadian veterans of the Korean conflict complained, often with good reason, that their war had been largely forgotten by the general public. The 50th anniversary of the North Korean invasion of South Korea has, however, rectified that situation to some extent. Along with Barris, see David J. Bercuson, *Blood on the Hills: The Canadian Army in the Korean War* (Montreal and Kingston: McGill-Queen's University Press, 1999). Manuscripts by Brent Byron Watson and William C. Johnston are scheduled to be published in the near future. The former is a study of the common soldier's experience in Korea, the latter a critical operational history.

8 Wood, *Strange Battleground*, p. 30.

9 Brereton Greenhous (ed.), *Semper Paratus: The History of the Royal Hamilton Light Infantry (Wentworth Regiment) 1862–1977* (Hamilton: RHLI Historical Association 1977), pp. 167, 247 and 343.

10 Ibid., pp. 343.

11 Ibid., pp 343–44.

12 Quoted in John Gardam, *Korea Volunteer: An Oral History from Those Who Were There* (Burnstown, Ont.: General Store Publishing House, 1994), pp. 30–31.

13 NAC, RG 24, Vol. 18237, 25 CIB War Diary, 5 Oct. 1950.

14 *Ibid.*, Vol. 18356, 2 R22eR War Diary, 1and 10 Oct., 10 Nov. 1950.

15 G. D. Mitchell, with B. A. Reid and W. Simcock, *RCHA – Right of the Line: An Anecdotal History of the Royal Canadian Horse Artillery from 1871* (Ottawa: RCHA History Committee, 1986), p. 165.

16 J. S. Moir, ed., *History of the Royal Canadian Corps of Signals 1903–1961* (Ottawa: Queen's Printer, 1962), pp. 288–89.

17 "Chronology of the Korean War," in Matray, ed., *Historical Dictionary of the Korean War*, Appx. C.

18 Hickey, *The Korean War*, p. 91.

19 NAC, RG 24, Vol.18237, 25 CIB War Diary, 30 Oct. 1950.

20 DHH, 112.3H1.001 (D 13).

21 Bailey to CO, 1 RCHA [?], 9 February 1989, letter in author's possession.

22 Gardam, *Korea Volunteer*, p. 59.

23 NAC, RG 24, Vol. 18340, 2 RCR War Diary, 20–21 Nov. 1950.

24 Quoted in Barris, *Deadlock in Korea*, p. 50.

25 Gardam, *Korea Volunteer*, p. 80.

26 John Marteinson and Michael R. McNorgan, *The Royal Canadian Armoured Corps: An Illustrated History* (Toronto: Robin Brass Studio and the Royal Canadian Armoured Corps Association, 2000), p. 349.

27 Michael Hickey, "Have We Learnt the Lessons of Readiness from Korea?" in *RUSI Journal* (June 2000), p. 64.

28 Ibid., p. 65.

29 Holmes, *The History of the Canadian Military Engineers*, p. 215.

30 NAC, RG 24, Vol. 18340, 2 RCR War Diary.

31 Ibid., Vol. 18237, 25 CIB War Diary, 26 Nov. 1950.

32 Quoted in Barris, *Deadlock in Korea*, p. 51.

33 Stevens, *Princess Patricia's Canadian Light Infantry*, Vol. 3, p. 354.

34 Quoted in Mitchell, *RCHA – Right of the Line*, pp. 165–66.

35 NAC, RG 24, Vol. 18237, 25 CIB War Diary, 8 Jan. 1951.

36 Wood, *Strange Battleground*, p. 88.

37 NAC, RG 24, Vol. 18238, 25 CIB War Diary, 6 Feb. 1951.

38 Ibid., 17 Feb. 1951.

39 DHH, 410B25.013 (D 4), 25 CIBG Weekly Summary No. 19.

40 Ibid.

41 Ibid., Nos. 20 and 21.

## CHAPTER IV

1 Stevens, *Princess Patricia's Canadian Light Infantry*, Vol. 3, p. 282.

2 Robert Hepenstall, *Find the Dragon: The Canadian Army in Korea 1950–1953* (Edmonton: Four Winds, 1995), p. 46.

3 NAC, RG 24, Vol. 18317, 2 PPCLI War Diary, 20 and 21 Dec. 1950.

4 Robert S. Peacock, *Kim-chi, Asahi and Rum*, (no place: Lugus, 1994), p. 88.

[5] DHH, 145.2P7.013 (D 6), "Report by Lt-Col J. R. Stone on activities of 2 PPCLI, 18–23 Dec 1950."

[6] Matray, *Historical Dictionary of the Korean War,* p. 521.

[7] DHH, 145.2P7.013 (D 6).

[8] J. R. Stone, "Memoir: Kapyong," *Infantry Journal* 23 (Autumn 1992), p. 13.

[9] DHH 145.2P7.013 (D6).

[10] Mel Canfield, "Memories of Korea: Early Lessons," in *Legion Magazine* (Jan/Feb. 1998), p. 49.

[11] 2 PPCLI War Diary, 2–8 Jan 1951.

[12] Stevens, *PPCLI,* Vol. 3, p. 285.

[13] Hastings, *Korean War,* p. 227.

[14] Ibid., p. 229.

[15] 2 PPCLI War Diary, 19–21 Feb. 1951.

[16] Canfield, "Memories of Korea: Grim Caution," in *Legion Magazine* (Mar/Apr., 1998), p. 15.

[17] 2 PPCLI War Diary, 24 Feb. 1951.

[18] Wood, *Strange Battleground,* pp. 65–66.

[19] 2 PPCLI War Diary, 8 Mar. 1951.

[20] DHH, 410B25.065 (D 15), "Return of Casualties...by Category, Unit and Date."

[21] Stone to CGS, quoted in Wood, *Strange Battleground,* p. 67.

[22] Canada, House of Commons, *Debates,* 1951, Vol. 2, p. 1443, 20 Mar. 1951.

[23] Stevens, *PPCLI,* Vol. 3, p. 295.

[24] 2 PPCLI War Diary, 28 Mar. 1951.

[25] Matray, *Historical Dictionary of the Korean War,* pp. 265–66 and 269–70.

[26] Ray Bordeleau, "We Regret to Inform You...", *Esprit de Corps,* Vol. 6, No. 8 (Sept. 1998), p. 10.

[27] 2 PPCLI War Diary, 23 Apr. 1951.

[28] Stone, "Memoir: Kapyong," *Infantry Journal* (Autumn 1992), p. 13.

[29] DHH, 145.2P7.013 (D 5), "2 PPCLI Action Kapyong Area – 23 to 26 Apr 51," p. 5.

[30] Ibid., p. 38.

[31] Stone, "Memoir: Kapyong," *Infantry Journal* (Autumn 1992), pp. 13–14.

[32] DHH, 145.2P7.013 (D 5), "2 PPCLI Action Kapyong Area," pp. 7–8.

[33] O'Neill, *Australia in the Korean War,* Vol. 2, p. 157; Wood, *Strange Battleground,* pp. 74–76.

[34] Stevens, *PPCLI,* Vol. 3, p. 300.

[35] 2 PPCLI War Diary, 24 Apr. 1951.

[36] DHH, 145.2P7.013 (D 5), "2 PPCLI Action Kapyong Area," p. 11.

[37] DCM citation quoted in Wood, *Strange Battleground,* p. 77.

[38] Hepenstall, *Find the Dragon,* p. 96.

[39] DHH, 145.2P7.013 (D 5) "2 PPCLI Action Kapyong Area," p. 27.

[40] Ibid., p. 12.

[41] Hepenstall, *Find the Dragon,* p. 96.

[42] DHH, 145.2P7.013 (D 5), "2 PPCLI Action Kapyong Area," p. 12.

[43] Quoted in John Melady, *Korea: Canada's Forgotten War* (Toronto: Gage, 1983), p. 77.

[44] Hepenstall, *Find the Dragon,* p. 94.

[45] DHH, 145.2P7.013 (D 5), "2 PPCLI Action Kapyong Area," p. 18.

[46] 2 PPCLI War Diary, 25 Apr. 1951.

[47] Ray Bordeleau, "The Fight at Kapyong," *Esprit De Corps,* Vol. 6, No. 9 (Oct. 1998), p. 10.

[48] Hepenstall, *Find the Dragon,* p. 99.

[49] Stone, "Memoir: Kapyong," p. 13.

[50] Wood, *Strange Battleground,* pp. 165–66.

## CHAPTER V

[1] Marteinson and McNorgan, *The Royal Canadian Armoured Corps,* p. 349.

[2] C Sqn, LdSH newsletter – mid-April to end of May [1951], copy in author's possession.

[3] NAC, RG 24, Vol. 18238, 25 CIB War Diary, 11 May 1951.

[4] DHH, 145.2R13013 (D 2), "Report on battle of Chail-li...," p. 2. All quotations regarding the fight at Chail-li are from this report unless otherwise noted.

[5] DHH, 681.013 (D 76), "Periodic Reports of Comd 1 Comwel Div..." (No. 2), May 51/Aug. 53, Appx. D, p. 7.

[6] Wood, *Strange Battleground,* p. 101.

[7] DHH, 145.2R13013, "2 RCR Report on Battle of Chail-li (Korea), 30 May 51," p. 4.

[8] Ibid., p. 8.

[9] C Sqn, LdSH newsletter...., pp. 5–6.

[10] NAC, RG 24, Vol.18264, C Sqn, LdSH War Diary, 30 May 1951.

[11] DHH, 145.2R13013 (D 2).

[12] 25 CIB War Diary, 9 June 1951.

[13] 2 RCR War Diary, 21 June 1951.

[14] Holmes, *History of the Canadian Military Engineers,* p. 218.

[15] DHH, 410B25.013 (D 4), "Hist Offrs Weekly Summary," No. 36.

[16] Ibid.

[17] NAC, RG 24, Vol. 18318, 2 PPCLI War Diary, 25 June 1951.

[18] NAC RG 24 v. 18239, 25 Bde War Diary, 2 July 1951.

[19] 2 PPCLI War Diary, 26 June 1951.

[20] DHH, 410B25.013 (D 4), "Hist Offrs Weekly Summary," No. 37.

[21] Hastings, *Korean War,* pp. 283–84.

[22] *Globe and Mail,* 12 Jan. 2001, p. A10.

[23] 25 CIB War Diary, 24 June 1951.

[24] 2 PPCLI War Diary, 3 July 1951.

[25] G. R. Stevens, *The Royal Canadian Regiment.* Vol. 2: *1933–1966* (London: n.p., 1967), pp 228–29.

[26] Ibid., p. 229.

[27] 25 Bde War Diary, 6 July 1951.

[28] Ibid., 10 July 1951.

[29] Ibid., 11 July 1951.

[30] NAC, RG 24, Vol. 18357, R22eR War Diary, 19 July 1951.

[31] DHH, 681.013 (D 93), "Canadian Operations in Korea – 25 Jun 50 to 31 Mar 52," pp. 31–32.

[32] Jeffrey Grey, *The Commonwealth Armies and the Korean War* (Manchester: Manchester University Press, 1988), pp. 192–195.

[33] 25 Bde War Diary, 31 July 1951.

[34] Stairs, *Diplomacy of Constraint,* p. 233.

[35] Quoted in David Rees, *Korea: The Limited War* (London: Macmillan, 1964), p. 285.

[36] Hastings, *Korean War,* p. 276.

[37] Matray, *Historical Dictionary of the Korean War,* entries under Battles of...

[38] Serge Bernier, *The Royal 22e Régiment 1914–1999* (Montreal: Art Global, 2000), p. 203.

[39] Stevens, *PPCLI* Vol. 3, p. 316.

[40] DHH, 96/47, Vol. 1, folio 2.

[41] Ibid.

## CHAPTER VI

[1] NAC, RG 24, Vol. 18312, 1 PPCLI War Diary, 6 Oct. 1951.

[2] DHH, 681.001 (D1), 'Report by A.R. Menzies, DEA, 12–17 Oct. 1951, p 7.

[3] Wood, *Strange Battleground,* p. 149.

4 NAC, RG 24, Vol. 18240, 25 Bde War Diary, 23 Oct. 1951.

5 DHH, 410B25.013 (D 99), "Hist Offrs Weekly Summaries," No. 53.

6 Stevens, *RCR*, Vol. 2, p. 235.

7 NAC, RG 24, Vol. 18343, 2 RCR War Diary, 2–3 Nov. 1951.

8 Gardam, *Korea Volunteer*, p. 105.

9 DHH, 410B25.013 (D 99), "Hist Offrs Weekly Summaries," No. 57.

10 Ibid.

11 Wood, *Strange Battleground*, p. 153.

12 NAC, RG 24, Vol. 18357, 2 R22eR War Diary, 22 Nov. 1951.

13 Peacock, *Kim-chi, Asahi and Rum*, p. 18.

14 DHH, 681.013 (D 76), "Periodic Reports of Comd 1 Comwel Div," May 51/Aug. 53, (No. 2), p 3.

15 NAC, RG 24, Vol. 18357, 2 R22eR War Diary, 23 Nov. 1951.

16 Bernier, *R22eR*, p. 208.

17 Ibid., pp. 206–209.

18 Chinese camp commandant, quoted in Anthony Farrar-Hockley, *The British Part in the Korean War*, Vol. 2, p. 267.

19 Ibid., Appx. G, pp. 443–48.

20 "Speech delivered by Major William E. Mayer, MC, US Army Medical Service School, before the students at the Chaplain School and the Army Information School" (undated), pp. 7–8. Copy in author's possession.

21 Ibid., p. 9.

22 Ibid., p. 11.

23 Hickey, *Korean War*, p. 341; DHH, 410B25.065 (D 9), "List of Cdn PWs in Korea."

24 Quoted in Wood, *Strange Battleground*, p. 250.

25 Mayer speech, loc. cit.

26 G. W. L. Nicholson, *The Gunners of Canada: The History of the Royal Regiment of Canadian Artillery*, Vol. 2: 1919–1967 (Toronto: McClelland & Stewart, 1972), p. 563.

27 DHH, 410B25.013 (D 102) "54 Transport Coy report," 1–31 July 51.

28 NAC, RG 24, 83-84/167, Box 7718, 20-1-1, pt 4, "Extract from the Minutes of the 58th Meeting of Defence Council, 27 May 1952."

29 DHH, 410B25.013 (D 102) "54 Transport Coy report," 1–31 July 51.

30 Ibid., 1–31 Oct 51.

31 René Lévesque, *Memoirs*. Trans. Philip Stratford (Toronto: McClelland & Stewart, 1986), p. 113.

32 Rees, *Korea*, p. 298.

33 DHH, 410B25.013 (D 99), Vol. 1,"Hist Offrs Weekly Summaries," No. 58.

34 DHH, 681.013 (D 76), "Periodic Reports of Comd 1 Comwel Div" (No. 2), p. 4.

35 DHH, 410B25.013 (D 99), "Hist Offrs Weekly Summaries," No. 59.

36 2 RCR War Diary, 28 Nov. 1951.

37 NAC, RG 24, Vol. 18385, 37 Fld Amb. War Diary, Sep. 1952, Appx. 3N.

38 Peacock, *Kim-chi, Asahi and Rum*, p. 31.

39 NAC, RG 24, Vol. 18385, 37 Fld Amb war diary, Sept. 52, Appx. 3N.

40 DHH, 681.013 (D 76), "Periodic Reports of Comd 1 Comwel Div" (No. 2), Appx. A, p. 12.

41 NAC, RG 24, Vol. 18344, 2 RCR War Diary, 7 Dec. 1951.

42 Stevens, *PPCLI*, Vol. 3, p. 332.

43 DHH, 681.013 (D 76), "Periodic Reports of Comd 1 Comwel Div" (No. 2), Appx. B, p. 4.

## CHAPTER VII

1 *National Post* obituary, 18 Oct. 1999, p. A13.

2 Quoted in Stevens, *RCR*, Vol. 2, pp. 243–44.

3 Bernier, *R22eR*, pp. 217–18.

4 NAC, RG 24, Vol.18242, 25 Bde War Diary (Ops Log), 7 May 1952.

5 NAC, RG 24, Vol.18243, 25 Bde War Diary, 13 June 1952.

6 Bernier, *R22eR*, p. 218.

7 Ibid., pp. 218–19.

8 General Staff, *Canada's Army in Korea* (Ottawa, 1956), pp. 74–75.

9 Peacock, *Kim-chi, Asahi and Rum*, p. 78.

10 S. Dunstan, *Flak Jackets: 20th Century Body Armour* [Men-at-Arms series] (London: Osprey, 1984), p. 19.

11 Ibid., pp. 19–20.

12 Peacock, *Kim-chi, Asahi and Rum*, p. 79.

13 Dunstan, *Flak Jackets*, pp. 18–19.

14 DHH 681.009 (D 11), Major W. H. Pope, "Infantry Defences in Korea," 19 Sept. 1953, p. 2.

15 Ibid., pp. 3–4.

16 Hugh Halliday, "Khaki in the Blue," *Journal of the Canadian Aviation Historical Society*, Vol. 1, No. 4 (Autumn, 1963).

17 Ibid.

18 Ibid.

19 Hickey, *Korean War*, pp. 348–49.

20 Wood, *Strange Battleground*, p. 192.

21 Donald Barry (ed.), *Documents on Canadian External Relations*, Vol. 18, 1952, p. 66.

22 Ibid., p. 71.

23 Quoted in Wood, *Strange Battleground*, pp. 195–96.

24 Canada, House of Commons, *Debates*, 1952, II, 2101.

25 Peacock, *Kim-chi, Asahi and Rum*, p. 21.

26 Mitchell, *RCHA – Right of the Line*, p. 179.

27 Quoted in W. B. Fraser, *Always a Strathcona* (Calgary: Comprint, 1976), p. 209.

28 Ibid., p. 210.

29 NAC, RG 24, Vol. 18316, 1 PPCLI War Diary, 6 Sep 1952.

30 NAC, RG 24, Vol. 18338, 1 RCR War Diary, 30 and 29 Sep 1952.

31 Ibid., 16 Oct 1952.

32 Quoted in Nicholson, *The Gunners of Canada*, Vol. 2, p. 567.

33 Mitchell, *RCHA – Right of the Line*, p. 181.

34 Quoted in Melady, *Korea: Canada's Forgotten War*, pp. 132–33.

35 Ibid., pp. 137–38.

36 General Staff, *Canada's Army in Korea*, p. 65.

37 NAC, RG 24, Vol. 18323, 3 PPCLI War Diary, July 1951, Appx. 3.

38 NAC, RG 24, Vol. 18324, 3 PPCLI War Diary, 15 Nov. 1952.

39 Ibid., 19 Nov. 1952.

40 Ibid., 3 Dec. 1952.

41 Ibid., 16 Dec. 1952.

42 General Staff, *Canada's Army in Korea*, p. 67.

43 Mitchell, *RCHA – Right of the Line*, p. 182.

44 General Staff, *Canada's Army in Korea*, p. 68.

## CHAPTER VIII

1 RCN destroyers carried out six more tours after the Armistice, and the final deployment by HMCS *Sioux* did not end until 7 September 1955.

2 Director Naval Plans and Operations (DNPO) to Vice-Chief of Naval Staff (VCNS), "Reduction of RCN Korean Commitment," 25 Feb. 1952. DHH, NHS NSS1650-40 Vol. 3.

[3] DNPO to VCNS, 15 Dec. 1950, DHH, NHS 1650-1, Vol 3, and Naval Staff Minutes, 18 Jan. 1952, DHH.

[4] Information provided by Michael Whitby from conversations with Admiral DeWolf.

[5] Peter T. Haydon, "Canada's Naval Commitment to the Korean War: Prudent Employment or Opportunism?", in Peter T. Haydon and Ann L. Griffiths (eds.), *Canada's Pacific Naval Presence: Purposeful or Peripheral* (Halifax: Centre for Foreign Policy Studies, Dalhousie University, 1999), p. 126.

[6] See Stairs, *The Diplomacy of Constraint.*

[7] DHH, 81/520 HMCS CAYUGA 8000, *Cayuga*, RoP, 13 Aug. 1951, pp. 1–3.

[8] DHH biog. file, interview with Commander Peter Chance, pp. 29–30.

[9] DHH, NHS 1650-239/187. CANCOMDESFE, "Korean War Report: Part One," p. 10.

[10] Naval Historical Center, Washington Naval Yard, Washington DC, Commander Task Force 95 Briefing for the Secretary of the Navy, "Island Defence," 31 Mar. 1952.

[11] DHH, 88/6, Commodore J. C. Hibbard, Inspection Report, May 1952, p. 6.

[12] *Cayuga*, RoP, 20 Sept. 1951, A Report of activities in the Choda and Sokuto area, 9th and 10th August, 1951.

[13] Ibid.

[14] Ibid.

[15] CANCOMDESFE, "Korean War Report: Part Two," undated. This part of the report was for Canadian eyes only.

[16] Ibid.

[17] DHH, 88/6, Hibbard Inspection Report, p. 7.

[18] CANCOMDESFE, "Korean War Report: Part Two."

[19] DHH interview with Lieut-Commander Chance, p. 35.

[20] Edward C. Meyers, *Thunder in the Morning Calm: The Royal Canadian Navy in Korea 1950–1955* (St. Catharines, ON: Vanwell Publishing, 1992), p. 170.

[21] *Cayuga*, RoP, 4 Nov 1951, App. A, pp. 2–3.

[22] Meyers, *Thunder in the Morning Calm*, p. 170.

[23] Thorgrimsson and Russell, *Canadian Naval Operations in Korean Waters*, pp. 77–78.

[24] Ibid., pp. 81–84.

[25] DHH, NHS 1650-239/187 Operations Korea, Flag Officer, 2 i/c Far East Station, "Report of Experience in Korean Operations, July, 1952 – April, 1953," 15 July 1953, p. 1.

[26] For Lieut-Commander Saxon's accomplishments see CANCOMDESFE, "Korean War Report: Part One," pp. 16–17, and Thorgrimsson and Russell, *Canadian Naval Operations in Korean Waters*, pp. 82–85 and 96.

[27] Malcolm W. Cagle and Frank A. Manson, *The Sea War in Korea* (Annapolis, MD: Naval Institute Press, 1957), pp. 204–207.

[28] Ibid., pp. 359–360. Ships destroying trains before July 1952 (of which there were several) were not included in the club.

[29] DHH, 81/520 HMCS CRUSADER 8000, Lieut-Commander J. Bovey, "HMCS *Crusader's* Report on Operations in Korean Waters, 18 June, 1952 to 19 June, 1953," 19 June 1953.

[30] John Bovey, "The Destroyers' War in Korea, 1952–53" in James A. Boutilier (ed.), *The RCN in Retrospect, 1910–1968* (Vancouver: UBC Press, 1982), pp. 254–262.

[31] *Iroquois*, RoP, 5 Nov. 1952, p. 1.

[32] *Crusader*, RoP, 18 Nov. 1952, p. 3.

[33] Cagle and Manson, *The Sea War in Korea*, p. 350.

[34] Bovey, "HMCS *Crusader's* Report on Operations in Korean Waters...," App. 4, p. 2.

[35] *Crusader* RoP, 18 Nov. 1952, p. 3.

[36] Ibid., pp. 3–4.

[37] Admiralty, *British Commonwealth Naval Operations, Korea, 1950–1953* (London: Ministry of Defence, Historical Branch [Naval], 1967), p. 243.

[38] *Crusader*, RoP, 18 Nov. 1952, pp. 5–6.

[39] Ibid., pp. 6–7.

[40] Ibid., p. 7.

[41] Ibid., 17 Feb. 1953, p. 4.

[42] Ibid.

[43] Ibid., 1 May 1953, p. 2.

[44] Ibid.

[45] DHH biog file, citation in RCN Press Release, 11 June 1954. See also J. D. F. Kealy and E. C. Russell, *A History of Canadian Naval Aviation, 1918–1962* (Ottawa: Queen's Printer, 1967), p. 124.

[46] DHH, NHS 1700 VF-871 (Signals), CANAVED to CANFLAGLANT, 14 May 1953,

[47] *Crusader*, RoP, 1 May 1953, p. 4.

[48] F.L.P.R., "Ace of Train Busters," in *The Crowsnest* (July 1953), p. 5.

[49] For *Huron* running aground see Meyers, *Thunder in the Morning Calm*, App. J, pp. 224–230. Unfortunately, given the superb navigation record established by the other RCN ships, *Huron's* grounding was the result of carelessness, not circumstance.

## CHAPTER IX

[1] Larry Milberry, *Air Transport in Canada*, Vol. 1 (Toronto: CANAV Books, 1997), p. 415.

[2] K. M. Molson and H. A. Taylor, *Canadian Aircraft Since 1909* (Srittsville, ON: Canada's Wings, 1982), pp. 298–304.

[3] Ron Pickler and Larry Milberry, *Canadair: The First Fifty Years* (Toronto: CANAV Books, 1995), p. 63.

[4] Ibid.

[5] Ibid., pp. 162–63.

[6] Stairs, *Diplomacy of Constraint*, p. 48.

[7] Milberry, *Air Transport in Canada*, p. 415.

[8] Quoted in ibid.

[9] DHH, 681.001 (D1), "Report by A. R. Menzics, DEA, 12/17 Oct. 1951.

[10] Lévesque, *Memoirs*, pp. 106-7.

[11] DHH, Payne biog. file.

[12] *London Gazette*, 5 June 1952; *Canada Gazette*, 7 June 1952; AFRO 406/52. This and most of the following *Gazette* citations can also be found in the relevant DHH biog. files.

[13] *London Gazette*, 5 June 1952 (Queen's Birthday Honours); AFRO 406/52, 13 June 1952.

[14] *Canada Gazette*, 30 May 1953; AFRO 360/53, 12 June 1953.

[15] *Canada Gazette*, 7 Aug. 1954; AFRO 448/54, 13 Aug 1954.

[16] DHH, McNair biog. file.

[17] Richard P. Hallion, *The Naval Air War in Korea* (Baltimore: Nautical and Aviation Publishing Company, 1986), pp. 28–29.

[18] Robert Jackson, *Air War Over Korea* (New York: Scribner's, 1973), p. 117.

[19] Thomas C. Hone, "Korea," in Benjamin Franklin Cooling (ed.), *Case Studies in the Achievement of Air Superiority* (Washington: Center for Air Force History, 1994), pp. 469–72.

[20] DHH, 181.003 (D 3235), "RCAF Air Intelligence Summary, June 1951," p. 14.

[21] Ibid.

[22] Hone, "Korea," in Cooling (ed.), *Case Studies in ... Air Superiority*, pp. 488–89.

[23] Jackson, *Air War Over Korea*, pp. 171–72.

[24] Ibid., p. 88.

25 H. A. Halliday, "In Korean Skies," Pt. I, in *Roundel* (Dec. 1963), p. 17.

26 DHH, Levesque biog. file.

27 DFC citation quoted in RCAF Press Release, May 1951.

28 Halliday, "In Korean Skies," p. 18.

29 Halliday, "In Korean Skies," Pt. II, in *Roundel* (Jan. 1964), pp. 16–17.

30 Halliday, "In Korean Skies," Pt. I, p 18.

31 DHH, Lafrance biog. file.

32 DHH, Hale biog. file.

33 NAC, RG 7, Group 26, Vol. 58, file 190 1, dossier 6 (Governor General's records).

34 DHH, Hale biog. file.

35 Ibid.

36 DHH, Glover biog. file.

37 Ibid.

38 DHH, Lindsay biog. file.

39 DHH, Mackenzie biog. file, "I Was a Prisoner of the Chinese Reds" manuscript, pp. 6–7, 53, *passim.*

40 Ibid., Toronto *Sunday Star* cutting, 21 Dec. 1980.

## CHAPTER X

1 Quoted in Gardam, *Korea Volunteer,* pp. 177–78.

2 Ibid., p. 178.

3 General Staff, *Canada's Army in Korea,* p. 69.

4 J.V. Allard with Serge Bernier, *The Memoirs of General Jean V. Allard* (Vancouver: UBC Press, 1988), p. 173.

5 DHH 96/47, Vol. I.

6 Ibid.

7 Allard, *Memoirs,* pp. 176–77.

8 Quoted in Wood, *Strange Battleground,* p. 247.

9 Harry G. Summers, *Korean War Almanac* (New York: Facts on File, 1990), p. 215.

10 Wood, *Strange Battleground,* p. 249.

11 Allard, *Memoirs,* p 180.

12 Quoted in Wood, *Strange Battleground.*, p. 243.

13 Allard, *Memoirs,* p. 182.

14 Quoted in Wood, *Strange Battleground,* p. 254.

15 Ibid., pp. 255–57.

16 Ibid., p. 257.

17 Ibid., pp. 257–58.

# INDEX